Acknowledgments

I continue to be perplexed as to how I got to this point, but I know I didn't do it alone. Enormous, heartfelt thank-yous go to:

My editor, Alice Levine, whose eagle eyes I would trust with any document.

My readers for the original edition, Gay Pogue, Lisa Call, and Patricia J. Velte.

The squad of artists that generously helped me nail the "look" of my book in exchange for a meal: Daniel Bahn, Lisa Call, David Castle, Jim DeLutes, Jan Fordyce, Cynthia Guajardo, Laura Tyler, and Denise West. A special thanks to Ann Cunningham, who went beyond the call of duty by sharing her publishing knowledge.

Ronnie Moore of WESType Publishing Services, Inc. Ronnie made this book look good and is a joy to work with.

Rachelle Disbennett-Lee, without whose encouragement I would not have succeeded and without whose advice there would be no Art Biz Coach.

Eric H. Anderson, Patricia J. Velte (who wears many hats for me), Mel Ristau, and Michael and Kathleen Redwine, whose design opinions I can always count on.

David L. Boren (now president of The University of Oklahoma), who gave me the experience of a lifetime working in the U.S. Senate. During my time on his staff, I shook the hands of many of our country's leaders. As a result of Senator Boren's example, I learned how to treat people in order to build lasting relationships.

Jean Cassels Hagman, the best museum director I ever worked for—and I worked for a lot. Jean instilled in me the value of bringing artists into the fold of the museum.

My coach, Cynthia Morris, who walked beside me during the two-year journey of writing this book and continues to be a friend and confidante.

All of my art teachers, from grade school through grad school. In particular, the late Mary Ruth Mayfield, who cheered me on, and the current Susan Havens Caldwell, who always challenged me intellectually.

Hilary Pfeifer, who gave Art Biz Coach its name.

Shari Cornish and Kelly Johnson, who help me in the virtual office each and every day.

My nephews, Heath and Jes, because this is my book and I want to applaud the little artists that they are and the bigger artists I know they will become.

All of my newsletter subscribers, blog commentators, Facebook fans, Twitter followers, and class and workshop participants from whom I've learned so much. And infinite thanks to those artists who have agreed to share their stories on the pages of this book.

A very special debt of gratitude goes to all of the clients who trust in me to help with their careers and dreams. I'm amazed every day at how fortunate I am to have you in my life.

Finally, to my husband, Robert J. Harrington, who stabilizes my boisterous enthusiasm with his voice of calm and reason. I didn't know there was another side before we met.

Congratulations ...

on deciding to take responsibility for your art career

As an artist, you probably relish your freedom to paint, draw, sculpt, sew, cut, glue, throw, blow, or carve all day, every day. After all, that's why you became an artist. You love having the freedom to create whenever you want and as much as you want. You can't imagine a day in your life without art.

You may be one of the many, many artists who are happy simply making art for yourself. But if you want to sell your work—consistently and to an ever-widening audience—you must distinguish yourself from the crowd. Artists are a dime a dozen. Everyone knows an artist or is related to one, although the truly remarkable artist is rare. However, if you are an artist trying to sell your work, you are no longer only an artist. You're a businessperson as well. The stakes are high when you have to make a living from your art and the pressure mounts to become one of the truly remarkable artists who stand out. You can't do that with a suitcase full of excuses.

I've listened to more excuses from artists than I care to recall. In the spirit of full disclosure, I've made up plenty of my own. However, my excuse-making days necessarily ended when I started my business and realized I had control over my destiny. I was now the boss. I had an even more frightening thought: *There's no one to blame but me.* If I had not accepted 100% responsibility for my actions, I would have continued making excuses, complaining about circumstances, and not learning from missteps. The same holds true for you. You must accept the responsibilities that go along with being a professional artist.

If you want recognition and compensation for your work, you need to stick your neck out and start telling people about your art. You have to put yourself out there! Stop making excuses and start cultivating collectors for your art. On one or more occasion, my students, subscribers, clients, and workshop participants have been exposed to my favorite quote.

> *Behold the turtle.*
> *He makes progress*
> *only when he sticks his neck out.*
> —James Bryant Conant

No doubt you will stick your neck out at various stages in your career. You first share your work with friends and family, then with other artists, then with strangers at arts festivals and galleries, and finally with critics and curators. At each stage of your career you need to take a leap of faith and answer difficult questions.

Are you more afraid of failure or success? If you fail, what does that mean? That you can't try again? If you succeed, will the demand for your art be more than you can handle?

What is the worst thing that might happen if you stick your neck out? Can you live with that result and learn from it?

What is the best possible outcome of sticking your neck out? What impact will that have on your life and career?

Given the possible consequences, is it worth sticking your neck out?

Once you decide it's worth sticking your neck out, you are ready to get out of the studio and dive into self-promotion. Note that I used the prefix *self* in the previous sentence. The practice of selling art through intermediaries is rapidly disappearing. Today artists are able to sell directly to patrons. Witness the phenomenal growth of the eBay auction rooms, through which artists reach buyers and collectors in record numbers, and the plethora of online (and offline) co-op galleries. The possibilities can't be ignored. Even artists who sell directly through these relatively new markets should be creating good old-fashioned buzz, which is the thrust of this book. The focus is on communicating about your work—to patrons, curators, critics, gallery dealers, and the general public.

This book can't make you into an art superstar. It can, however, help you make changes in how you approach promoting yourself and your art. When used consistently and with integrity, and when backed up by strong work, the ideas and practices within these pages can have an enormous positive impact on your career by helping you start or maintain the buzz. You want people to be talking about you and your art, but they can't talk about you if they don't know you exist. You should always be around the next corner to remind them of your art.

Principles of No-Excuse Self-Promotion

The first step in self-promotion is to accept and "own" six principles. These principles have become the foundation for my classes, writings, and workshops.

1. You are in charge of your career. You have control over words, prices, artwork, and your image. People will take as much from you as you give them, so guard this power to remain in charge of your destiny. Accept 100% responsibility for your actions and make no excuses.
2. Connections are critical to your success. To succeed, you must make an effort to meet new people and to maintain relationships.

3. Life isn't fair, the art world isn't fair, and no one owes you anything. Building a successful career and reputation is hard work. There are no shortcuts, no easy ways out.
4. If you ignore the latest technology, you'll quickly fall behind.
5. Your artwork doesn't speak for itself. The right language can help you sell your art. Sure, some art sells itself, but have you ever heard of marketing anything without words?
6. No one can promote your work better than you. No one believes in it more than you do. No one wants you to succeed more than you do. Motivation and ambition must start within you. Unless you are working with a coach or business mentor, no one is going to ask you to set goals; no one is going to tell you that you have to make a certain amount of money or achieve a certain level of success in order to be satisfied. You *must* set your own goals.

Need to be reminded of these principles every day? Get the Principles of No-Excuse Self-Promotion poster at IdRatherBeintheStudio.com.

Once you accept and own these principles, you are on your way to no-excuse self-promotion. Now it will be a cinch for you to tackle the sixteen No-Excuse Actions that form the heart of this book.

WHAT DOES IT TAKE?

In order to promote yourself successfully as an artist, you need to possess certain qualities. Self-confidence, the first requirement, is the hardest to attain. Because your art is personal and comes from deep within you, you have to get beyond self-doubts and be prepared to accept criticism and rejection. The other qualities on the list are likely to be easier to come by.

- Loads of self-confidence
- Passion for your work, for sharing it with others, and for art in general

- Emotional support from friends, family, or other artists
- Money—enough to get you through the slow times
- Good language skills
- Initiative, ambition, and determination
- Persistence
- A recognizable style and the talent to make it remarkable
- Good habits, routines, and rituals
- Integrity, reliability, and dependability

WHY ME?

I have the coolest job in the world and it happened quite accidentally. When I left the world of art museums after ten years, I tried to start an art-consulting business. I soon recognized that the artists with whom I had connected in my roles as a museum curator and educator continued coming to me for help and advice. Everyone wanted an agent!

After a little research, I discovered that being an artist agent wasn't in the best interest of the artists. Galleries, curators, and collectors like to deal with and know the artists. A third party only gets in the way. No, I decided the best way to help artists was to teach them skills so they can help themselves. Simultaneously, I was building my own business. What I have learned through experience has been incorporated into my consulting. As I said, this book is not the answer to all of your questions, but it contains solid advice that has already benefited thousands of artists.

HOW TO USE THIS BOOK

Here is how to get the most from these pages.

1. Break the spine. The book is to be used, not worshipped.
2. Read the chapters as needed, freely skipping from one topic to the next. This book is not intended to be read cover to cover, all at once.

3. Whatever you do, though, do not skip Actions 1, 3, 4, 13, and 15. These should be reviewed at least once a year and even more frequently if things are changing rapidly for you.

4. Keep a notebook or journal as you're reading. Better yet, use sticky notes, underline, and write in the margins of sections that speak to you the loudest. Make your book a personal resource.

5. Use the material available to you at IdRatherBeintheStudio.com and in the Resources section at the back of this book.

6. Form an art-marketing salon with like-minded artists, using the book as a guide. For marketing plans and guidance, visit artbizconnection.com.

I hope this book will give you the tools and routines that will make your time out of the studio more enjoyable. I hope you pick and choose the techniques that work for you at this moment in your career—saving the rest for your next step. Above all, I want you to delight in the process of sharing your art with the world. Are you ready to start?

"I'd rather be in the studio!"

I'd Rather Be in the Studio! is the perfect title for this book because I hear that excuse more than any other from artists who are not promoting their work consistently. It's usually uttered with an annoying whine, but only once within my earshot. My subscribers and clients know I won't stand for whining and I won't work with whiners. I am tough when it comes to this topic. In other parts of the book, I'll mention the importance of setting boundaries. "No whining" is just one of the boundaries I've set for my business. Life is too short to work with people full of excuses.

I understand that you would rather be making art than marketing it. Who can blame you? Creating new work and building on your ideas is much more fun than the rest of the stuff you must do for your business. Let me be clear: Your studio time should be your most sacred, nonnegotiable routine. Neglecting your studio is unacceptable. You're an artist and artists make art. Successful artists usually make some kind of art every day. When they're not in the studio, they're thinking about making art, looking at other art, and taking notes. You must work at this level to compete.

After you have set your nonnegotiable studio time, you can decide when you'll get out of the studio, where you'll go, and for how long. This time away from your studio, which feeds your creativity and leads to new connections and opportunities, is also nonnegotiable. No one is going to magically appear in your studio, wave a shimmering wand, and give you the success you want in your art career. *You* have to get out of the studio and make *it* happen.

But what is "it," exactly? What do you want to happen?

Action 1

Define Success
for Yourself

What is it that will get you out of the studio and into marketing mode? What's your vision? What is your definition of success? Do you know what you want to achieve? If you don't, how will you know when you get it? And how will you know what you're supposed to be doing to get it? I can identify with those who prefer to stay in the studio. Life outside can be rough—especially for those who don't know where they're headed.

I talk constantly with artists about achieving success. They know they want it, but most don't know what "it" is. They picture themselves producing artwork, entering exhibits, and trying to sell their work. They hope that something good will come from their efforts, but are not sure what "good" means. They're frustrated by lack of recognition, too little time, and overwhelming obligations. Most of their frustrations, however, stem from the fact that they haven't defined their true ambitions or determined which actions it will take to achieve those ambitions.

Everyone defines success differently. To some, success is producing the perfect sculpture. To others, it might be making $100,000 a year from the sale of their art or seeing their work enter a museum collection. What does your vision of success look like? Define it. Make it uniquely yours. Own it. I encourage you to be specific enough that you can visualize your dream and make it come true.

Whatever you do, don't let someone else define success for you. Remember that the first principle of no-excuse self-promotion is that you're in charge. Only you can decide what it means for you to be successful. Don't accept anyone else's definition.

VISION OF SUCCESS

Use the table below to think about success in the various areas of your life and career. Not all the categories will apply to you, but complete those that do. Define your success in terms of . . .

Production of art (number of artworks you create each month or year or number of hours you spend in the studio each week)	
Quality of artwork (improvement, mastery)	
Exhibition venues	
Teaching venues and opportunities	
Travel	
Home, studio, and environment	
Spirituality	
Health	
Leadership roles	
Published work	
Visits to your website or blog	
Subscribers to your newsletter	
Social media connections	
Sales of your book	
Sales of your art	
Grants received	
Articles by you	
Public or private collections	
Commissions	
Licensing	
Other	

In addition, write in your journal for each of the areas using the format *I will feel successful when.* . . . For example:

I will feel successful when my work appears on the cover of Art in America.
I will feel successful when I am awarded a Pollock-Krasner grant.
I will feel successful when . . .

We work on creating a career vision and habits that will sustain you in the Art Biz Coach Blast Off online class. If you need support in these areas, take a look at the class contents at artbizcoach.com/bo.html.

APPEAR SUCCESSFUL

As you see, success has many different definitions. You have to know how to define it for your personal, professional, emotional, and spiritual life. Only you can decide what it means to you and whether or not you're willing to go after it. It will not happen overnight. In the meantime, you can *appear* more successful than you are by using these four tricks.

1. **Psych yourself up.** People are impressed by an artist who exhibits confidence—not arrogance, but confidence. Feeling confident is the most important thing you can do. If you believe it, you can become it. Start envisioning the success in your future. Write about it, speak about it, tell others, envision it, and make art about it. Listen to self-esteem CDs, read self-esteem books, or repeat a mantra. Do whatever it takes to make you believe. You have to believe before you expect others to buy into your dream.
2. **Dress nicely.** Yes, that's right! Starving artists—or artists who look like they're starving—rarely attract a crowd. Everyone loves a winner. Savvy collectors want to buy art from artists who are going places. If you don't radiate success, how will you attract a following?
3. **Speak kindly about others.** Don't talk out loud about how lousy the festival organizers are (especially in front of potential

customers). Successful people like you don't have time to complain about your lack of recognition or poor sales. You're too busy figuring out your next step. In other words, no whining allowed.

4. **Splurge on your presentation.** Buy the very best paper you can afford for your letterhead and printed matter. Hire the best photographer and Web designer. Your paper and electronic portfolios must stand in for your artwork. They often create the first impression people have about you. They have to be at least as good as your work.

NO-EXCUSE PRINCIPLE

Don't let anyone define success for you. You are in charge. What works for some artists may or may not work for you. It's up to you to forge your own path.

NO-EXCUSE ACTION

Define success for yourself. Look over the list of various areas of your life from the table in this chapter and decide what it means to be successful.

My definition of success is . . .

If after defining success, you still believe you can attain it by staying in the studio all of the time, there's really no reason to read further. However, if you decide you need to get your work out so it is seen by more people, read on! In the next two chapters, I'll help you get organized for success.

"There aren't enough hours in the day to do it all."

Everyone is busy. Everyone has to juggle a personal life, creative time, and work. Every person who has ever made and wanted to sell a product or service has to devote time to marketing and running the business. And we all have only twenty-four hours each day. In case no one has ever told you, I'll break it to you now: *There will never be enough hours in the day, or days in the week, to get everything done. Never. You'll always think of more you want to do.* Your focus should be on setting priorities and boundaries.

The flip side of this universal time limitation is that you are free to set your own schedule. Except for family and other personal obligations you're free to get up when you want, work when you're inspired, run errands or exercise when it's convenient, and take a nap when your eyelids are heavy. Herein lies the irony. It is easy to feel overwhelmed by these choices. It's also easy to get off track and lose focus. Likewise, you can become so consumed in work that you lose balance. It is unacceptable to neglect health, family, friends, and recreation in your eagerness to succeed. You must vigorously maintain the balance that helps your art flourish.

If your business is going to become what you envision it to be, you have to work hard while practicing self-discipline. People who succeed—including artists—do not succeed simply because they are the best at what they do. They do so because they have a combination of passion, commitment, focus, self-confidence, and fortitude. They know how to get things done! In this section, I'll share organizational tips and tricks that have made being self-employed easier for my clients and for me.

Action 2

Organize Your Information
It All Has to Go Somewhere

Staying organized and prepared is a terrific way to save time. If you're constantly disorganized and throwing things together at the last minute, you're wasting valuable time that could be spent making art or cultivating art collectors.

It's convenient to have your office and studio space near one another. If your materials are toxic, your office space should be separate. Otherwise, combining office and studio space should be a goal, as long as there is plenty of room for everything. Setting yourself up in one space prepares you mentally for your art career and allows you to move seamlessly between your roles as artist and entrepreneur.

In this Action, I'll concentrate on how to store and organize information for your marketing efforts.

Getting Organized Empowered Him
Enrolling in your Get Organized course was a big step for me, but it turned out to be very worthwhile. Before I participated in the class, clutter was rampant around my house. Now, I have reclaimed my tabletops. Your class inspired me to go through all

*the piles and either organize or recycle the papers. I created a
new filing system. Currently, my mail and other documents are
read when they arrive and then either placed in a file or
recycled. Every night I now make sure the newspapers and other
items are recycled and counters and desks are neatly organized.
The biggest benefit is my workspace. I feel more exhilarated in
the morning when I come down to my office, which is now
much more inspirational.*—Bruce H. Morrison, Short Hills, NJ

CHOOSING (AND USING) A DATABASE SOFTWARE

As an artist, you need to maintain a great deal of information: sales
records, inventory, photographs of your artwork, patrons, and potential
collectors. A computerized database will help you quickly locate information without having to sort through pages or to alphabetize records
constantly. With coded entries, you will be able to send mailings to the
appropriate people or specific places on your contact list. For example,
you might not always want to send a newsletter to a gallery or curator.
Or you might want to locate contacts in a certain geographical region.
Both of these tasks can be accomplished if you have a coded database.
For the first situation, you can easily send to certain recipients by
pulling up your newsletter list with a single checkbox. For the second,
you can do a simple search of states, provinces, or zip codes rather than
wading through a box of index cards or a notebook filled with chicken
scratches.

There are several database options to keep track of all your contacts. Since my museum days, I have been a big fan of the FileMaker
database because it's flexible. However, this flexibility means it must be
formatted. If you have the time to do that and if you think you could
use it for other aspects of your life in addition to your art, FileMaker
might be a good choice. You can read about it at filemaker.com. My
numerous self-formatted FileMaker databases include ones for blog
entries, newsletters, personal and business mailing lists, and artist
quotes—all from one piece of software. If you don't want to spend
hours and hours developing your own system, you can invest in a

ready-to-use program designed specifically for artists. All you have to do is plug in your information. I've included a list of software options in the Resources section. Most of these options can handle every aspect of your art business except the detailed financial reports that a program like QuickBooks can provide.

As you consider the options, plan for the future before purchasing a database. Develop a list of everything you need in a software program at this time and then think beyond the present. What might you need in the next year or two? Will you ever need to use the data in another program? Can you easily import records from a program like Excel? If you upgrade to a more comprehensive software program in a couple of years, what kind of work will be required to switch over? What difficulties will you encounter? Only you can decide what is the best solution. Try them all out! The extra effort to get a program that you will be satisfied with for years to come will be time well spent.

YOUR CONTACT LIST

Your contact list is your most valuable tool for cultivating collectors. Let me say that again: Your contact list is your most valuable tool for cultivating collectors. It's your #1 asset. You will work hard to create your list and it will work even harder for you. Once you have your software in place, you can begin to build your contact list.

In the simplest terms, a contact list includes names and information for people you know or might like to know. For the artist, a contact list usually begins with friends and family, and then expands to buyers, potential buyers, arts writers, art consultants, gallerists, and curators. Use your contact list to keep these people informed of your goings-on. Your contact list is something unique to you and your career. No one has this same list. Nobody! It is the primary tool you use to share your art with the world. As you'll discover in Action 13, sharing in a sincere way is much easier and much more effective than trying to sell.

The artist's contact list holds brick-and-mortar addresses along with email addresses and phone numbers. You need all three types of information in order to keep your name in front of people and to conduct critical follow-up. But your list might also store Facebook business pages, Twitter names, and other social media data.

Think of your contact list like an old paper address book. (Remember those?) Your contact list is simply a place to store names and contact information for safekeeping. Just because you have someone's email address doesn't mean it's okay to add them to a list to receive bulk newsletters and blasts. It isn't at all appropriate to do that. You're keeping their information for possible future use and personal contact.

Bottom line: Your contact list stores potential. It's current—with all data in one place when you need it.

Your contact list should:

1. Be easy to access at a moment's notice. A computerized database gives you this advantage.
2. Contain about 150 names at the bare minimum. That's how many people you probably already know and everyone you know should be on your list. I'll talk more about building your mailing list in Action 13.
3. Be updated regularly. The frequency of your updates depends on how many new people you meet and how much activity you generate. I update mine weekly, although monthly or quarterly updates are probably sufficient for many artists.
4. Be used. Your mailing list is worthless if it's not used! You can send out email messages once a month and send print items by mail three or four times a year. If you don't continue putting your name in front of people, you are likely to be forgotten.

The self-promotion efforts outlined in the rest of the book depend on the strong foundation of your mailing list. Try building a business without that foundation.

I'm often asked if it's okay to buy mailing lists. Sure, it's okay, but it will be like throwing money out the window and hoping it lands in your bank account. No purchased mailing list can take the place of building your own list. Your career is unique: no one makes art like you do; no one knows the same people as you do; and no one has the exact same vision as you do. Your mailing list will reflect all of these. Replete with people you know, have met, or have some connection to, your contact list is almost worthless to anyone else, yet it's invaluable to you.

Don't let the fact that I said you should have no fewer than 150 people on your list stand in your way of getting started. You have to begin somewhere—and that might mean your list has only 30 entries at first. You might add 20 names each week. Keep that pace up and, before you know it . . . presto! Two hundred names! After you have finished reading this book, you'll see how easy it will be to double that number. With practice, you will devise methods of getting the most out of your contact list.

When you design your database, you may find it useful to record information that will help you personalize your relationship with patrons. You can record which works of yours people own, which other artists' works they collect, and whether they have expressed an interest in a certain piece or style of yours. You can also record the mailings you have sent them (and which ones you sent holiday cards to), the community committees they serve on, and where they work. If you think that some individuals might become key collectors of your art, keep track of their family members' names, birthdays, and so on, so that you can personalize your correspondence and conversations later. Very few artists (or businesspeople, for that matter) keep records of this nature. You will stand out in the crowd because you have gone to the trouble of getting to know them.

In order to make it easier to update your list, create a paper file labeled "Contact List" and keep it handy in your file cabinet. Put all business cards and names you gather in this paper file. Make a note on your calendar to update your list on a regular basis. Then do it. Enter all new contacts from the paper file to your database. If you update your list regularly, the task will seem less overwhelming and more efficient than sorting through a pile of business cards and scraps of paper just before an important mailing.

STORING YOUR INFORMATION ELECTRONICALLY

Now that you have started your contact list—your most valuable self-promotion asset—focus attention on how you can also store other information electronically. Think of your computer storage as if it were a filing cabinet. You open a drawer, look at alphabetically organized files, pull out the one you need, and find the document you're looking for.

On your computer, you have a folder called "My Documents" or "Documents". You can create an infinite number of levels of folders in this larger folder. As the diagram below indicates, a folder called "Business" contains a file called "Contracts," which contains a document called "Standard Gallery Contract."

   📁 *Business* → 🗂 *Contracts* → 🗎 *Standard Gallery Contract*

The same "Business" folder can contain another file called "Correspondence," which includes a document called "Grant Cover Letter."

   📁 *Business* → 🗂 *Correspondence* → 🗎 *Grant Cover Letter*

Of course, this sort of "filing system" can go on and on. Digital images on your computer might be organized in a similar manner. In your folder of "Images of Paintings," you can create a file called "Still Lifes," in which you have a subfolder named "Apple and Pear"—the title of one of your paintings. In that subfolder, you have digital images of that work at various resolutions and distinguished by a number of details.

   📁 *Images of Paintings* →
     🗂 *Still Lifes* →
       📁 *Apple and Pear* →
            ☐ *appleandpear–300ppi.jpg*
            ☐ *appleandpear–300ppi.dtl.jpg*
            ☐ *appleandpear–150ppi.jpg*
            ☐ *appleandpear–72ppi.jpg*

Keep as much as you can in digital format in order to cut down on bulky paper and make it easier to retrieve data by searching your computer for titles and keywords. Just remember to have a reliable backup system in place and to use it frequently. Streamline your data by using consistent filing categories.

INVENTORY YOUR ARTWORK

I have an instructional story to share with you. I met with an elderly man (I'll call him Mr. Smith) whose wife had Alzheimer's. She had been a painter and was now in a nursing home. He was interested in selling off her works. It wasn't money he was after. He was simply trying to find nice homes for the paintings.

Mr. Smith showed me his wife's résumé along with slides (unlabeled) of her work. Her résumé revealed that she had exhibited in a variety of annual shows in her home state, but no dates were given. Mr. Smith wanted me to estimate a value for the paintings so that he could price them. I don't appraise artwork, but I often talk with artists about pricing their art and could have worked with him on that. However . . .

Mr. and Mrs. Smith may indeed have had many more records, but they were probably packed away without much order and it would have required a great deal of effort to get to them. It was effort he didn't seem willing to make. Without dates and sales records, it was difficult to devise a fair pricing scale.

There are three lessons to be learned from this story.

1. Keep a meticulous inventory of your art. If you don't have an updated inventory list, it's hard to tell what you have available. No one—not even you—would be able to tell quickly what titles you have, what the works are, what the dimensions are, and which works have sold.

2. Track your sales record. If you don't keep track of dates and prove that your reputation has grown and sales have increased, there is no reason to believe that your works would have gone up in value. (Try telling the IRS that you don't know where things are or what happened to them.)

3. Don't leave the dirty work for someone else to tackle when you're gone.

Keep this story in mind whenever you question spending time inventorying your artwork. If you're just starting out, keeping an inventory may seem like overkill. As your career blossoms, you'll be thrilled you set up systems to grow with you.

Categories for Your Inventory

Consider these categories for your inventory records, adapting to your specific needs.

Name of artist. Presumably you are the creator of all the works in your database, but add the names of any collaborators.

Title. Titling your works (1) differentiates them from one another; (2) makes it easier for others, such as critics, to identify them and to write about them; (3) helps people relate better to your subject matter or intent by giving them clues; and (4) allows search engines to find your subjects when they're online.

Location. Exactly where each item in your inventory can be found at any given moment.

Images of artwork. Just imagine printing off an information sheet for someone interested in one of your pieces. With the image on there, it will look like it's straight from a catalog.

Date. Keep track of the date you complete your work and make note of it on the artwork.

Foundry. Record the location of the casting and with whom you worked.

Print shop. If you work with a master printer, log that information.

Support. Is it on canvas? Board? Paper?

Primer. What did you use to prepare your surface?

Medium. Be specific. Someday a curator or conservator will come to you and ask you how to conserve one of your artworks. You should be able to exactly describe the medium you used so that the work is cared for properly.

Technique. For some mediums, this category will be more important than for others. A fiber artist, for instance, might note "hand-appliquéd, machine-quilted."

Varnish / Patina. Again, be precise.

Size. Art is always listed as height by width by depth in inches or centimeters (never width by height by depth). Keep a record of size both with and without the frame.

Sales price. Your sales price is always listed as the retail price.

Frame. Description and size. Note framer if other than you.

Materials cost. This category should be included since you need to keep track of it for tax and pricing purposes.

Provenance. The provenance of an artwork is its history. It includes when and where it was exhibited and who has owned it (in some cases, there may be a sequence of owners). Provenance is invaluable when determining ownership of disputed works of art.

Image availability. What images, views and details do you have of this artwork?

Related notes or stories about the work. Notes or accounts of the work will be impressive and be equally informative when you print it out next to the image in the same database.

CREATING AND KEEPING PAPER FILES

As I said earlier, life is somewhat easier if your paper and electronic files are set up in the same manner. It's a snap to create paper files. You don't even need to have a filing cabinet. You can begin by using file boxes or discarded liquor boxes, but I highly suggest that whatever you use is attractive. An aesthetically pleasing office area will make the work less of a chore.

If you already have a paper filing system, set aside time to clean it out once a year. Reorganize, combine, and discard. Throw out all extra copies of items (unless the documents are ones you give out often) and newspapers, as newsprint is not archival. Make excellent photocopies of the articles to keep on file and then discard the newspaper or at least keep it away from your files. Don't be stingy with files. Make as many categories as you need in order to find things quickly.

> Organizing expert Liz Davenport has one of the best secrets I've ever heard for creating order out of chaos. Rather than trying to find a place for every item that reaches her desk or mailbox, the first question she asks herself is "How can I get rid of this?" See orderfromchaos.com.

Get a labeling machine for your files. I confess that a label machine was the last thing I wanted to spend money on, but I would never do without one again. I started using one after reading David Allen's *Getting Things Done*, a book I highly recommend. Allen notes that having attractive files makes you think differently about getting and staying organized. The way your files look affects how you feel about working with them.

A Menu of Filing Categories

The categories you use for both electronic and paper filing will vary depending on the media you use and your career goals. What follows is a list of options for your categories.

Business / Legal

Bank Statements

Business Equipment

Contracts—For commissioned work, galleries, etc.

Copyrights & Trademarks (or Intellectual Property)

Correspondence

Expenses—Bills, materials, mileage, travel, etc. Filing according to the line item on Schedule C for the IRS will make it much easier at tax time.

Credit Cards

Goals

Insurance

Legal Issues

Licensing

Original Forms & Documents—Documents you use repeatedly: model release, copyright retention, prices, how to take care of art; also your artist statement (see more below), résumé, articles, and other items that are in your portfolio. Keep *originals*, items you might need to photocopy, in this file.

Receipts

Taxes

Warranties & Owners' Manuals

Website & Blog Hosting

Art

Articles About Me—Remember that newspaper is not archival. Photocopy newspaper articles and keep the copies in your files away from newspaper.

Artist Organizations & Communities

Artist Statement

Caring for Art

General Articles—You might be interested in keeping files of inspirational art or artists. You can categorize by style, medium, location, or date.

Ideas—Things you would like to do if you had the time, such as write an article.

Materials & Techniques

Newsletter—Items you want to include in your next newsletter or good examples from other artists.

Philosophy

Résumé & Bio—Record your accomplishments before you file them elsewhere so that you remember to add them to your résumé.

Teaching

Wish List—Art books, special materials, etc.

Workshops

Marketing / Publicity

Blog

Festivals

Galleries

Leads & Hot Prospects—It's a good idea to keep this file on top of your desk and follow up on leads immediately.

Mailing List

Marketing & P.R. Articles

Media Contacts

Media Releases

People I Should Know

Photography—Information on people who photograph fine art, costs, and articles on doing it yourself.

Public Speaking

Venues

Website Ideas

Website Projects

Sales

Articles on Sales & Selling

Inventory & Price Lists

Receipts for Sales of Artwork

If you're overwhelmed by organizing your art business, check out the Art Biz Coach Get Organized online class for artists at: artbizcoach.com/go.html.

NO-EXCUSE PRINCIPLE

You won't do an effective job of promoting your art and maintaining critical relationships if your records are a mess. Spend time on what's most important, not on looking for stuff.

NO-EXCUSE ACTION

Whatever else you do, get your contact list up and going. Make it your #1 priority.

Action 3

Live with Routines
to Free Your Creative Mind

As a creative soul, you are moved by inspiration. An idea strikes and you quickly lose concern for everything else in the world. You're in the flow. But, wait! What about all of the other things that need to be done? When will you get to them? As we've already noted, there will never be enough time to do it all. Part of being a creative soul is structuring your life to make the most of each precious minute.

In her book *The Creative Habit*, renowned choreographer and author Twyla Tharp makes a case for embracing routine as part of a creative life. If you structure your life around routines, your mind will be free to respond to your creative inspiration. When you have set yourself a specific routine, all of the pieces of your life fit together to make you whole and to make you a better artist. Conversely, when you are worried about having time to do something or you try to fit something (say, exercise) into an already busy schedule, you're using energy that should be spent on your art.

As an artist, your routine might include cleaning your brushes thoroughly at the end of each studio session or reading your favorite art magazine the minute it lands in your mailbox. One of my favorite routines is getting dressed and completely ready for the day before I enter the office, answer a phone, or check email. This type of routine can be significant for most people; it helps them feel like they're running a business. If you don't shower, brush your teeth, put on your makeup, do your hair, and get dressed, you might feel as if you've never left your bed. It's purely psychological, of course, but not getting dressed and ready for your day might lead to additional excuses for not doing what you might otherwise do: "I can't go to the bank because I'm not dressed"; "I can't meet for coffee because I don't have my makeup on." As we know, we're trying to overcome excuses, not make up more.

PREPARE TO IMPLEMENT ROUTINES

An effective routine is built on knowing *what* you have to do and *when* you have to do the things you know you *have* to do! Here are some ideas to help you implement your routines and free your creative mind.

Get Straight with Your Task List

Chances are that you already keep a "To Do" list. Maybe it's in a notebook. Maybe it's on a scrap of paper. Or maybe you keep it in your computer. It really doesn't matter as long as you have one and only one task list. It's hard to get things done when you have three or four lists and have to check all of them. If all your tasks are on one list, you can more easily assess your priorities.

After years of writing my tasks on paper, I adopted a system taught to me by productivity expert Leslie Shreve <productiveday.com>, which is part of her Productive Day Success System™. I put all of my tasks (personal and business) in my Apple Mail To Dos. Because this is a digital list, I can change do/due dates, alter text easily, and repeat the tasks. Tasks can be scheduled far in advance so that nothing in the future is forgotten.

The biggest benefit of the electronic task list is the ability to change it as your priorities change. This is cumbersome with a paper task list.

By putting everything you need to do on your list, you can look at each item and decide what needs immediate attention. Get rid of the unnecessary items on your list. As you look at your list each morning or night, ask yourself if you really need to do each task on your list or if you should focus your energies elsewhere. If something stays on your list for too long, you must question whether it's really necessary.

Learning what to tackle first is one of the hardest things to do. But if you review your task list, you'll recognize the most critical item. It's usually the one thing that will have the biggest positive impact on your career. Identifying this action doesn't mean you can't do anything else. It just means you can't afford to ignore it. It won't go away.

Honor the process of maintaining your task list. This action allows you to prioritize what you do and focus on what is most important at any given moment.

Let Technology Be Your Assistant

Use your computer calendar or smart phone to set reminders for your appointments and tasks. These technologies are a good reason for keeping your calendar on the computer rather than on paper. You can use them to prompt you to follow up with a potential customer or gallery or just to jog your memory for an upcoming appointment. I'll elaborate on this idea in Action 11.

Stay Focused

Once you have your tasks listed, stay on track by reviewing your schedule every evening for the following day. This simple act is probably the single most important thing I do to help me maintain clarity. It has worked for a number of my clients as well. Try it. Verify your appointments and decide how you will use the remaining time in the day. You will have a peaceful night's sleep and a more productive schedule the next day.

Trick Yourself into Tackling Tasks You're Avoiding

Attention all procrastinators! What chores, tasks, or jobs do you find yourself putting off or ignoring altogether? What do you dread so much that you neglect?

Making follow-up calls?
Writing thank-you notes?

Updating your mailing list?
Overhauling your inventory?
Cleaning your studio or office?
Balancing your books?
Researching your next series?
Dare I say it, creating art?

So, what is it? What task are you loath to tackle? After you identify *it,* trick yourself into completing *it* and getting *it* off your mind. Here are some techniques that have worked for me.

- **Take baby steps.** "Clean office by Thanksgiving" might be overwhelming. But you may be able to commit to these smaller steps: recycle ten things each day; organize drawers; buy new files; or touch each piece of paper in a stack only one time until it finds a new home.
- **Block out time on your calendar.** Having a vague idea that you need to get something done is one thing. Creating time and space for it is quite different. It's a commitment that you make to yourself.
- **Set your timer**. This technique is my favorite. If you promise to do something for just 15 or 30 minutes, you can make a game of it. It's amazing how hard you work to beat the clock before it runs out. It also generates a certain amount of momentum, so allow yourself the flexibility of going on after the timer buzzes.
- **Get out.** Sometimes I get past procrastination by putting myself in another environment. Plop down at a coffee shop to write your thank-you notes. Visit the library to research your next series instead of staying at your computer. Go to another room in the house to work on your statement.

After you have tricked yourself, treat yourself. Sure, you will always have other things remaining on your list, but bask in your small victories. Treat yourself to a new paintbrush or indulge in a manicure, an afternoon at the gym, or, my personal favorite, chocolate.

Keep Clutter Out

Clutter in your studio and office leads to clutter in your mind! Clutter drains your energy because it is always there to remind you of things you haven't done. If you're like me, you don't like to be reminded of things you haven't done! You should look forward to spending time in your office. As a visual artist, you undoubtedly respond to beautiful things, so you should have lovely surroundings when you work, whether it is less clutter, a fresh coat of paint, a plant, a work of art, or a wall of inspiration.

A ROUTINE FOR MARKETING

Although routine should be a critical part of all aspects of your life and art, I'm mostly concerned with your marketing routine. A solid commitment to regular marketing actions seems particularly important for the artist who would much rather dive headfirst off a cliff than do anything related to self-promotion.

Your marketing routine might include variations of the following activities.

- Review goals
- Post blog entry
- Comment on five other blogs
- Read art books and magazines for two hours at the library
- Read one motivational book
- Read one business book or magazine
- Read art columns in local papers
- Watch one art video
- Send email messages to five contacts just to stay in touch
- Update status on Facebook and Linkedin
- Write in your journal for 15 minutes
- Send five handwritten note cards with your art on the front
- Visit museums and galleries to nurture your creativity
- Attend two art openings
- Go to one networking event

- Have coffee or lunch with one artist or business contact
- Visit a nearby city for one day of gallery hopping
- Update your mailing list
- Check out five new galleries online
- Send two tweets a day on Twitter
- Have artwork photographed
- Send newsletter
- Call to check in with galleries or retail outlets
- Send media releases
- Update website
- Recommend a connection on Linkedin

Most of the above activities will be explained in more detail later in the book. How do these items fit into your current routine? What do you need to add to feel like you're doing a more thorough or well-rounded job? What do you have to do daily, weekly, monthly, or quarterly? Devise your own list and change the quota to reflect your goals.

In order to promote myself effectively, I need to do these things each day:

In order to promote myself effectively, I need to do these things each week:

In order to promote myself effectively, I need to do these things each month:

In order to promote myself effectively, I need to do these things each quarter:

Resist the temptation to make your list very long. As I said previously, there will never be enough time. You have to prioritize and make time for what is most important to you. Your must-do list should be reserved for things that are absolutely critical to your career.

In his wonderful motivational book *The Success Principles*®, Jack Canfield describes his 23rd principle: "Practice the Rule of 5." Just after the publication of *Chicken Soup for the Soul®*, Canfield and his co-author, Mark Victor Hansen, committed to accomplishing five specific things each and every day that moved them toward their goal of making the book a best seller. Think about the progress you could make if you implemented their Rule of 5. On one day, your list might look like the one below.

> *Send one follow-up note*
> *Post blog entry*
> *Write press release*
> *Give business card to one person*
> *Update Facebook fan page status*

There! Five things you've done to move your art career forward. See how easy it can be?

Put your routine in writing with the Self-Promotion Routines Planner at IdRatherBeintheStudio.com.

NO-EXCUSE PRINCIPLE

Building your art career is hard work. It takes discipline and dedication. Taking control of your time is taking control of your career and your life.

NO-EXCUSE ACTION

Commit to at least three solid routines for the next 30 days in order to make them stick.

"My art speaks for itself."

Your art has never spoken for itself. You might have thought it did, but art (perhaps yours) has always been written about, scrutinized, and categorized by others: arts writers, critics, gallery dealers, and curators. On occasion, you might find what others say about your art is to your liking, but more than likely you will wish you had found the words for yourself in the first place.

You can do more than simply react to what others say about your art. You do not have to feel frustrated because what others say is not what you want to hear or what you want your audience to hear. You do not have to clam up because it seems as if no one is listening. You do not have to be on the defensive, needing to respond to the person with the ball instead of calling the plays. You can choose to be on the offense.

Forgive the sports analogy, but it would be better if you had started the play. It would be best if viewers respond to your art as you had intended. Language—both written and spoken—can do this for you. You can have control of the ball from the start by speaking and writing about your art. Communicating about your art begins with your artist statement.

Perhaps you *have been* communicating about your art, but you lost control of the ball during the game. Perhaps you did not receive the response you would have liked. You can reverse the situation by assessing your plays—much like sports teams do after every game. They talk about what went right and what went wrong, they watch tapes over and over again, and then they change the playbook. They want to win and they'll do everything possible to improve their plan before the next game.

Assess your play by asking yourself these questions.

What can I say or do differently to get a more acceptable response?

What can I add to what I am saying? What should I omit?

Does my appearance and body language (smile, eye contact, gestures) work for or against me?

Do I emit confidence in everything I say and do?

After you've assessed your situation, change your playbook where necessary. Your artwork is your creation, but you can't let it down. You have to back it up—even enhance it—with spoken and written words. In your efforts to support it, try not to become too attached to the words you use; there's almost always room for improvement, so vary your approach. Communicating about your art is a never-ending process that begins with your artist statement.

Action 4

Differentiate Yourself

The Power of Your Artist Statement

The pensive and deliberate process of writing your artist statement can be a boon to your promotional efforts. Once you take the time to get to know your work better and learn to articulate more clearly, you'll find many uses for the language in all of your promotional materials. Writing your statement is the first step in marketing your art.

As you will soon realize, if you haven't already, your artist statement will be requested by everyone from gallery dealers to show promoters to curators. But what *is* an artist statement? In truth, there is no strict definition—and there are no exact guidelines for an artist statement. I suppose it would be a lot easier if there were a standard statement format, but there isn't. Within the art community, there are a multitude of ideas and beliefs about what a statement should look like. I have my own biases, reflected in the guidelines that follow.

YOUR STATEMENT IS . . .

Your statement has the potential to be one of your strongest promotional tools. It is the backbone of your promotions because it's all about your art. It's your chance to guide the perception of your work. It makes little sense to hang a show, send out a press release, or apply for a grant before you develop a meaningful statement. Why should viewers spend time trying to connect with your art if you haven't spent time trying to understand it for yourself?

In general, your statement is about the current direction of your work. You want readers to focus on the future and where you're headed, not how you got there.

A well-written statement empowers you. It helps you define yourself before others do it for you. It gives you back the ball and has you playing offense instead of defense.

Above all, your statement should compel readers to look at your art. If it doesn't do that, it hasn't done its job.

If you're like most artists, you despise writing your statement. In my experience, most artists are unhappy with their statements and most statements fail simply because artists rush through the process. I suspect you dislike the process so much that you procrastinate. Finally, with a deadline looming, you throw something together in preparation for an exhibit or entry; you don't spend any more time on it than absolutely necessary. Very little good can come of this approach.

It's difficult to stand back from your art and to think about it objectively. Your art comes from your soul. It's a challenge to put it into words. The process from which it evolves is complicated and words describing it rarely flow easily. I understand that you would much rather be making art than talking or writing about it. Just know that you are not alone. Many, many artists are in the same situation, but that's no excuse to blow off writing your statement. In fact, maybe you should think of it as an opportunity to excel where others are slacking.

You must (*must!*) make time to write your statement. It will not be any good if you don't work at it. You certainly wouldn't expect your art to improve if you didn't work at it. Language skills are no different. View your artist statement as an opportunity that should not be wasted. It's free. It costs you absolutely nothing to communicate these ideas to your viewers.

His New Statement Worked Wonders

I applied to a member gallery some months ago and was denied admission. At that time I submitted slides, résumé, and my old artist statement. A couple of months later I was part of a group show and one of their members saw my work and suggested that I apply. I advised her that I had and was rejected. She suggested I reapply and I did.

I submitted the same slides, résumé, biography and the new artist statement you helped me with. Well, I was accepted. I could only conclude that, since the submission was the same and that the artist statement was the only thing that changed, it was the statement that impacted on my acceptance. My first group exhibit with them is next month in New York's SoHo district.—Hank Rondina <hankrondina.com>

GENERAL GUIDELINES FOR YOUR STATEMENT

Write in the first person. It is a statement, after all. It comes from your lips (or pen or keyboard).

Keep it short. Stick to two paragraphs at most. Sometimes, a single paragraph will do. Always, always, always aim for brevity. If you decide to create a statement that is longer than two paragraphs, be sure that every word adds to your message. If not, leave it out.

Consider writing your statement as an opportunity to clarify your thoughts—for yourself and for others. You're too close to your work to mine a deeper meaning without a lot of effort. You might not even think twice about something that seems interesting to other people. A neutral party can help with the process. (See the Conversations exercise below.)

Stick to the current direction of your work. Let me emphasize that. Your statement should reflect your *current direction*, particularly what is unique about the methods and materials you use. Do not include anything about your influences or past lives. Just talk about where you're going and what you want viewers to take away. Any mention of other names will cause readers' minds to wander to someone else besides you.

Allow your statement to be organic. It should grow, change, and mature along with your work. Don't let it sit on a shelf and collect dust. Don't labor so much that you think you have the perfect statement and never need to look at it again. You shouldn't be afraid to change it and make it better.

Think of your statement as a connecting device—something that connects viewers' experiences with your art. Above all, it should compel viewers to look back at your work. This is the litmus test for a successful statement. Your statement has failed if people read the words you've written and then go on to the next artist without being intrigued enough to take another look at your work.

Resist including biographical information. Your biography (which is written in the third person) is not the same as your statement (which is written in the first person). They are two different documents. (See Action 6 for more on your biography.)

Avoid quotes from other sources. Use your own words to describe your art to avoid the reader's mind wandering to someone else.

Keep your philosophical dissertation to yourself. Your statement is an opportunity to connect with art viewers. Anything you write that is incomprehensible to the reader creates an unnecessary barrier.

GET READY TO WRITE

I sincerely want to help you find words that will boost your career to a higher level, and I have created a process to do that. And it is a process.

You can't expect the words to flow easily and just so. My suggested method is by no means the only way to go about writing your statement, but it has worked for the vast majority of my clients. If you approach the process with serious effort, you will be greatly rewarded with realizations you didn't even know about your work. Most importantly, the process should instill in you a desire to continue writing about your art and to find new ways to describe it.

Get your tools ready. In order to engage in this process seriously, you should be prepared at all times. You never know when genius will strike, and if you don't capture a thought immediately, it is often gone forever. Best-selling author Mark Victor Hansen said, "Don't think it, ink it."

1. Get a notebook. A writing teacher once advised me to write with a pen on paper rather than on the computer. "The hand," she said, "is closer to the heart." Although my fingers are practically glued to a computer day in and day out, I have benefited greatly from this advice and encourage you to explore the handwritten word as part of your routine. Something magical happens when you physically write things down, focus on your words, and believe in what is on the paper. Use an inexpensive spiral notebook. If you use a notebook that is special and precious, you may be constrained because you don't want to make mistakes. These practice writings are all about making mistakes!

   If a notebook seems too structured, write on scraps of paper as the thoughts arise. Throw the scraps in a shoebox for safekeeping until you are ready to patch them together for your writing.

2. Use a voice recorder to capture thoughts about your art as you are driving, on a walk, or working in the studio. Many artists who don't like to write prefer the voice-capture method as a starting point. I don't think a voice recorder can replace the handwritten word, but it can certainly help you make valuable contributions to your statement.

3. When the above are impractical, carry a small journal or send yourself an email or voicemail from your cell phone. You never know when you'll need to capture a brilliant idea.

4. Use a computer to refine your words. Some people take the time to transfer the content from their handwritten journal entries to a computer. You might find this two-part method helpful because it gives you the opportunity to reconsider word choices as you lay them out in a different format.

START WRITING: EXERCISES TO MAKE YOU THINK

The process of writing your statement—about finding better language for your work—is about discipline. It's about forcing yourself to put together thoughts in a way you might not have previously considered because you now know it's for the advancement of your career. You deserve this!

I have provided a series of thought-provoking prompts and questions that I hope will encourage you to write a great deal in your journal. But before we begin, here are some guidelines for the exercises.

Discover your best time to write, without limiting your writing to that particular time. Write when the mood strikes. Some of your most creative thoughts may come outside of your designated writing time. Go with the moment. That's why you have the notebook, voice recorder, or cell phone with you at all times.

Prepare yourself mentally for your daily writing. If you are hurried or feel pressured because of something else you should be doing, put your writing aside for later in the day. When you are ready to write, light a candle, meditate, or do whatever it takes to open your mind.

Stick with one body of work. If you have two or more very different bodies of artwork, you can repeat these exercises for each one. You might end up with a very general statement that is applicable to all of your work, and then add or subtract sentences for specific purposes.

What you don't want in the end is a statement that is so general it could be applicable to almost any artist's work.

Ignore grammar, facts, and proper punctuation. For now, the focus is on getting ideas down. You are writing for yourself until the very end, at which time you can add, delete, and make corrections. Just keep writing.

Time yourself. The first time through, aim to spend at least 30 minutes responding to each journaling prompt.

Expand on the prompt. The prompts are just to get you started for your writing time. It's up to you to go beyond them. Get as many words down as possible. If you like, go through them again—rewording what you previously wrote or trying something new altogether.

JOURNALING EXERCISES

"The subjects and style I choose are _____ because _____ ."

EXAMPLE: "The subjects I choose are landscapes because I have always wanted to bring nature indoors and to make it a part of my life."

EXAMPLE: "I choose to work as an abstract artist because I have always been intrigued by pattern and color. My interest may have started when my grandmother taught me to quilt when I was a child."

"I am most inspired by _____ ."

EXAMPLE: "I am most inspired by non-art materials that have had a previous life."

As a general rule, do not mention other artists in your statement. You can, however, be inspired by the same things as another artist, so focus your writings on the ideas—not the person who inspired them.

What inspires you to create? The materials you use? The places you see and visit? The people you know and meet? Your emotional state? Other artists' work?

The mark you make on the page? Note that I didn't ask why you create. This question usually elicits a response such as, "I don't know. I just have to make things," which says nothing about your work. I want you to form specific ideas about the act of making art, not generalized phrases that appear in so many statements. What makes you say "I have to make this specific piece of art now"?

How do you begin an artwork? What inspires you to start a piece of art? Is it a drawing? A photograph? A single mark? What is the first step you take in making an artwork?

"I choose my materials because _____ ."

EXAMPLE (rephrased): "I work with fabric because it already exists. Pre-printed and vintage fabrics, unlike a blank canvas, provide a starting point and initial inspiration."

Is your process understood by the majority of people? Or would it be helpful for you to define it somehow? If so, try to find the words for it.

One of the things I learned from talking to museum visitors day after day is that they are often fascinated by the way things are made. Artists sometimes take their crafts for granted. After all, they are routine for you. You forget that not everyone does what you do and very few people understand how you do it. Consider your work as if you were talking about it to someone who knows nothing about art. Do you approach a traditional medium in a unique way? Explaining your approach will help you stand out in a sea of artists. (Use the Conversations exercise that follows to help you with this process.)

"I think viewers are most interested in my _____ ."

EXAMPLE: "I think viewers are most interested in my technique. Most have never seen an etching being made and are fascinated by the acid eating away at the metal and the resulting plate."

What would you like people to say about your art?
Note that I didn't ask what they are already saying about it. I want you to think about what kind of comments and responses you want to receive. It goes back to playing offense. When you understand this, you will know which words to use in your statement. Why wait around for people to respond to your art when you can nurture their responses? A vague statement like "I hope my art brings joy to

those who view it" is unlikely to get the response you desire. Be specific. Write about the aspect of your work that you think might bring joy to viewers.

Are there any emotions you are trying to elicit?

What are the formal qualities (line, shape, color, texture, and so on) you would like people to recognize?

What do you want them to say about your use of materials? Or your subject matter?

What can you write to elicit that response as they read your statement and look back at your work?

EXAMPLE: If you want people to notice use of color in your work, you might write "I challenge myself by first selecting two colors that don't seem to go together. Then I add other elements and manipulate them with the original two colors until the composition is harmonious." Viewers who read that statement will look back at your art to try to figure out which two colors you started with, which is exactly what you want them to do.

Experiment with descriptive language. Use words that you have not used in the past. Try putting down your thoughts in more than one way.

CONVERSATIONS EXERCISE

The true locus of creativity is not the genetic process prior to the work but the work itself as it lives in the experience of the beholder.

—Monroe Beardsley

Viewers complete the work. If you want to sell your work . . . if you *really* want to connect with art viewers and collectors . . . don't ever forget them. Viewers won't play a prominent role in the creation of the work, but they will complete the work for you. Your art lives in the minds and memories of so many people whose appreciation or lack thereof is colored by their experiences. Those people bring entirely new meaning to what you do—meaning you probably never even considered. That's powerful stuff!

Because the ultimate goals of self-promotion are to expand your audience, gain more recognition, and/or sell more art, you should realize how valuable the opinions of others can be.

You must acquire a certain level of comfort when talking about your art regardless of whom you are speaking with. I developed the Conversations exercise when I was teaching a university class in aesthetics. My students, who were learning how to teach art and who would be responsible for the art education of a vast number of young people, had never actually sat down and had a one-on-one conversation about art with anyone. I quickly learned that having such a conversation is a valuable process for each and every artist to go through. Artists have told me this is the single most enlightening exercise they completed for their statement. They further admitted that they never would have done it if I hadn't assigned it.

In a nutshell, the Conversations exercise provides a format for you to engage in a discussion about your art with someone (anyone!). It is preferable that the person is not someone who is too close to you; the person should remain objective. The individual needs to provide you with constructive criticism. It is also preferable that, at least on your first attempt, the person is not an art expert and does not know much about how you make art.

The structure for your conversation is up to you. Do you want to invite your guest to your studio or gallery? Meet at a coffee shop and show images? Offer to come to the guest's home?

Rules for the Conversations Exercise

You are the host(ess). The individual is your guest and should be treated as such.

Be organized, prepared, and respectful. You are asking for someone else's time. Value that contribution, and begin and end on time.

Put the other person at ease immediately. Encourage your conversation partner to be totally open and to ask questions. Reiterate: There is no such thing as a stupid question or an incorrect response.

Prepare yourself for criticism and do not allow yourself to become defensive. You are showing your work and exposing your ideas to the public, however private this conversation might seem. Be open to new interpretations. Consider it a learning experience or market research.

Remember: Your guest knows about 150 people. There's no telling when those contacts might come in handy. If your guest likes you and your work, many others may be told about it.

Record the conversation so that you don't have to take notes throughout and can concentrate on the dialogue.

You might begin the conversation (in person or on the phone when you ask the guest to meet you) in this way.

"I have just completed a new body of work and I am trying to describe it so that people can understand it better. It would help me if I could get some feedback from you and I only need about 30 minutes of your time. I am not looking for anything in particular. This is not a test. There are just certain things I forget to talk about when I write about my work. Talking with people who are not 'in' on my creative process is helpful to me."

Ask only open-ended questions. Do not ask questions that require correct answers. You don't want to make your guest uncomfortable.

Ask questions like those that follow to encourage dialogue.

Do you have art in your home? Tell me about it and why you selected it.

(The answer to this question will tell you about their knowledge of and enthusiasm for art. It will also tell you if they seek out art, if they purchase it from people they know, or if they buy it to match the sofa. No answer is better or worse than the others, but the answers ought to help structure follow-up questions.)

What do you find most interesting about my work? What are you attracted to?

What do you find least interesting? Distracting? Puzzling?

What would you like to know about how it was made, framed, and so on?

Does it remind you of anything in your life? Or recall a memory for you?

Is there anything you would like to know about me or my background?

Pay close attention to the answers. Be prepared to ask follow-up questions.

After your meeting, go back to your journal and write what you learned. Listen to the recording you made during your conversation. Did it make you think about anything new? Or perhaps shed light on something not so new? Explore these thoughts in your journal.

I suggest you practice the Conversations exercise on a regular basis. Try it with someone who is knowledgeable about art and then someone who is closer to you. If you do this exercise often enough, you will soon be able to talk about your art with anyone and everyone.

A Simple Meeting Paid Off for Her in Unexpected Ways
The assignment for my artist statement was to meet with and show my paintings to a non-artist in order to get some feedback.

I made an appointment with the two real estate women who had worked with me to sell my house. We had a very invigorating, lighthearted and engaging discussion about my artwork. This dialogue led to an invitation from the women to coordinate a monthly artist reception in their office. Needless to say this meeting opened the doors for more creative marketing possibilities right here in my own community.
—Joann Wells Greenbaum <joannwellsgreenbaum.com>

PUT IT ALL TOGETHER

In the previous exercise, I asked you to write about what you want people to notice, so you should have the answers in hand. Those answers are critical. You must know the response you're seeking from viewers before you put everything together. Otherwise, your goal is unclear. When your goal is unclear, your message is also unclear.

Every word you use in your statement should guide viewers toward a better understanding and appreciation of your art.

You've written a lot, but now you need to go through all of your writings and find out what is best. Admittedly, this part is the hardest. There is no easy way for me to teach you how to write, but I can suggest the following steps.

1. **Start by rereading what you have on paper and circling or highlighting good, meaty thoughts that define who you are and what you're about.** Allow yourself to rewrite or use more colorful language.
2. **Find the best opening sentence you can.** Look for a sentence that will grab your audience. Your choice may not be perfect, but you have to start somewhere—and you can improve it throughout the process. Your opening sentence should make people want to read more, not scratch their heads and wonder what you are talking about.
3. **After you have an opening sentence, fill in the paragraph with additional thoughts you want to convey.** Again, your text doesn't need to be perfect at this point. Simply write a

paragraph that is interesting and coherent. Along the way, remember my General Guidelines for Your Statement.

4. **When you think you have a solid draft, set it aside for a while.** Getting away from it and letting your mind rest are essential for clear, objective thinking.

5. **After several hours, or even a day, look at it again.**

6. **Delete unnecessary words.** Ask yourself which words aren't needed. (Be sure to get rid of words like *really* and *very.*) We all seem to have shorter attention spans than we used to. We like bullet points and appreciate brief email exchanges. Think about your own attention span. Load as much punch into the delivery as you can. Combine sentences and delete ones that aren't vital. Henri Matisse said in his treatise on painting, "All that is not useful to the picture is detrimental." The same could be said of your statement: "All that is not useful in your statement is detrimental to your message."

7. **Explain and simplify.** Decide which words require explanation or simplification. The clearer you are with your word choices and sentence structure, the more quickly people will relate to you and your work.

8. **Add words.** Decide which words are missing that would help define your work for the viewer.

9. **Double-check what you have written against my General Guidelines for Your Statement** found earlier in this Action.

10. **Recall the Conversations exercise from above.** Consider which of your guest's questions and answers will help you refine your writing.

EDIT YOUR STATEMENT DRAFT

Take your one- or two-paragraph statement and look it over. Make sure it is in good form. You can enlist help at this stage, but don't ask anyone to help you until you have done your absolute best by double-checking grammar, punctuation, and spelling. Anything less makes you look lazy and wastes the time of the person trying to do you a favor (unless you're paying for that help, of course). Why should anyone help you if you haven't checked the spelling?

If you are satisfied with your statement, ask a friend to read it and offer an opinion. As with the Conversations exercise, it is preferable to find someone who doesn't know much about art and with whom you haven't talked much about your art. It can be anyone who has never seen what you have written. The aim is to work with someone whose honesty you can count on and whose opinions you value.

Ask your friend's help with any of the following, leaving the remainder to tackle on your own.

Opening. Does your first sentence intrigue and lead to further reading? Or would one of your other sentences be a better opening?

Overuse of personal pronouns. Are there too many "*I*"s, "*me*"s, and "*my*"s? Rewrite sentences to get rid of as many as possible. Restricting the number of personal pronouns will help viewers see themselves in your statement. It's no longer just about you, but about them, too. (Thanks to Harriete Estel Berman for her insight here. I think it's a valid point. See harriete-estel-berman.info.)

Clarity. Is it easy to understand what you're trying to say? Is there a better way to say it? Would changing certain words or phrases make it easier to follow?

Grammar, punctuation, and correct word usage. Not everyone is a grammarian. We can all use as much help as we can get in this area.

Repetition. Have you used the same or similar word too often? Because your statement is short, you should seek variety in your vocabulary.

Redundancy. Have you overly described your work? Beware of lists, which are used too frequently in artist statements and seem a lazy way to get more words on the paper. Example: "I seek morning light that is clear, unfiltered, and bright." *Clear, unfiltered* and *bright* are similar ways to describe the same type of light. A better way to say this might be "The clarity of unfiltered morning light is a favorite starting point for the landscapes."

Focus. Do you stick to the point or do you jump around? Are you trying to cover too much territory?

Purpose. Does your statement lead to a higher appreciation of your art? Or are there questions left unanswered?

The litmus test. Do the words in your statement compel readers to look at your work again and to find out more about you?

Repeat this process with someone who knows more about art than the first reviewer of your statement. It is likely that another person will have a different take on your work than the person who doesn't know much about art. Of course, you want your statement to appeal to both.

For further inspiration and ideas, check out the chapter entitled "Your Creative DNA" in *The Creative Habit* by Twyla Tharp.

As I said before, your statement should be organic. Don't let it sit on a shelf. Use it. Be proud of it. But most of all, don't treat it as sacred. Allow it to grow and change. You wouldn't allow your artwork to stagnate, would you? Likewise, using old words to describe new ideas doesn't make sense. You do your work an injustice when you ignore the language needed to describe and explain it to others.

There are links to good artist statements and more to help you with your statement on IdRatherBeintheStudio.com.

NO-EXCUSE PRINCIPLE

Your artwork doesn't speak for itself. The process of writing your statement will give you the confidence (and words) you need to connect with new audiences as you promote your work in formal and informal situations, as well as through text on your website, blog, applications, and in media releases.

NO-EXCUSE ACTION

Get to know your art. Spend time on your statement, put it away for a while, and then spend more time on it. Learn to love the process of writing just for yourself—before you have to share your thoughts with others.

Action 5

Fill the Rooms
Speak and Teach to Become an Expert

Imagine this scene . . .

Your work is being included in the art museum's biennial exhibition for the state's artists. As part of the programming, the curator asks if you would be willing to give a gallery talk about your art. Do you jump at the chance? Or do you freeze out of fear? My hope is that after reading this chapter, you jump. You dive headfirst! You realize it's an incredible opportunity and embrace it enthusiastically.

If you seek a certain level of success, you must learn to speak to groups of all sizes that want to hear about your art. Perhaps more importantly, you should recognize public speaking as a powerful tool that helps you define yourself and stay in control of your career. It's a natural outgrowth of the process of writing your statement. Once again, your art does not speak for itself.

Public speaking can occur in several types of venues.

Gallery talks occur in a gallery space and are often shorter than a formal talk. You might be asked to comment on your work in an exhibit or other work in the gallery. Guests may be standing, in which case a shorter presentation is better. Gallery talks are usually given in conjunction with an exhibition. In other words, it's a built-in venue—you don't have to seek out an audience. Because gallery talks are predetermined for the most part, I'll be concentrating on two other kinds of talks in this chapter.

Formal talks are usually arranged at a museum or by an organization in your niche market. They most likely last 30 minutes to an hour and include visual aids like slide presentations.

Instructional talks include demonstrations, classes, and workshops. While formal talks can be a form of teaching, teaching art media and techniques in instructional talks is quite different.

She Overcame the Fear of Public Speaking

As a big confession to you, I was terribly nervous about doing gallery talks about my art. However, now that I have done so many, I am actually enjoying public speaking. Somehow, I was able to break through that fear. I have talked to a number of large groups throughout my month-long exhibit and enjoyed every minute. The groups were very attentive and asked great questions. It was a major breakthrough for me. I feel liberated!—Margret E. Short <margretshort.com>

IS ANYBODY LISTENING?

Some time ago, I read an article that encouraged artists to get out in public and speak about their work. The author was thorough in his discussion of planning and organizing artist talks, but he left a giant hole in his argument: He didn't mention the audience. I won't make that mistake.

Public speaking is all about your audience. Below, I'll discuss what you'll say to people and how you'll go about saying it, but let's first look at how you're going to find an audience.

There are at least two ways to go about finding a speaking gig. The first is something like playing darts. Come up with an idea for a talk. Then throw the idea out there in an effort to reach a wide audience. Mention your availability on your website and blog. Send a press release. You might also post flyers at churches, gyms, coffee shops, libraries, and other places that get a mixed crowd.

The second way to find an audience for your artist talk is to make a concentrated effort to approach a specific audience. Contact organizations and groups of people you would like to speak to and with whom you see a good fit with your art. (We'll get to specifics shortly when I cover how to pitch your idea.)

Plan in Advance for Speaking Opportunities

Groups and organizations that engage speakers need time to prepare their newsletters and programs, which usually have strict deadlines. It would not be uncommon for a well-organized group to have speakers lined up at least a year ahead in order to be able to print seasonal schedules. Nevertheless, it is possible for you to find organizations that work on shorter schedules and those who are seeking fill-ins for speakers who have had to cancel.

Once you have a topic, put all of your ideas and planning into a nice package in order to "sell" it to prospective venues. Have these materials available in both print and electronic format.

Contents of Teaching or Speaking Promotional Packet

Cover letter
Description of your presentation
Bio
Photos
List of books you've written
Testimonials
Ideas for how to promote the event
Media clippings
Interview (see "Interview Yourself" under Action 12)
All of the above in appropriate format for a website

(See Action 6 for more help with putting together a promotional packet.)

Now, let's look at some general venues and organizations that schedule a variety of programs, which are different in every community.

- Women's organizations
- Rotary clubs <rotary.org>
- Lions clubs <lionsclubs.org>
- Libraries
- Churches
- Recreational centers
- Business and professional groups
- Brown bag lunch groups (which often meet in botanical gardens, art centers, art museums, history and natural history museums, and zoos)
- Adult and continuing education programs
- Outdoor and environmental organizations

Of course, if you have a niche market, you'll be able to look at even more venues and organizations. Below are three examples of artists whose talks can be targeted to specialized audiences.

The wildlife artist naturally looks to clubs and organizations that focus on the outdoors and hunting, as well as zoos, natural history museums, and maybe even botanical gardens. If your subject is the Bengal tiger, and it just happens to be the Chinese Year of the Tiger, combine the two and instantly double your possible venues by adding Asian centers and more general venues like libraries, schools, and churches.

You don't have to go it alone in looking for an audience. Consider teaming up with a local expert in a discipline that relates to your subject matter. For instance, a zoo curator might give the background of the tiger before or after you talk about painting the tiger. This concept doubles your potential audience as the curator has a set of contacts to invite to the event.

The feminist artist is in luck! Women's organizations are everywhere. Conduct a Web search for women's chambers of commerce, women's support groups, and associations that support women's causes (for example, breast cancer research, equal pay, or reproductive rights).

The landscape artist is usually passionate about the beauty of the environment. Guess what? There are a lot of other people around with a similar enthusiasm for the same landscape. Seek out environmental and ecological groups as well as tourist venues. You might also have luck with local history museums, which seek to preserve and interpret the environs.

Get the idea? Now, think of where you can find an audience.

TEACH TO LEARN, EARN, AND CREATE RAVING FANS

Turn your speaking skills into teaching to become a true expert. There are a number of reasons why you should teach.

Teaching forces you to learn more. You must be current and more efficient when you teach. They say if you want to remember something, repeat it and teach it to someone else right away. In order to be more proficient at your art, teach it to another. In order to be more articulate and confident about your art, teach it to another.

> *I hear, and I forget.*
> *I see, and I remember.*
> *I do, and I understand.*
>
> —Chinese Proverb

Teaching builds your audience. Do you remember how devoted you were (or perhaps still are) to your favorite teachers? A good teacher breeds a flock of eager, loyal students who become raving fans and help spread the word. Before you know it, you're famous and much in demand!

Teaching establishes you as an expert. You become the go-to person in your town, city, region, or niche market. You can't buy advertising that valuable.

Teaching brings in additional income. The main motivator for most artists to teach is the extra money. If you have made a name for yourself, if your price point is right, if you have a unique offering, and if you are able to keep a high percentage of your enrollment fees, you could do very well for yourself.

Of course, not everyone is cut out for teaching. You must be patient, generous, kind, and confident. You must also be organized and willing to promote the heck out of your classes and workshops.

Think about teaching as an extra job. You're going to market your classes and workshops differently than you do your artwork. That means one job is your art and the other is your art teaching. They're not necessarily mutually exclusive, but they have different timelines, schedules, and audiences. Your third job is to make sure your art isn't lost in your teaching. In other words, don't let the teaching consume your long-term dreams, unless teaching itself is the dream. Keep up your art career and be a prime example to your students by continuing to produce and promote your work.

Where do you teach? Teaching encompasses a wide range of formats and, therefore, venues. You can mentor or tutor a small number of students in your home or studio, be a faculty member at an existing institution, demonstrate your technique, or lead workshops and adventures all over the world. There are many teaching venues.

- Colleges and universities (require graduate degrees in art)
- Artist communities and retreats
- Art centers and museums
- Art supply stores
- Schools
- Galleries and co-ops
- Your studio
- Private homes
- Recreation centers
- Empty office spaces
- En plein air

Where do you find students? The last five locations on the above list may require you to do most of the promotion to bring students in, but you should be seeking your own students no matter where you teach. After all, you know the people who are interested in what you do better than anyone else. (We'll discuss promoting your classes shortly.)

The longer you teach, the more rewarding it will be. Like everything else, it's a commitment. Make sure you're cut out for it.

PITCH YOUR IDEAS

If you have decided to make a concerted effort to find an audience for speaking or teaching, do not do it blindly. Behave as businesslike as possible. Research, research, research! Find out about the venues, their members, and their calendars before you contact them. Visit websites, ask people about them, and read articles that reveal what they're up to. After you have narrowed your list, send out postcards, letters, brochures, or emails. Your contact person at the venue will likely have the title of program director or educator, or you may just ask for the name of the person in charge of lectures and classes. Include items from your promotional packet that you think are appropriate. Follow up your mailings with phone calls.

The pitch in your cover letter should have this rhythm.

- *Opening:* Say something nice about the organization and why you want to talk to the group. Schmooze a little.
- *Content:* What can you offer their audience that uniquely qualifies you to speak and gives them an irresistible reason to book you? If you don't expect payment, say so. Funds may be a deciding factor in organizations with little or no budget, and they might appreciate having a speaker who doesn't charge.
- *Closing:* Thank them for their attention. Add that you'll call them in a couple of weeks to see if they are interested.

After you send your material or when you call, be prepared for questions that will come your way for which you'll need answers. The contact person might ask some of these questions.

> *How much is your fee?* (Be prepared to give an amount, even if it is only to cover your transportation. For a public talk, you will probably have to charge nothing or very little, depending on the venue—especially when you're starting out. Instructional talks, however, are another matter. Everyone expects to pay teachers who are seen as experts on a subject—even if it's only a small amount.)
>
> *How long is your talk?*
>
> *What dates are you available?*
>
> *Can you send me your résumé?*
>
> *What type of equipment will you need?*
>
> *Do you have references?*
>
> *Can we videotape your presentation?*

Likewise, you may want some information from the venue.

> *What are possible speaking dates?*
>
> *How much time is allotted for your speakers?*
>
> *Will people be eating while I am speaking? Or would I speak before or after a meal?*
>
> *Is anyone speaking before or after me?*
>
> *Is there also a business agenda for this meeting?*
>
> *Will people be at tables or will the chairs be in rows?*
>
> *What is the setup of the room? Does it allow for PowerPoint presentations (dark enough, electrical outlets, LCD projector)? Can I do a demonstration?*

How many people usually attend your meetings or similar events? What are their backgrounds and interests?

How do you advertise your speakers?

Can you mail to my mailing list?

PREPARE YOUR PRESENTATION

Audiences are used to good and bad speakers. Be one of the good ones. Before you begin to organize your thoughts, ask yourself: "What are the one or two things I want my audience to remember at the end of my talk?" That powerful question should guide your content and clarify what you say. Whatever your answer, it should be stressed at both the beginning and end of your presentation and backed up by content in the middle.

How many times have you sat through talks, lectures, and speeches that had nothing to do with you? When the speaker was just listening to the sound of his or her own voice? Or when the entire presentation was a sales pitch intended to boost the credibility of the speaker? The only times people want to hear all about you are (1) if your story is absolutely captivating and filled with adventure, or (2) if you are famous and being paid handsomely to speak. If you can be captivating with a story that's all about you, by all means do so. Otherwise, you should prepare a talk that relates your work to the interests of the audience. If you can do this, you will shine.

You don't have to use a fancy multimedia production in order to be a hit. In fact most slide presentations are ineffective because people put all of their energies into the slide and nothing into the content and delivery. But because you are scheduled to talk about your visual art, you will need some visual aids. Most people find it easy to put together a PowerPoint (or similar) presentation with slides of their work and any other relevant material—without fancy graphics or distracting text. You will need an LCD projector, which should be provided by the venue. I strongly suggest practicing with the projector or at least a remote control and your computer before your talk. Based on my experience, I further suggest that you arrive at your venue early and test the equipment with plenty of time to spare.

Become adept at using PowerPoint, Keynote, or a similar software program. These are easy to use and much easier to put together than the old slide presentations. Whatever you do, though, don't get caught up in the PowerPoint styles. You don't need all of those fancy graphics and templates. You have your art! Start each slide with a blank page, adding your art so that it is the only design element.

As you plan your talk, write your text, get away from it for a day or two, and then look at it with fresh eyes. This technique works even better if you are part of a group and can have someone else review your talk. You might even find it helpful to use a voice recorder to practice your talks. The spoken word has a much different rhythm than the written word. Therefore, piecing together a talk orally makes more sense for some people. Don't forget to add humor, plan transitions, and figure out how your visuals will fit in. Another good way to include subjects of interest to your audience is to incorporate famous artists—names that they know—into your talk.

Practice your talk out loud. As I said, the written word doesn't always work when read aloud. Rehearsing can make even a speech that is read from a script sound interesting and natural. Practice it again and again. Practice with your visuals. Time it, knowing that when the engagement date arrives you might either speak faster or perhaps interject additional information that makes your talk longer. There is little worse than ill-prepared speakers who do not know their limits. If you don't want to read from a script, you must know your material well and be aware of your timing. Make your host happy and your audience even happier by not being long-winded.

Promote yourself! If you are planning to sell a book, reproductions, note cards, or anything else at the venue, learn how to subtly weave references to those items into your talk. Ditto for an upcoming exhibit of your art or a workshop you're leading. It works!

PROMOTE YOUR PRESENTATION

Speaking of promoting, you're going to have to talk up your talk and get people to come hear you. Unless your presentation is for a members-only group, don't rely on the organization or venue to promote your talk. Plan on doing some promoting of your own.

10 Ways to Promote Your Formal or Instructional Talk

1. Post the time, location, and description of your talk to your website or blog schedule. If teaching is a large part of your career, you might even consider getting a website just for your classes and workshops.
2. Blog about your preparation for the event well in advance. Don't worry about giving away content. Sharing juicy information establishes you as an expert.
3. Create a Facebook Event on your fan page. Target invitations to guests living near your presentation.
4. Start tweeting about your presentation long before the event date. Use Twitter more frequently as the event date gets closer.
5. Create a packet of information for your speaking or teaching. Make it available as both an e-document (sometimes people can't wait to get it!) and a hard copy. Provide juicy descriptions for websites and blogs. Not only does this packet make it easier for your venue to promote your talk, it also gives you more control over the language that is used for getting the word out.
6. Save a special place for teaching announcements in your newsletter.
7. Send enticing email blasts to your list. Ask people to forward the messages to everyone they know who might be interested. (Read more about enticing language in Action 10.)
8. Write a terrific press release and email it to art organizations, institutions, and groups within your niche market. Ask people to forward it. Make sure it gets a listing in the paper and is posted to your online media kit (Actions 10 and 12).

9. Post the event on craigslist.org.
10. Hang up flyers at coffee shops, art schools, art centers, bookstores, and other relevant places. Give stacks of flyers to venues or shops that attract your target audience.

Use all of the other tips in this book to promote your presentations as you do your art. As with all of your marketing messages, say more than "Come hear me speak." Give people a reason to get dressed, get in the car, and drive to hear you talk. What are they going to hear that will be worth their while?

SHOW UP AND DELIVER

Below is a list of basic considerations for your presentations.

- Arrive early. Arrive even earlier if you need to test equipment.
- Set up handouts and sales materials before the audience arrives.
- Meet as many people in the audience as possible before your talk. It's easier to speak to a crowd of friendly faces than to a crowd of anonymous ones.
- Ask someone to take photos of you while you're presenting.
- Be ready for the speaker to introduce you. Stand nearby so you don't have to walk a long way to the stage or podium.
- Start on time.
- Have a clear focus and be organized.
- Respect the mission, needs, and time of the group or organization to which you are speaking.
- Ask engaging questions of your audience. The questions can help put you at ease while making your audience feel like they're involved.
- Use humor to your advantage.
- Plan coherent transitions between the various sections of your talk.
- Call your audience to action. When you conclude, don't forget why you're there: You're there to promote yourself and your

work! Don't be shy. You won't ever get anything until you learn how to ask for it. At the end or in private conversation, add any of these invitations.

> *Please tell all of your friends to come see my show!*
> *I would love it if you could drop by my studio sometime.*
> *Take one of my cards and call me when it's convenient.*
> *Let me know if you belong to other groups who might like*
> *to hear me speak.*
> *If you know of anyone who might be interested in my*
> *work, I would appreciate your telling them about me.*

- End on time.
- Take photos with audience members before everyone leaves. You'll want these pictures for your fan page on Facebook or for your blog.

Finally, follow up. Send thank-you notes to anyone who helped you organize or set up for the event. Write notes to special people in the audience who were interested in your art. Call anyone who wants to visit your studio. Do it soon! (See Action 11 for more on this topic.)

For a more detailed checklist, download the Presentation Organizer at IdRatherBeintheStudio.com.

IMPROVE YOUR PRESENTATION SKILLS

If you enjoy speaking or teaching, or if you just recognize the value these activities add to your career, you'll want to get better. I've provided some ideas to help you improve your skills.

Start evaluating yourself by recording your presentations on film or on audio. It isn't always easy to see or hear yourself speaking, but it is comforting to know your public speaking is a work in progress. You can constantly make improvements and become a better speaker by accepting more and more invitations. In fact, don't just move on to the next speaking engagement. Evaluate, revise, and improve as you go along.

If you really want to be a better speaker, practice, practice, practice. Join a local Toastmasters club to practice your public speaking. Toastmasters stresses technique and style. Because Toastmasters is international, it has groups in many places. If you don't find one near you, you can always form your own group—even one that caters to artists only. See toastmasters.org.

Speaking Circles, based on the book *Be Heard Now!* by Lee Glickstein, appears to be an excellent alternative to Toastmasters for those who fear public speaking or just want to get better. The emphasis in a Speaking Circle is on connecting with everyone in the room—*really* connecting— through eye contact. It's all about being present and authentic rather than being perfect. As we all know, most communication is nonverbal. I think this concept could be a powerful tool for artists who are uncomfortable speaking in public. Read more at speakingcircles.com. Or pick up Glickstein's book, which I believe will change your outlook about speaking.

Study other speakers. Here are a few assignments to get you thinking.

- Go to an artist's talk—formal or informal—and critique it for yourself. Try to be an objective observer and consider presentation and content as well as the art you are shown.
- Attend a non-artist's talk on a subject about which you know next to nothing. The presentation might be at a public library, botanical garden, museum, bookstore, or civic center. Just make sure the talk is not about art. Critique (by taking notes or by observing) the speaker. Was the information presented coherently? Was it interesting? Did it make you want to learn more about the subject? Did the speaker connect with the audience?
- Watch the free videos from the TED conferences. TED speakers are the best, most polished speakers and their presentations are free for all to see at ted.com.

Write about your experiences in your journal. Note what you liked about the speakers and how you could emulate them in your artist's talk. Describe what you did not like about the speakers and how you can avoid similar pitfalls. If you don't write it down soon after you attend the talk, chances are you will forget your points by the time you need them most. One of the most beneficial aspects about being a part of a group like Toastmasters is that you not only receive feedback, you give it. So, you're constantly telling others how they might improve their presentations. You can't help but get better when you do this!

NO-EXCUSE PRINCIPLE

Speaking and teaching spotlight you as the leading advocate for your art. A room full of people means a bigger audience. Those who see and hear you in person are more likely to be raving fans that will help you fill rooms in the future.

NO-EXCUSE ACTION

Conquer your fear or trepidation about public speaking. Don't wait for someone else to say something about your art that you don't like. Speak up now!

"I don't know where to begin."

Artists who utter "I don't know where to begin" usually fall into one of two camps. They either haven't thought through the process of building a business or they (at the other extreme) have conducted a lot of research and are overwhelmed by the amount of work before them. It hasn't escaped my attention that an excuse about where to begin might be better off at the opening of the book instead of introducing Action 6 and Action 7. I've put it here because marketing materials are often the first thing you think of when you begin promoting your art. That's where most artists begin—or don't begin (because they say "I'd rather be in the studio").

These days, you have an entire cadre of tools available for your marketing arsenal. There are traditional printed materials, some of which are also available as electronic items. To them, add the possibilities that exist because of the latest technology and you could spend all of your time producing new marketing materials. I'm not advising you to devote all your days to creating marketing strategies. However, you shouldn't ignore any of the tools available to you. You just have to be selective.

Artists usually start by creating their statements (Action 4, check!), bios, and business cards. After that, the desire for a website takes root and more and more promotional pieces are added as needed. I've broken down the Actions to address your marketing materials into hard "stuff" (items you can hand to people—Action 6) and virtual "stuff" (formats that exist on the Internet—Action 7).

Action 6

Create a Portfolio

That Impresses the Right People

Got stuff?

Every promotional campaign has to have printed and electronic "stuff" that trumpets the message to potential buyers. An artist's promotional efforts are no different. Yes, you have the words, but you also need "stuff" to hand out, post, share, mail, email, and stack.

This chapter describes a number of standard items in the artist's portfolio of marketing materials. Chances are you will eventually end up with most of them as your career progresses. If you have been selling your work for some time, the advice on these pages will help you revamp your materials and message. If you are starting out, you just need to select a few of these. You don't need them all at the beginning of your quest to promote yourself. In fact, I heartily discourage you from spending a lot of money on marketing materials at the outset. I offer this advice because you're going to want to change the materials periodically. As you use them, you'll discover what works, what doesn't, and, I'm afraid, the enormous mistakes you have made. It's hard to justify reprinting if you've spent buckets of money on the first batch. Despite the cost for even a limited array of marketing pieces, you should always have a handsome selection of printed materials of which you can be proud. If you want to know which elements from this Action should be in a portfolio headed for a particular gallery or curator, ask! Be guided by the recipient's preference.

Before you make all kinds of mistakes on your stuff, let's look at the big picture.

POLISH YOUR IMAGE

You have exactly two seconds to make an impression, according to business author Malcolm Gladwell's groundbreaking book *Blink*. And you only get one shot at it. People might give you a second chance, but you'll have to work a lot harder the next time to overcome the judgment already formed about you. Two seconds. What will you do with it?

Everything you do sends a marketing message. Because you represent yourself, you also represent your art, your business, and your career every time you tell someone you're an artist. Your brand is the message—in the broadest sense of the word—that you send out to the world. It's a combination of your art (the most important part), you, marketing materials, and your venue or booth. Each piece of the branding puzzle should transmit the same message on the same frequency. If you're confusing people, you're more than likely losing potential collectors.

When you think of a well-branded artist, you recall a steady style along with consistent, classy marketing materials and messages. Likewise, when your collectors see your work, visit your website or blog, or receive your latest postcard, they should know immediately that they're looking at your work. They shouldn't be thinking of other artists or wondering if they're looking at an array of artists. They should know it's *your* work. They will be able to make this instant connection if you have been consistent with your message. In business terms, this concept is called branding.

If the word "brand" is too commercial for you, I understand. I, too, was first introduced into an art world that doesn't like to talk about commerce and art in the same breath. If thinking about your "brand" doesn't serve you, try thinking of it as style or image. Whatever you call it, you—like everyone who is trying to sell anything in today's crowded art marketplace—need it.

Artists of yore (not too yore ago) didn't have to worry about these things. In fact, there are many artists today who still don't. A gallery dealer nurtured their brands and they've never had to worry much about marketing. Most of us aren't that fortunate. We're trying to stand out not only among other artists but also among the estimated 600 to 3,000 marketing messages that we're exposed to each day. Each DAY!

Today's art buyers are sophisticated and busy. As noted, they're bombarded with visual images and messages. They browse—or even shop—purposefully. If they are not intrigued by what they see or, as is often the case, if they are confused, they'll move on. They know there are other artists out there. They suspect something better is probably right around the corner. Your job is to do everything possible to ensure that doesn't happen. It's up to you to strengthen your image in a way that makes your work memorable and desirable in the eyes of art buyers.

Branding allows you to position yourself in the art market rather than waiting for others to do it for you or overlooking you altogether. It gives you control over how you are perceived. Above all, branding leads to (1) enhanced credibility because it makes you look more professional, and (2) increased recognition because you are easier to pick out of a crowd. Both result in more sales. The more people who know you, the more people there are to buy your art, and the more sales you make.

It doesn't matter so much that you know a lot of people, although that certainly doesn't hurt. What matters is that people know you, like you, and remember you. Branding helps accomplish the knowing and remembering. It's up to you to make sure they like you.

START WITH YOUR ART

In order to have a successful career, you should be able to define yourself and your art in a sea of artists. To do this, you must first find your style. There is no sense worrying about marketing or selling your work on a large scale until you have produced a large body of work of high quality, which looks like you did it.

He Returned to His Art

*Your self-promotion class made me realize the tremendous
number of people out there who are working at their art and
trying to sell. I discovered that, on the whole, artists are an open
and friendly group of folks who respect the unique and unusual.
It also led to the realization that what I see as high quality
artwork and commercially successful art don't necessarily match
up. Probably the most important lesson for me was the
recognition that I have a lot of work to do to improve the work I
produce and to create pieces that I am proud of in sufficient
number to make approaching a gallery worthwhile.*

—Jas Atkinson <aestheticmollusc.com>

When I tell artists they need to focus and build a cohesive body of
work, I often meet resistance that sounds like yet another excuse: "But
I like to do so many different things." (This topic could be the subject
for a whole book.) Yes, you can work in as many styles as you want, but
two very different bodies of work require twice the effort to market
them. For three different bodies of work, you will exert three times the
marketing effort. And so forth. Each body of work that looks like a
different person did it will be marketed to a different audience.

> 3 different styles of art = 3 different audiences =
> 3 times the marketing effort

Style is a word that is often thrown around carelessly. But what does
it mean? We say someone "has style" or so-and-so just got a new hair
"style." If you're an emerging artist, you are no doubt in search of a
style, but how do you know when you find it? In short, your style is a
combination of the mediums, technique, and subject matter you
choose. It's not just that you make contemporary quilts, but what you
do to distinguish your work from that of other artists. Two quilt artists
might each create abstract, colorful compositions using the same traditional block. If both were mature artists, however, we'd probably be
able to tell one artist's work from the other. For example, a fiber artist

might employ one or more of the following attributes in creating the quilt in order to differentiate her work from other fiber artists.

- Hand-dyed fabrics from organic dyes
- Loose threads hanging on the surface (rather than hiding them)
- A particular fabric that becomes a signature of sorts
- Text written with ink on top of the quilt

In other words, the artist becomes *known* for having works that contain a certain characteristic. Spend time developing your artistic style. Nurture it until it becomes your very own—something no one else can lay claim to. In her book *Living With Art,* Rita Gilbert noted: "*Artistic style* is the sum of constant, recurring or coherent traits identified with a certain individual or group." I think this is a good definition. An artist's style is neither good nor bad, it just *is.* The execution might be criticized; the colors might be perceived as ugly; or the composition seen as weak. But the style is what it is.

Picasso had a number of styles, ranging from his Blue and Rose Periods to Cubism to Neo-Classicism; yet everyone who has studied art history can spot a Picasso. Monet's broken brush strokes are slightly different than those of his Impressionist contemporaries, but we often recognize his paintings by the subject matter: haystacks, Rouen Cathedral, and, above all, water lilies. This is what you want from your work: a style to call your own.

Everyone is looking for the next new thing, the next new discovery. And it had better be different from the old thing. We want to be blown away—not just by technique, but also by ideas. You can hammer away all you like against conceptual art, but the fact is that ideas are just as important, if not more so, than technique. What can you do to make your art different from that of other artists? What can you do to stand out in the crowd?

To begin to answer those questions, start with how you make art. Learn to use your materials in a new way. If you are a watercolor artist, your circle can include other watercolor artists, from whom you may learn some new techniques. However, it is important to expand your circle beyond those who work in the same medium. For example, a fiber artist can cause you to look at the world with new eyes. It will improve your "brand" (and your sales) if you become a watercolorist whose work doesn't look like every other watercolorist. As you're learning to use your materials, try combining your medium with other media. Apply your watercolor skills to your own handmade paper. Turn the flat surface into three dimensions and suddenly you're a watercolor-sculptor. Think you're a landscape painter? Try painting with twigs and leaves and things found only in nature—nothing manmade.

Next, look at how you're presenting your art and frame or install your work in an inventive way. I've seen large black-and-white photos hung with only Plexiglas over them and adhered to the wall with what appeared to be giant shiny bolts. I presume the bolts were just for show and weren't really the main means for hanging. In other words, the bolts and Plexiglas were a gimmick that distinguished the work from other photographers who use standard white mats and thin metal or wood frames. Working in three dimensions? Maybe, like Constantin Brancusi, you carve bases for each of your sculptures to ensure they are shown exactly as you had intended.

It might sound a little counterintuitive, but in order to make your work truly remarkable, you have to look at a lot of art. You have to know what's out there before you know how you'll set yourself apart. If you have a niche market, chances are that other artists have also discovered that market. How will your art be different from theirs?

DESIGN

The unique qualities of your art should dictate the image projected in your marketing materials. Whether it's serious and professional or fun and funky, develop a list of two or three words that describe how you want others to perceive you. Memorize those words. Post them where you can see them. Regardless of how many items you use from your marketing arsenal, make sure each one promotes your brand as best it can. Colors, typefaces, and your message should be consistent and reflect your mission. Your name should be spelled and written the same way (if you use a middle initial, use it every time). Any tag line ("Con-temporary Southern Landscapes") should be precisely the same on every promotional piece, whether it's printed or electronic. Always get a second set of eyes—critical eyes that you trust—to proofread for these things. There should be no doubt that you're professional, that you'll be in business for a long time, and that you are going places.

With the advent of desktop publishing, we all think we are graphic designers. I'm guilty of that thought myself! Sometimes I just don't want to spend the money to pay someone else to do it for me. If you can come up with the money or finagle a trade to hire a graphic designer, the results will be well worth it. Visual artists have talent and expertise in their field, but graphic designers know much more about computers and graphics. Graphic designers are also experts in visual communication, which is very different from being proficient in fine art. If you look over several designers' portfolios and talk with satisfied clients, you will find one you can trust with your branding.

You may think your marketing materials are up to snuff, but how do they rate next to what other artists are sending out? Look around. Don't ever forget your competition! Find out what they're up to and what their marketing materials look like.

Up to this point, we've been talking about you and what you want. What about the person on the other end? With each promotional effort, think about and answer this question: *Whom do I want to act on this promotional message? Buyers and collectors? Gallery dealers? The media?* Your marketing message may vary slightly depending on your answer. Just be aware of the subtle differences that might be necessary.

My Rules for Artists' Marketing Materials

I am fully aware that these rules reflect my biases. That's why they're called "my rules" and not "THE rules." They have, however, served my clients well.

- Nothing upstages the art—it must be the focus of attention for all of your marketing material.
- Unless you do cutesy work, don't use a cutesy typeface or logo.

- Develop a standard "look." Use the same typefaces and paper for everything. Use good-quality white or off-white résumé paper for your cover letter, résumé, statement, and biography. Avoid colored paper or paper with a background pattern. Plain white photocopy paper is appropriate for any other paper that goes into your portfolio (for example, image lists and article reprints).
- Splurge on the highest quality photographs of your art. Print color photos on glossy white paper, which makes the images look best. Do not add copyrights or watermarks in the center of your images. Period. It ruins the first impression of them and just isn't appropriate in the fine-art world.
- If you have a good picture of yourself, use it when appropriate. It will help people relate to you.
- Put your name, address, phone number, email address, and URL (website address) on all of your materials. These are the basics. You should also add your social media accounts wherever possible.
- If you're uncomfortable putting your address on printed material, consider getting a post office box. You need a standard address in order to look professional. It demonstrates that you intend to be in business for a while.
- Don't want to share your phone number? Try the free service at Google Voice <google.com/voice>. You can get a phone number that rings on any or all of your other phones or sends you a text message. Daniel Sroka recommends Maxemail <maxemail.com> for a phone number, voicemail, and faxing.
- Give me something I can relate to! Develop good stories about you and your art that can be added to various marketing pieces.
- When you post your prices, do so discreetly. Use a smaller font or lighter text.
- Get a second set of eyes (besides your mother's). Edit! Spell Check! Grammar Check! Cut out everything that is redundant or unnecessary.

Now that you know my rules, we can look at individual items in your marketing arsenal.

RÉSUMÉS

All of your accomplishments should be listed on a master résumé. This document, which an academician would call a curriculum vitae, or CV, is a document that outlines all of your accomplishments from your first public showings at the local coffee shop to art festivals to museum exhibitions. Put it all on there. Why *all* of your accomplishments? Because one day you might want to look back with fond memories of every success and, yes, every bumble. You'll want to see how far you've come. And, when you're famous, curators will want to know. Trust me when I say that curators dive in to the minutiae of artists' careers. It's in their blood from their training as art historians.

I'll admit there are some things in your career that you might not want to be reminded of later in life, but I encourage you not to edit them out of your master résumé. Your job here is simply to record—knowing that no one but you ever has to see this document. Even curators should receive a slightly edited version. For example, curators don't really want to know about each calendar listing that was in your hometown paper.

Here are a few tricks for updating your résumé.

- Add each accomplishment as it occurs.
- If you can't do the above immediately, keep a file folder titled "résumé." Drop in your announcements, articles, honors, and public collections so that everything is in one place when you're ready to update.
- Put a reminder on your calendar to update your résumé at least twice a year.

The most important categories go at the top of your résumé. For most artists, these are exhibitions—in particular, solo exhibitions. A suggested order follows.

1. Solo exhibitions
2. Group exhibitions
3. Public collections
4. Corporate collections
5. Recent publications
6. Grants and honors
7. Lectures / Public speaking engagements
8. Teaching
9. Related activities
10. Education
11. Birthdate

If you are in academia, seeking a teaching position, you would put teaching and education at the top, followed by the rest.

> Make sure your name is in the title of any solo exhibit.
> Your name in the title screams Solo Show!

Tweak Your Résumé

1. Make your résumé easy to read. Use a business-like typeface—nothing decorative or playful.
2. Put everything in reverse chronological order, acknowledging that your most recent accomplishments are your most important.
3. Don't forget dates. I have been astonished to see artists' résumés without dates. Put months and years for your exhibitions, articles, and other accomplishments on your master résumé for your own records. However, the year alone is sufficient for dates on your public résumé.
4. Use accurate exhibition titles. Artists often fail here. Either they didn't title their exhibitions in the first place or they didn't keep track of the titles. Exhibition titles are very important—particularly if you have a number of exhibits at

the same venue. (Titles distinguish one exhibit from another.) Take time to title all of your exhibits. Make sure your name appears in the title of solo exhibits.

5. If you are a fine artist or fine craft artist, opt for the word "exhibit" if possible over the word "show," especially if your work is displayed in gallery spaces and other fine-art venues. It's a classier word that connotes "fine art" rather than a form of entertainment.

6. Do not use the word "Artist" below your name on your résumé. Your résumé will spell out the fact that you're an artist.

7. Private collectors are usually not named on a professional résumé. If your résumé is sparse and you insist on adding private collectors, obtain the collectors' consent. Be especially mindful when adding individual names on your website résumé. When you post information on your website, it's there for all to see. The individual names become an invitation to unscrupulous "visitors" who make note of private homes that house valuable art. Protect your patrons at all costs.

8. If you have only one item under a category, consider grouping it with another. For instance, you might only have one work in a public collection and a couple of awards. Make a heading titled "Honors and Collections" so single entries don't look so lonely.

9. Check your punctuation for consistency. Either use periods at the end of all entries or don't. Use quotation marks or italicize exhibition titles, but don't do both. Abbreviate states or write them out. Again, don't mix them up. Double-check to make sure all items are presented in a uniform format.

BIOS

If you're just starting out, a biography might be a better choice than a résumé. When there are a lot of holes in your résumé, it looks strangely empty when your sparse accomplishments are in linear order. A bio hides the holes. You will also, at times, be asked to submit a biography instead of a résumé. Bios are far preferable to résumés for telling your story. They're more user-friendly and media-friendly, particularly when made interesting.

Think of this document as your résumé in paragraph form. It is written in the third person. In your bio, you are highlighting the most important items on your résumé. Add a short description of your work in the opening paragraph and keep it in reverse chronological order. You can use the same language on websites, in grants, press releases, and other written materials. In addition, a gallery or exhibition venue may ask you to provide biographies for handouts.

When writing for public consumption, you may want to spice up your bio. What do I mean? I mean that your bio shouldn't read like everyone else's bio. It's sad, but true: Almost all bios read like the one below.

> *He's an artist. He makes this. He shows his work here and there. It can be found in these collections. He studied here and got this degree. He was born in this city, but now lives here.*

Do you think I'm exaggerating? How many artist biographies have you read? How many are memorable? Most will put you straight to sleep. Artists vying for gallery and museum attention have the most boring bios of all. Those bios are, quite understandably, straight from academia. They consist of just the facts, related dryly. All fine and good except that the information is a real snoozer to read and wouldn't tempt anyone into writing a profile about you. Some curators and galleries might prefer the straight-laced, just-the-facts bio. But when you're marketing to the media and to the general public you have to craft a more interesting story. Most people have a sense of humor. And everyone enjoys being entertained. Think about it. Don't you tend to remember people when you're drawn into their stories? Incidentally, just because they often bow to tradition, I can't believe that—given the choice— curators and high-end gallery dealers won't bend a little to accommodate better storytelling from artists.

Let me show you how to spice up your bio. Using the every-artist example above, create a framework.

1. Description of your art: Jamie Alison is an artist who makes _____ .
2. Exhibits and venues: She shows her work in _____ .
3. Public collections: It can be found in these collections.
4. Education: She studied here and got this degree.
5. Born/lives: She was born in this city, but now lives here.

Updating your résumé is the first step to creating a spicier bio; then you have to tell a better story. What is quirky about you? What can you say about yourself that will set you apart from other artists? Or how can you give just the facts using colorful language and storytelling techniques? Let's try expanding on the five sentences above.

1. Description of Your Art

A description of your artwork in the first paragraph will set the tone for what is to come. It shows the reader what your current direction is. You should not be too creative with this paragraph because you need to describe your work clearly.

2. Exhibits and Venues

Just the facts: *She is represented by Zenker Gallery in Denver and Anderson Fine Art in Tulsa.*

Spicier: *If you like to end your gallery hopping with a good meal, you're in luck. After visiting Jamie's work at the Zenker Gallery in Denver, walk two doors down for the best Cuban food west of the Mississippi. When you're in Tulsa, don't miss Café Olé, which is just around the corner from Jamie's work at Anderson Fine Art.*

Spicier (if you're not showing publicly yet): *She shows her work to anyone she can get to look at it in the shining metropolis of Golden, Colorado. If you're lucky enough to have her cook you her famous vegetarian chili, you'll surely be treated to a studio tour before dinner.*

3. Public Collections

Just the facts: *Jamie's work can be found in public collections that include the City of Boulder (Colorado), Baptist Hospital (Kansas City, Missouri), and Charles Schwab Investments (Denver, Colorado).*

Spicier: *If you make a quick tour through Colorado, jump on I-25 and take the downtown exit to Denver to find Jamie's work in the lobby of Charles Schwab Investments. Hop back on the highway and get on 36 to Boulder. At the intersection of Table Mesa and 36, you'll see Jamie's Windmill Goddesses. If you hit a stoplight, you're in luck. Viewing is easier when you're not whizzing by it at 45 mph. Remember: Safety first.*

4. Education

Just the facts: *Jamie has her B.F.A. from the University of Oklahoma and her M.F.A. in sculpture from the University of Texas.*

Spicier: *Jamie tried to live the cowgirl life by spending two years at the University of Wyoming at 7,200 feet altitude in Laramie. Not cut out for that life, she returned to her home and graduated with her art history degree from the University of Oklahoma just in time to see the Oklahoma Sooners win another national football championship. Yep, Jamie loves Oklahoma football. It's one reason people are so perplexed as to why she attended grad school at the University of Texas (the Longhorns are the Sooners' #1 rival).*

5. Born / Lives

Just the facts: *Jamie was born in Great Falls, Montana, and now calls Chicago home.*

Spicier: *Jamie was born at an Air Force base in Great Falls, Montana (longer story) and grew up in the red earth of Oklahoma, which will always have a huge place in her heart. After living in Laramie, Wyoming, Washington, D.C., Austin, Texas, and Tulsa, Jamie could no longer resist the lure of the big city. She's lived in the Windy City since 1991.*

Anyone can create a more interesting story about themselves and their art. It just takes time and imagination—and a desire to stand out in the crowd.

BUSINESS CARDS

A business card is one of the first marketing pieces for all in business. Having that petite piece of paper with your contact information on it seems to impart to the world that you're serious.

What should go on your business card? You may include an image of your art, which helps people remember you. If you have a logo, which I don't usually advise for fine artists, it can be featured in place of an image. But a logo and an image together might compete with one another, which is why I usually don't advise creating a logo. (Remember, we're talking about a very small space!) In addition, you need to include your name, address, website URL, phone number, email address, and social media accounts. Your business card should include more than one way for potential patrons to reach you. It is risky to give only an email address, as spam filters and delivery problems have made email unreliable. I have often been frustrated when I tried to reach an artist who has given me only an email address. If my email message doesn't get through, I have no other way to contact the artist.

The standard size of a business card is $2'' \times 3.5''$. Although it may be tempting to use a nonstandard sized card, I encourage you to resist the temptation. For those who avidly keep track of contacts with business cards, nonstandard sizes can be terribly annoying. Either the cards don't fit neatly in stacks or business card holders or they fall out of holders because they're too small. Recipients may not be able to store them in their usual place, which means that you are not found or "remembered." If you insist on using a nonstandard size, it would be in your interest to use a smaller rather than larger card—or at least offer a size that folds to $2'' \times 3.5''$. A smaller card can at least fit within holders made for standard-sized cards.

If you've been in business for a while and go through a lot of business cards—say, at art festivals—it's usually a good idea to have them printed in bulk quantities. However, if you're just starting your business, large quantities don't make sense. Batches of ten or fewer might be best. Trust me, in a month—after you have lived with your first card and passed it around a bit—you'll want to make changes.

Because so much of my business is online, printing mass quantities of business cards is wasteful. I'd be stuck with them for years. Like many artists, I print my business cards on my home printer. It is easy to print your own cards because the paper companies have now come up with clean-edge cards. Messy perforated edges are a thing of the past. Just print and separate when the ink is dry.

In addition to being easy and economical, printing your own business cards can be to your advantage. Artist John T. Unger prints multiple images of his sculptures and allows his patrons to choose the card that shows a work they admire. He describes his technique on his blog, johntunger.com.

The text stays the same for each card, but I change the images every time I print a new batch. When I do an art show, I have cards with the image of every piece in the show. When I make new work, I make new cards. I keep some images in constant circulation, either of custom work I've done or of my "greatest hits," but basically, they're always new. This system works for me on a couple of levels. The most important is that when someone is interested in a particular piece or style of work, I can give them the card that features that item. That way, they always remember why they wanted it. The side bonus is that everywhere I go, I always have a mini-portfolio of my most recent work. When someone asks me what I do, I can show them. And then I let them pick their favorite card.

Did you get that? Business cards with an image of everything in his shows. Letting people pick their favorites—giving them choices—involves them in his work. We all like to have choices.

Regardless of whether you print your cards at home or use a printing service, make sure they meet professional standards. Use good quality paper. No flimsy stuff. If they're cut by hand, get the lines straight. Don't scrimp on ink and print on the setting for highest quality. (If you don't know how to adjust the print quality settings, learn.)

LETTERHEAD

Although we write fewer and fewer traditional letters, you still need to have stationery for situations that require it. Following the rules for your marketing materials, your letterhead should look very much the same as your business cards. An image of your work may be an acceptable element on your stationery, and it's certainly preferable to any other graphic. If you use an image on your letterhead, keep it small and easy to read by selecting one that is graphically strong rather than muddy. Use very good white paper for the best print quality that shows off your image.

With so much correspondence being conducted through email, there's really no reason to get 500 sheets of letterhead printed at a time. You can print your own on your printer. Keep a letterhead template on your computer. Print your letters on high-quality paper and at a higher resolution for a more polished look than if you were printing something for your records or files.

NOTE CARDS

Handwritten notes are invaluable for nurturing personal relationships. Taking the time to write thoughtful personal messages will set you apart from other artists. For this reason, you should stock up on note cards with images of your art. Many artists print their own note cards; if you do so, be sure to use high resolution and good quality paper. If you prefer to engage a printer, check out the list of printing companies in the Resources at the back of the book or talk to your local printing store. Many offer card printing. (There's more advice on using and composing handwritten notes in Action 11.)

BROCHURES

Brochures aren't a necessity, but they can be useful—particularly if you are marketing yourself outside of your local area. They can be viewed without an electrical source, which means that recipients can see them as soon as they open the envelope. There is no need to turn on a projector, hold them up to a light source, or slip a disk into a computer. A brochure gives you instant impact—if, and only if, it's a *good* brochure.

Before you start work on your brochure, collect samples from artists and other businesses and study the contents and the layouts. What do you like and dislike? Consider the impact those brochures have on you before starting on yours.

Make sure you know how you will use your brochure before spending any money on it. Who is your target recipient? What do you want to happen when the recipient receives your brochure? Will you mail the brochure, hand it out, or simply add it to your portfolio? Your answers to these questions will determine the design and content of your brochure. I learned the hard way that people would be happy to include my brochure in their mailings if only I had made it slightly smaller so it would fit in a standard Number 10 envelope.

The content of brochures varies from artist to artist, although the art should always be the focus. Underneath all of your images, add small subtle text with titles, media, and sizes. Insert a very brief statement and/ or bio (shorter is better here) along with your contact information. If you're using your brochure for wholesaling or direct sales, include a price list.

Artists who design their own brochures risk having the product look exactly like what it is: a self-published document printed on a substandard printer. Spacing is off. Layout is unpolished. Typefaces are inconsistent. Brochures like these do nothing to enhance your reputation or to promote the work. If you're going to create a brochure, do it right and consider hiring a professional. Otherwise it's an enormous waste of time and money, not to mention a potential roadblock for your career.

CATALOGS

Catalogs usually illustrate a cohesive body of work. They contain some narrative about the art, which might be an introduction by an art critic or a story you want to tell about your work. Additional stories can be placed alongside individual works of art. Include a biography or complete résumé in the back and price list if pertinent and you have a substantial promotional piece. Like brochures, catalogs are not a necessity. However, they can show your work in its best light when they're designed and printed professionally.

Although being included in a good catalog from a gallery or museum is a fantastic promotional tool, many venues don't have the budget to produce them. More and more artists are setting aside funds to create their own catalogs; however, some—certainly not all—galleries and curators might be put off by catalogs that are self-published by the artist. Because it's a costly undertaking, you might want to test the waters with a very small print run. If you decide to do so, look over the list of printers in Resources at the back of the book. Print-on-demand outlets can run single copies for you.

Are you beginning to see how the same information (your résumé, your bio, your stories, your statement) can be used and recycled for all of your marketing material?

ARTICLES

Make sure that news about your career finds its way to your collectors—both private individuals and public institutions. Your collectors take as much pride owning your work as you do in making it. Articles written by you or by someone else about your work can be photocopied and sent with a letter or as part of a promotional packet. Whether it's a review, a juicy story, or something instructional you've written, don't hesitate to add articles into the marketing mix. Now you understand why it is important to keep your mailing list updated. You never know when something will come out that you are dying to share with people immediately.

Newspaper print, which is full of acid, turns yellow over time. A really good photocopy that is made when the article is new will last a lifetime. While you're at it, make extra copies to have on hand. Always photocopy newspaper articles on a lighter setting so that the print on the back of the article doesn't bleed through to the front. Also, for best reproduction, copy documents in color—even if the original is black and white. Don't forget to include the publication data on your copy. Add the title graphic from the front page of the publication alongside your article for a polished look.

Don't despair if you are an emerging artist without articles to your credit. They'll come in time.

IMAGES: PHOTOGRAPHS, CDS, AND DVDS

Whether you're trying to sell your art or are focusing more on building a reputation, the photographs of your images must be as good as or better than the originals. They must stand in for the work itself. The color must be true, the focus excellent, and there should be no shadows or hotspots. Go through your portfolio of images and discard all photos of your artwork shown on stockade fences, in the grass, or against your grandmother's quilt. You want an invisible (or next-to-invisible) background. For two-dimensional art, that means cropping all images to the corners of the work. For three-dimensional art, an invisible background usually means a neutral, gradated backdrop (keep an eye on what the current photo trends are for your type of art). Ask an impartial witness: "Does this photograph do justice to my work?"

Unless you are a photographer, don't try to shoot your own work, particularly if your art is three-dimensional. Photographing sculpture, glass, jewelry, and shiny objects requires a special set of skills. In order to do it right, you would need to purchase thousands of dollars worth of equipment, invest numerous hours in educating yourself, and devote lots of time to practicing and re-shooting the images that don't turn out right. Even then, you won't see what the trained photographer can see. You have other things to think about. Do your genius and let others do theirs.

Hire a photographer for the best results, but not just any photographer. It must be someone who photographs art. If you don't know of such a photographer, contact other artists, a local arts council, or artist organization and ask for help. Museums, too, would know where to find art photographers and might even have someone on staff who freelances in that role. After you have the names of a few reputable photographers, compare their work and study their portfolios to ensure you are satisfied with the quality of their work.

The art world is transitioning away from 35-millimeter slides and toward digital submissions. But until galleries, festivals, museums, and expos agree we no longer need slides, you might have to shoot in both formats or convert one or the other. In the meantime, you should call the venue you are submitting images to and ask for the preferred format. You can never go wrong by asking. It shows you are concerned about the proper mode of submission. Furthermore, it puts your name in front of the venue one more time.

Include a copyright notice with your images along with a credit to the photographer. The format includes the copyright symbol or the word "copyright" followed by the year and your name. (You can learn more about copyright and protecting your images at copyright.gov.)

©2011 Heath Lewis. Photograph by Robin Harvey.

Many artists view CD ROMs and DVDs as cost-effective solutions for sharing images. This is true in theory. While a well-produced digital presentation can be impressive, it can also be an enormous waste of money. In order to reap the results you seek from a digital presentation, you first have to get recipients to look at the disk. They must be interested enough to stop their work, pop your disk into their computer, and watch the show. Because this is highly unlikely if the recipients do not know who you are, I strongly suggest you submit printed components in addition to a disk. Include a brochure, 8"×10" prints, disk cover art or a case insert, and other items that are instantly impressive. Think about the mail you receive from people or companies you don't know. What makes you want to open it and spend time with it?

SIGNS

There will be times when you need signs. For example, you might post signs on your art festival booth, at the entrance to your exhibit, or on the outside of your open studio. You also need them at the sales table of a workshop or on the door of a class you're teaching. Make sure your signs are easy to read and project the same image as the rest of your marketing materials. Go over my rules for marketing materials and apply them to all of your signage.

PUT TOGETHER A P.R. NOTEBOOK

Once you've gathered a decent array of marketing materials, put together a P.R. notebook. Call it a brag book if you like. The goal is to assemble something for the general public that reveals your activities and accomplishments. It's a little bit different than an official portfolio because it is intended for public consumption, which means you can stuff it with whatever you like and however many things you like.

Use a three-ring binder with sheet protectors, but don't stop there. Make it special. You're an artist, after all! Create a cover that looks like your work and helps promote your artist's brand—something that makes people want to touch it, pick it up, and read all about you. Fill it with your statement and biography, articles about you, postcards and flyers from exhibitions and workshops, photographs of you, your art and your studio, and letters containing testimonials. Put your notebook out at art openings, festivals, exhibits, and classes. Take it with you to anywhere you think you might be asked about your work.

NO-EXCUSE PRINCIPLE

The marketing materials in your portfolio reflect the image you want to project to the world. Maintaining control of how they look means you're in charge of your image, which is a good place to begin.

NO-EXCUSE ACTION

Polish your image. Make sure all of your marketing materials are well branded and professional in every way.

Go to IdRatherBeintheStudio.com to get the Marketing Materials Planner.

Action 7

Claim Your Online Presence
with a Quality Website or Blog

Having an Internet presence is essential. I'd even go so far as to say you almost don't exist if you're not online, which explains why securing a website is one of the first steps artists take toward self-promotion. To get your art online, you need to be involved in any one or a combination of the following online activities.

- You have a website built from scratch with your own domain name as the URL (website address).
- You develop your site through a site-hosting service just for artists, such as FineArtStudioOnline <fineartstudioonline.com> or ArtSpan <artspan.com>. These services are great ways to get a website quickly. They offer valuable support to their members, which is an additional benefit. However, their design layout options are currently limited. If you use one of these services, be sure to secure a separate URL with your name in it so that your address is robertjharrington.com instead of artspan.com/robertjharrington. It helps with your branding.

- You use a blog instead of a traditional site. Having a website used to be non-negotiable, but a lot of artists are now using blogs as effectively as or even more effectively than most websites.
- You have a blog in addition to a website and it's updated at least twice a week. It's about your art and/or your niche market.
- You have a couple of pages on an online gallery. This presence is often a benefit of membership in an artist organization. The artist pages at the Oklahoma Visual Arts Coalition <ovacgallery.com> and the Chicago Artist Coalition <chicagoartistscoalition.org/galleries> are examples.
- You sell your art on eBay, Etsy, or other commercial site.
- You have an image portfolio on a site like Flickr.com.
- You have a business page on Facebook and a portfolio on your LinkedIn profile.

All of the above options give people an opportunity to see your work online. But nothing can replace the image you create for yourself and your art through a personal website and/or blog. Social media expert Chris Brogan refers to your website as your home base. No other online platform can promote your art the way you like to present it on your own site. In this chapter, I'll show you how to build your online presence to serve you best.

She Took Control

With your advice, I revamped my website. I would never have known what a difference an innovative, well organized website could make. I now receive three times the monthly hits from search engines, and my sales have increased.—Deb Trotter <debtrotter.com>

YOUR WEBSITE

I want to suggest a few guidelines for the creation of your site. I'll begin by asking an obvious question—one that very few people consider: What would you like your website to do for you? Is it a place you send people so they can see images of your work—an online portfolio? Will you use it for aggressive e-marketing (e-newsletters, blogs, and so on) to generate website traffic and, ultimately, enthusiasm for your work? Or will you use it to sell directly to customers? Maybe it's a combination of all the above.

> Don't leave your visitors wondering how to find what they are looking for on your website. If visitors are confused, they'll leave the site. People don't have time to guess what they're going to see when they click on an ambiguous word.

Navigation Menu

After you know what you want your site to do for you and how much you can or should spend, you can select the pages and layout you'll need. There are five categories that must be on the navigation menu of your website. The navigation menu, which is composed of your major links, should look the same and appear in the same place on every page of your site. Try to keep the number of major links to as few as possible so that your site isn't cluttered and you aren't confusing visitors with too many options. On the Art Biz Coach site, I have six major navigation tabs at the top of each page, with a drop-down menu under each. These links take visitors to critical pages. However, I have created a hierarchy by differentiating the link styles. Minor links are deeper within a site and might be linked only from one or two of these major pages. We'll get to those next, but first, the five categories for your navigation menu.

Home. Every site must have a HOME page where people land when they type in your website address. Your name should be prominent and links to pages inside your site should be easy to navigate. Your HOME page should feature the most impressive and graphically interesting of all your artworks. Ask yourself: What can I put on this page that has a *wow* factor and will draw people in? You have to capture Web surfers' attention immediately.

Artwork. Devise a system to organize your artwork online that makes sense to visitors, such as categorizing by subject matter or media. I caution against using the word GALLERY to denote where your artwork can be seen on your site. Instead, use a heading such as ART, ARTWORK, PORTFOLIO, or even PAINTINGS, SCULPTURE, or POTTERY—all of which are more descriptive than GALLERY. Save GALLERY for a page listing your gallery representation. But don't break down your ART pages by date or by generic terms like "Gallery 1" and "Gallery 2." Visitors won't know where to click. It's like having to choose between door #1 and door #2 on *Let's Make a Deal.* They won't know what to expect. When visitors don't know where to click, they leave, so do what you can to keep visitors on your site and looking at your art.

Position your artist statement next to your art so that people can read about and see your work on the same page. If you have additional short stories or statements to make about the work, use them next to your art as well. Insert keywords into your stories and titles to help the search engines find you. If you want to know more about attracting Web traffic, check out the resources at IdRatherBeintheStudio.com.

You wouldn't install your art without an identification label, so why would you post images of your art online without the same information? Whenever you add images to your website, blog, or social media profile, make sure the credit line is visible. A credit line consists of the following: your name, title of artwork, media, dimensions, and copyright notice. You may think adding your name to every image is redundant. It may be, but it is necessary. Visitors can land on any page on your site. It needs to be clear that the images are yours and that you own the copyright to them.

"Older" artwork presents a dilemma when designing an artist's website. On one hand, it's nice for visitors to see your progression as an artist, you're proud of the work, and the art is still for sale. On the other hand, you want your current work to be most prominent, and you want visitors to know what you're working on now.

If someone were opening your website as they would open a portfolio, you could guide them through a tour of your career—showing them the works in the order you prefer. In a portfolio, this is usually front to back. But the Internet doesn't work that way. Thanks to search engines, visitors might land on any number of pages on your site before they see your HOME page. You have to be ready. Every page has to be a landing page.

So how do you show "older" art on your website? Your main menu would have a link titled ART or PORTFOLIO. Clicking on that link would take site visitors to a page with your most recent work or with categories of that work. Your primary art pages (meaning the pages that display the art you want people to see first) would be the fewest clicks away from the HOME page. On the primary art pages, you feature your most recent work, while also providing a link to older art. At the bottom of the page or in the sidebar, you could link to "Artwork 1995-2005" or "Artwork Prior to 2011." You could also be more descriptive: "Midwestern Landscapes 1995-2005" or "Bronze Wildlife Prior to 2011."

Try to avoid the phrases "Older Work" or "Archived Work" on your website. Both of these sound like the work is either unwanted or unavailable and you never know when someone will land on one of these pages. Every page has to be welcoming. Every page has to have your name on it and show visitors exactly where they are. Every page has to provide context.

About. The ABOUT page is home to your biography or résumé and your photograph. The most intriguing photographs of artists are those taken in the studio with the artwork or actively participating in something related to their artwork. For example, artist Glen Robert Hacker specializes in angler trophy portraits. His picture at anglertrophyportraits.com depicts him at high seas with a catch of his own. He's no longer just another artist, but a fisherman who can readily relate to people who might want portraits with their trophy fish.

Contact. Add your contact information to every page of your site so that it's easy for people to find you. Post your email address, making the link "hot," which means it will launch a self-addressed e-mail message for your visitors' convenience. If visitors have to type out your email address, you've created a barrier. However, some people who visit your site from their workplaces may be prohibited by their corporate systems from sending an email generated by the link on your page. As a courtesy, always provide your complete email address on your CONTACT page. Include a phone number as a backup to your email address and a conventional mailing address. And don't forget to add your social media accounts to your contact information. Your CONTACT page might also be combined with ABOUT.

Blog. Your blog might be hosted on your website or just linked, but it should be prominent. If you have a blog, it should be a major link and on every page.

Optional Pages and Minor Links
After you have decided on the basic pages of your site, you can begin to explore optional pages or minor links.

News. You might include a newsletter you write on a regular basis, upcoming workshops you're teaching, and an online media kit.

Testimonials. It's a good idea to include testimonials from happy patrons, particularly if you welcome commissions. Testimonials can also go on your ABOUT page or COMMISSIONS page.

Shopping Cart. You need a shopping cart only if you plan on selling a great number of items on the Internet. In fact, it shouldn't even be a consideration until you have already built up an online audience. Without the amplified online presence, a shopping cart is an enormous waste of money and virtual real estate. Even if you get one sale every day on your website, you will find it is fairly easy to process those yourself. You might consider adding the cart to do the work for you when you start getting a substantial number of orders.

Pricing or Purchase Information. If you are selling directly to customers, it should be easy for them to make purchases. If you don't sell a great deal online, a pricing page doesn't have to be a major link. It can be linked from within your artwork pages. If you sell only through galleries, this page might be called "Purchase Info" or "Galleries" or "Where to Find My Work."

Guestbook or Mailing List Sign-Up. Many artists include sign-up forms on their sites in order to collect email addresses, which is a good business practice. To encourage people to sign up, indicate what they're going to get when they do so; also be sure you tell them what you will do with their addresses. Create a privacy policy that says you will not share information with anyone—ever. See Action 13 for more on collecting email addresses.

Visit. If your studio is open to the public, post the hours, give readers directions (a link or a map), and indicate where they should park. This page can be combined with your CONTACT page.

Resources. This page includes links to information available on other sites—a useful service you provide your visitors. If you teach, give teaching resources and links. Your links might also include art centers, galleries, museums, local art organizations, and other artists. Don't add links from random sites simply to get your site listed on theirs and to have more links on your site. This practice is passé. Trade links with sites that are meaningful—ones that relate to your work. Adding a sentence that describes the information that will be found on the linked site is a helpful courtesy, and search engines may reward your effort by increasing your ranking.

Gift Ideas. You can sell reproductions of your art, note cards, or other items on your site or through a link to a storefront like CafePress <cafepress.com> or Etsy <etsy.com>. These lower-priced items are usually separate from your fine art pages.

Website Design Guidelines

After you have decided what you want on your site, you can begin to have fun: It's time to consider the image your website will project. Return to the list you created under "Polish Your Image" in Action 6. Unless you are an expert in creating a website, I strongly suggest you work with a professional on your website instead of doing it yourself. Homemade websites—created by people who are usually working on their first and only site—usually don't work properly. If you don't know code and how to use it, I beg you not to try to design your site yourself. Your website is a key to your livelihood! Nurture your genius in the studio and let others take care of the areas they know best. In the long run, it will save you time and money—not to mention headaches.

> Web guru Patricia J. Velte <whitewingdesign.com> says you should avoid the three biggest mistakes artists make on their websites.
>
> 1. Bad photographs of artwork
> 2. Clunky design that detracts from the art
> 3. Not enough text or stories to connect with visitors or to get picked up by search engines

Here are some guidelines for your website (some of which are repeated for emphasis from My Rules for Marketing Materials in Action 6).

- Don't spend a fortune on your website in the beginning. You may have heard it takes $2,000 or more to set up a website, but that just isn't true. Places such as FineArtStudioOnline.com can get you started inexpensively. And there are very good Web designers who are affordable. Shop around! Most importantly: know what you want, what you must have, and what you can add later. You're in control. Don't let anyone talk you into anything you neither need nor want.
- Unless you do cutesy work, don't use a cutesy domain name. Stick with your own name. Again, your domain name is a way to brand yourself. For most artists, it's more important that

patrons remember your name than your company name or a clever website address. If your name is already taken as a .com, try adding "art" or "studio" at the end of it: davidcastleart.com, annesart.com.

- Temper the background of your site. Start with a white background for everything. If you absolutely can't stand it, switch to off-white or light gray before you try darker colors. Black, in particular, has a negative psychological impact on people and tends to be too harsh for most artwork. Light text on dark backgrounds is also difficult for people with astigmatism and other eye problems to read. Patterned backgrounds almost always compete with the art.

- Feature images on your home page that capture attention. Your best work should be on this page. Make sure every other page on your website does an equally good job of showing off your art. Why wouldn't you put your art on every single page? You've got the real estate—use it.

- Make sure your name is prominent on every page. Since about half of your visitors will land on one of your other pages first, you don't want to leave any doubt as to your identity.

- Nothing should compete visually with your images, which should always be the focus of attention. This point leads to my next four.
    - No funky fonts unless your site and work are funky. Stick with basic fonts for your text. If viewers don't have the same font that you used on their computer, the page won't display correctly and your site will look amateurish. Limit the number of fonts on your site to two or, at most, three. Pick a standard font size and stick with it.
    - No background music—no matter how much you like the song! Music can be annoying and can startle visitors if they're not expecting it and their speakers are turned up. Musical tastes, like art, are very personal. Why risk offending someone's ears?

- ◦ No flashing graphics or scrolling banners. Ever. Period. End of discussion.
- ◦ No logos or other images besides your own, except on your RESOURCES page.

- No bad photographs. Make sure you have the highest quality photographs of your art. If it doesn't pass the test, don't put it online for the whole world to see.

- No tiny pictures. Use small, but not too small, thumbnails and good-sized (but quick-loading) larger images. My favorite thumbnail size is about 100-140 pixels for the smallest dimension. If you have a very long or a very wide artwork, your larger dimension might exceed that range.

- Protect your intellectual property as best you can without letting it become an obsession that keeps you from sharing your work with the world. Keep the images at a low resolution (72 pixels per inch) to discourage digital theft and make sure you show them in the best light. No copyrights or watermarks should be visible on top of your images since they ruin the appreciation of the work itself. Put your copyright information below each image; on a separate page describe the rights and the terms under which others can use the images, if you like. As an alternative to copyrights, look into a free Creative Commons license at creativecommons.org. This tool is being used more and more frequently by authors, scientists, educators, and artists for the sharing and advancement of intellectual property, both online and offline.

- If you have gallery representation, link to the gallery instead of trying to sell works yourself. This creates goodwill between you and your dealers.

- When you post your prices, do so discreetly. Use a smaller font and lighter text or place prices on a page separate from your images.

- Do not use big "Add to Cart" or "Buy Now" buttons—another graphic that takes away from your work. Buttons make your site look like a tacky infomercial rather than a place for high-class art.

- If you're actively trying to sell your work from your website, you'll have to update it regularly. Most artists update two or three times a year, but many are adding new work far more often than that. The frequency depends on how prolific you are, how many sales you are making, and who is doing the updates for you. Make sure these and all other expenses are accounted for in the budget in Action 15.

START A BLOG

If you really want to claim your online presence, start a blog. It's easy to do! In contrast to all of the coding that goes into a website, the major blogging platforms provide templates that do most of the work for you. If you feel comfortable writing just a few paragraphs and can crop and size photos, you have all the skills you'll need.

To get started, you have to answer a few questions, sign up, and then start posting entries and adding pictures. Once you hit "Submit," your blog entry is instantly posted for the world to see. But it gets better. If you decide you don't like what you've posted or want to change it, you can delete it or make the changes and then republish your site. It takes just minutes.

She Witnessed the Power of Blogging

Within the first three weeks I was completely surprised by the amount of interaction I was having with people who had visited my blog and then clicked through to my website to see more of my work. Overall my monthly website hits have doubled and most importantly these click-throughs led to sales and some really great exhibition opportunities.

—Kesha A. Bruce <keshabrucestudio.com>

Blogs help you build an audience by connecting with readers on a very personal level. Whereas websites are mostly static, blogs are ever-changing (or should be) and more personal. They give you a platform for a more intimate dialogue with your viewers and patrons. If you have a focused subject matter, blogging is that much easier because you know what you're going to write about. More importantly, you'll know who your readers are.

Sign Up for Blog Hosting

There are three primary options for blog hosting.

1. Blogger, brought to you by Google, is free. It is a Web-based blog hosting service that requires no software. Your blog can be viewed from a blogspot.com address, a unique domain name, or from your website. See blogger.com.

2. WordPress, an open source software, is extremely popular and can be used one of two ways. WordPress.com is just like Blogger in that you're provided a free blog on the WordPress server and you select the template, which can be customized to some extent. With the other method, wordpress.org, you install the software on your own Web server. This second method requires a little more technical savvy, although you can pay people to install it for you and teach you how to use it. WordPress.org is the clear winner among professional bloggers. All of the traffic from a wordpress.org blog goes to your site rather than a third party's site.

3. TypePad was my original choice for a blog-hosting service and I was never disappointed, although I've since migrated to WordPress. TypePad is not free, but does come with very good customer support. Adding your unique domain name (e.g., artbizblog.com) is also an option with TypePad. Pricing packages vary. See typepad.com.

What to Write About

One of the most frequent excuses I hear from artists who haven't started a blog is that they don't necessarily want to share their personal lives with the world. Guess what? You don't have to! Yes, I said that blogs are personal, but the notion that a blog is a journal about your private life is erroneous. Some, indeed, are, but most are highly edited, focused journals. They consist of selected thoughts intended for public consumption. The majority of blog readers don't care what you had for breakfast or what you're watching on TV. People want to read about subjects that interest them. You'll build a following if you write about something that your likely readers can relate to or something they want to know about.

If a blog is too personal—if it focuses too much on the author—visitors won't return. Likewise, they will soon become bored or irritated if they are bombarded with sales messages. Fresh content that spotlights items of interest to your audience will keep them coming back again and again.

Most importantly, write! And learn to write better. Writing is a critical skill for promoting your art online. You can't excuse yourself from the task of writing by saying "I'm not a writer." That's a cop-out. You must write. The longer you write, the better at it you will become. Blogging regularly will help you become more confident sharing your art in other formats. You'll have plenty of words ready for your artist statement, gallery talks, brochures, or grant applications.

So . . . write! Perhaps Margret E. Short's story will inspire you.

Margret, an artist in Portland, Oregon, started her blog to document a project related to the 400th anniversary of the birth of Rembrandt and a special exhibit commemorating this auspicious occasion that was scheduled to tour the United States. In a stroke of genius, Margret resolved to create a series of new works based on the color palettes of specific paintings in the exhibition. The result was to be an exhibit of her work at Portland's Lawrence Gallery, which coincided with the blockbuster exhibit at the nearby Portland Museum of Art.

When she contacted me nine months prior to her exhibit, Margret sought guidance and support to see her through this project. In reviewing her thoughts on promotions, she wouldn't have dreamed that I would tell her to start promoting it immediately—before her paintings were even begun. To her surprise, I encouraged her to start a blog that would document the process. She could gain followers and enthusiasts over many months if she shared her process. I hope you can see that this idea is much better than sending out a press release and invitation a couple of weeks before the opening!

I have to give Margret all the credit. She had heard about blogs, but wasn't exactly sure how they applied to her or what she could do with one. I coached her along. Just start the blog, I said, and we'll worry about the rest later. As I recall, it was up within a week or two and branded to look just like her website. Her focus on Rembrandt's pigments provided a framework for her posts.

Margret let people in the secrets as she was discovering them. People love secrets and obscure facts! Here is one of Margret's entries on the color green: "If jars glazed with celadon had a clear pleasing tone when struck, people would consider the jars as homes of gods." Who knew? And from another entry, she confided that epidot, a pigment from Russia and Austria, is unpleasantly gooey and that it "must be used immediately after making it or it turns gummy and is not brushable at all." Since the completion of the Rembrandt project, Margret has concentrated on ancient Egyptian pigments. You can check it out through her link at margretshort.com.

Make your blog successful by homing in on a focus as Margret did. There is a list of content ideas in Action 9 to get you thinking.

The best blog content comes from listening. What questions are people asking you about your art? Take each question and turn it into a new blog post. What are people saying in their comments on your blog or Facebook page? What are people tweeting about on Twitter? Pull out the juicy ones and make them into new posts. What ideas are engaging people on other blogs? What has your attention? Make a post about it! By staying on top of current conversations, you are inserting your thoughts into a bigger dialogue. This instantly makes your blog more interesting.

To ensure a continuous flow of content, keep a number of ideas in the works. I do this in multiple programs on my computer.

- I use Evernote <evernote.com> to "clip" interesting discussions and passages on websites and also to save questions from my followers.

- I use FileMaker as a software database for my posts before they are inserted as drafts on the Art Biz Blog.
- I use a WordPress plugin called Editorial Calendar to plan and schedule my posts on the blog itself. I'm relying more and more on this feature and less on FileMaker.
- I start a draft directly on the blog and save it.

With all of these, I am capturing ideas so that I can go back and add, delete, and move around content. Ideas have time and space to percolate with this process. The pressure of trying to write the perfect post in one sitting disappears.

Before getting too caught up in perfecting your writing skills, remember that images of your art are critical to your blog posts. Readers must be able to see your art quickly, so it should be a goal to include one artwork with each blog post you write.

As soon as your blog is off to a strong start and you are comfortable with its direction, you can begin thinking about how you will attract more visitors and subscribers.

A Quick-Start Manual for More Blog Visitors

It took me five or six months to get the rhythm of my blog going and to figure out what in the heck I was doing with it. I encourage all of my clients to get started on their blogs immediately. Don't wait for your content ideas to be well-informed or your layout to be perfect. You can change those things later. When you're starting, you need practice time. You need to be able to make mistakes before the whole world sees them. After you get the kinks worked out, you can start telling people about your blog and, presto!, the content will be there for all to see. This Quick-Start Manual outlines the key areas you need to work on if you want more blog visitors. And who doesn't want more blog visitors?

She Experienced the Value of Blogging

I was rolling my internal eyeballs last fall when Alyson started talking about blogs in her workshop. "One more thing to keep track of" was my first thought. But my second thought was that it might be a good way to focus some of my ideas for a future book project, and to stay in touch with friends and clients. I launched my blog, Brush and Baren, about a month after the workshop. Was I ever surprised when three weeks later I discovered my website coming up second after Wikipedia in a Google search for "linocuts"! (Previously I had been buried somewhere on page 15.) Traffic to my website has grown exponentially, and my blog is directly responsible for new clients and new followings in markets I never would have found otherwise.

—Sherrie York <brushandbaren.blogspot.com >

Focus on content. More than anything, good content will attract people to your blog. Create a regular schedule so that readers can depend on you, and commit to writing and posting images of your art. Reread what I said above about focusing your blog and generating ideas.

Post consistently. Don't get overwhelmed by the idea that you have to blog every day; however, the more often you write, the more frequently visitors will return. Above all, you want to be reliable for your readers. If you blog whenever you feel like it, you'll find it difficult to gain loyal fans for your blog.

Use keywords and phrases throughout your website and blog. If you want to be found by those people searching for "American Indian sculpture," you'd do yourself a lot of good by using those three words together as often as you can and by linking them to other blogs and websites when the occasions arise.

Link to other blogs in your posts. Linking shows you in a favorable light to those bloggers. By linking to other blogs in your postings or through trackbacks, you are doing them a favor. Good deeds are usually rewarded.

Create meaningful text links. Don't create hotlinks with text that only says, for instance, http://www.artbizblog.com. Instead, make a link to "art marketing advice" and then link those words to http://www.artbizblog.com. Why? Because searchers don't look for complete URLs (Web addresses) in their online searches. They might, however, look for "art marketing advice," so those are the words that the search engine will pick up from your blog. It's a courtesy to those you mention on your website or blog to provide them with a meaningful text link. (And I would certainly be grateful any time you'd like to link to artbizblog.com!)

Ask people to leave comments on your blog. Whenever someone sends you an email about something that was on your blog, ask if they would please leave it as a comment on your blog. I had to do this when I first started the Art Biz Blog, as many of my subscribers were unfamiliar with how blogs work. When you receive an email message with a comment, be kind and accommodating. Explain that it would help you out if your correspondent would leave a comment on your blog. Another way to encourage comments is to ask questions at the end of your posts— questions that are relevant to the posts' content. People love to share their opinions and you don't get what you don't ask for!

Read and comment on other blogs. Every time you comment on another blog, you leave your blog address in the comment form. The more you leave your virtual footprint all over the Internet, the "hotter" you will become. It's like leaving flyers all over town or passing out your business card to everyone who visits you at the art festival. You're telling people that you're here. (See "Get Google Alerts" below.)

Make your blog visible on your website. Add a link to your blog from your home page and on every other page you can think of. It should be one of your major links.

Add an email subscription form to your blog. Not every blog reader is as tech-savvy as those who know how to set up RSS feeds for their blog favorites. Those who aren't might prefer receiving notice through email updates. You can do this through FeedBlitz <feedblitz.com> or FeedBurner <feedburner.google.com>.

Use your newsletter to drive people to your website and blog. Don't just include a mention of your blog in your newsletter. Instead give your newsletter readers a compelling reason to visit your blog. For instance, let's say you include a top-ten list in your newsletter. Instead of giving away the final item on your list, post it on your website or blog. In its place: "And the number one reason people are coming to the art festival is posted at artbizblog.com." Alternatively, you can ask a question like "What is the highest price ever paid for a painting? Find out and see a picture of it on my blog at . . ."

Recommend like-minded blogs in your sidebar. If you're a ceramist in Arizona, you might have links to other ceramic artists, other Arizona artists, ceramic organizations and websites, and sites about clay or geology. It wouldn't serve you to trade links with a blogger who is documenting global warming unless your work was also about global warming.

Artist and prolific blogger Lisa Call advises you to start your blog with a list of links to blogs that you feel have great content. She says, "You don't have to ask to link to someone's blog. Blogging is a form of social networking, so don't be stingy with your links—it is how you build a network. However, unlike static websites where asking to trade links is common, in the blog world it is considered less appropriate to ask someone to link to you. Write great content and people will link to you in due course if you are out there leaving quality comments and getting known." See blog.lisacall.com.

Bottom line: You will attract more visitors to your blog by committing to rich, useful content and by being generous to others. One tool you'll want to take advantage of in this quest is Google Alerts.

Get Google Alerts

Who could have imagined ten years ago that the word *Google* would be so ingrained in our vocabulary? We use it as a noun to refer to the company and website. It's a verb when we're looking for something on line. And it transforms into an adjective when we talk about making our sites more search-engine friendly or "Googleable." (Heck, my spell check is even okay with that word!)

But Google is much more than a search engine. There are all kinds of cool tools on google.com that you should be aware of. Go to images.google.com and see if your images show up. In addition to using the Google Images site and pulling up your images on the Worldwide Web, you can also use Google Alerts to see where your name might be popping up in the virtual world.

Visit google.com/alerts to sign up free of charge. Select the name or search terms you want to track and Google sends you a report when it shows up in their search engines. For instance, I have alerts set up for "art marketing," "Alyson Stanfield," "art biz coach," and several other phrases. Because of these alerts, I have come across articles about my workshops, sites that are linking to me, and, most importantly, blogs that mention Art Biz Coach or me. This information is invaluable because then I can go to those sites and leave a relevant comment. Voilà! I just left another footprint, claimed my online presence, and made a new friend.

Google lets you select how often you receive the alerts (as it happens, once a day, or once a week). Google Alerts are free and you can change or cancel them any time you like. As an artist you might set up alerts for any or all of the following items.

- Your name (and variations and misspellings of it)
- Your competition (keep an eye on what they're up to!)
- Your niche market ("healing jewelry" or "corporate art" or "public art")
- Your medium or particular interest ("New England landscape painting" or "contemporary quilts" or "pet portrait artist")
- Your location ("artist in Illinois" or "Chicago art")
- Your Twitter @Name
- Titles of your artwork
- Names of galleries or venues where you'd like to show your art

When you set up your alerts, enter your alert terms in quotes and Google Alerts will deliver citations only with the full search term. If you leave the quotes off, you'll get all kinds of responses with your words appearing in no particular order. For instance, if you leave off the quotes for *New England landscape painting*, you might get articles about a "New England landscape" businessman (landscaper) who also does some house "painting" on the side. But "New England landscape painting" would call up articles and references that included those four words in that order.

NO-EXCUSE PRINCIPLE

The Internet is an amazing tool that artists 15 or 20 years ago didn't have. It has given artists more control over their careers than ever. Learn how to use it to your benefit. Ignore it at your peril. Technology isn't slowing down. Yes, it takes time to learn, but so do all things that are worthwhile.

NO-EXCUSE ACTION

Follow the steps in this Action to claim your online presence instead of waiting for people to visit your website and blog. Visit artbizblog.com to stay up to date.

"I don't want to bother people."

E X C U S E

As you're going through this book, you're undoubtedly realizing that self-promotion is putting your name in front of people and keeping it there. A number of my clients ask how much contact is too much. This question is immediately followed by the comment "I don't want to bother people." Here's my theory on that concern.

You're not bothering people IF you give them something they want.

Bothering people is clanging pots and pans in their ears. Bothering people is calling them on the phone during dinnertime and asking them to listen to your pitch for switching Internet providers. And bothering people is sending out two emails a month telling people only that they should go see your website because you have new stuff there. You won't be bothering them if you write something that is interesting and valuable to their lives.

I'm shocked by the number of artists who give up promoting themselves because they sent out 500 postcards one time two years ago and never sold anything as a result. (You can almost hear the whining that goes along with that.) Anyone in advertising or marketing will tell you that it takes at least seven exposures before people get your message and act on it. Seven! That's a lot of contact with your mailing list.

With the next three actions, I'm giving you permission to connect with your contacts frequently through social media and monthly with email or newsletters. But, and this is a big but, you only have permission if 50% of your messages are thoroughly interesting and contain information of value to the recipients. Ask yourself: Would I like to receive this in my inbox or mailbox? If it came to me, would it encourage me to act?

Action 8

Amplify Your Online Presence
with Social Media

As an artist, you are often alone in your studio. You create your work alone. You leave the studio and head to the computer (again, alone), where you work on your mailing list, blog, and digital images, and then perhaps catch up on accounting chores—all alone. You get the picture. You're alone a lot!

You may be resigned to the life of a loner, but even the most solitary artist benefits from staying connected to a community. Of course, you should get out and have lunch with friends, attend art openings, and take classes. Nothing can replace the face-to-face contact of these experiences. But only social media offers you a unique benefit: instant access to large numbers of people. Suddenly, you don't feel so alone. You're connecting to other artists, gallerists, museum personnel, and art buyers.

Today, our get-togethers aren't bound by geography. We can share ideas in virtual space, which can lead to more face-to-face connections than you might imagine.

"Social warmth," the term *Time* magazine used to describe social media, is the biggest reason to give it a try. Social media is another way to connect with friends and build new or stronger relationships, which also happens to be the focus of this book. It's about making new contacts, giving, and receiving. In fact, social media represents the highest form of marketing because (1) most of us are more comfortable with connecting, building relationships, making new contacts, giving, and receiving than we are at "selling" and (2) it works! We buy things—including art—from people we know, like, and trust. Oh, and did I mention that the basic social media platforms are free? Dang, you're lucky to have these tools!

This chapter assumes that you're already set up on each of these social media platforms, but if you are not, there are plenty of resources to help get you started. If you do a Web search for your query, you'll find all kinds of guidance.

A follower once told me that he'd "rather have a life" than be on Twitter. Well, guess what? Twitter is part of many people's lives—just as the Internet is now but wasn't 20 years ago. Our reality is constantly changing. I'm going to show you how to use Twitter and other social media to build relationships in order to more effectively promote your art. If you're ready to embrace this new reality, read on.

A STRATEGY FOR THE BIG THREE

Not too long ago, I was using the Art Biz Blog to post short snippets of information. I'd mention an interesting blog entry and encourage you to read it or I'd add a reminder about one of my upcoming classes and hope you'd click on it. I wouldn't do that today. Instead, I'd probably update my status on Facebook and Twitter because these formats are conducive to brief messages. Alternatively, I might write a blog post that is more of an in-depth look at the post I recommend: what is good about it, what I disagree with, and so on.

Social media has evolved and changed the way we use the Internet as part of a business strategy. There are numerous social media sites you might benefit from, including LinkedIn, but the three I think are most important are your blog, Facebook, and Twitter. In this Action, I'll show you how the big three can work together.

Your Blog

As I noted in Action 7, your blog is home base. You might be all over the Internet, but *your* blog is *your* space. You control the way it looks and the content. No independent social media site can top this advantage. Your artist blog has a mission: to share your art with the world. Stick to that mission as best you can. Your blog is about your art. (There are many blogs that are not about art. Those bloggers have another purpose.) The blog is where you conduct business.

Facebook

Use your personal profile on Facebook to connect with people you know and let them in on more about you. You don't have to focus exclusively on art. Instead, talk about your other interests from time to time: food, football, exercising, and anything else that makes you human and interesting. It's important to be yourself and to be personable—not 100% business—on your Facebook profile. Your profile gives your friends an opportunity to feel more a part of your life.

On the other hand, people "Like" your fan page on Facebook (a.k.a. your official page or business page) because they like your work. This page is about your art and your life in art, and yet it is still more personal and social than your blog. Use your fan page to post images of your art and to invite fans to your events. As you'll see, you can also connect your blog to your fan page.

Twitter

Twitter gives you an opportunity to build a reputation as a friendly, trustworthy, and helpful person. Some people think that Twitter is a waste of time because it is the least promotional of all these sites. But you should think of Twitter as a "good old boys" game of golf. You know they're playing a game, but you also know that the people who don't get invited to join the game are missing potential business deals.

Twitter is called a microblog because it allows only 140 characters for updates and for responses to others' updates. Use this platform to make brief announcements in real time, to link to new blog posts and resources, to suggest tips, and to retweet (repeat) interesting things you read from other people on Twitter.

The Big Picture

When you investigate and set up your social media sites, consider how they will work together. It's best not to have a Twitter account here, a blog there, and a Facebook page somewhere else. All three should exist in harmony. After you've been using a site for a while, you'll get a better sense of its strengths and weaknesses and how it will become part of a larger social media mission. You'll see how you can drive traffic among the various platforms. We covered blogging in the previous Action, so let's focus on Facebook and Twitter.

FRIENDS AND FANS ON FACEBOOK

If you want to get your art online quickly and inexpensively, establish an official page on Facebook. Official pages, in their original incarnation, were known as fan pages, and many people still refer to them as such. They're also known as business pages. I prefer the term *fan page* to *official page*, so I'll use it more frequently. (Just remember that a *fan page* is the same as an *official page*.) You do not need a personal account to set up a fan page—only a business account. Facebook warns, however, that functionality is limited without a personal account.

I can think of five reasons why Facebook should be your first step toward an online presence and why you need a fan page in addition to a personal profile.

- As of this writing, Facebook has over 600,000,000 users. SIX HUNDRED MILLION. But . . .
- Unlike personal profiles, fan pages are public. You don't have to be a member of Facebook to view a fan page. Anyone can see the content—which brings me to my next very important point.
- Facebook fan pages are indexed by Google and appear near the top of search engine results.

- Facebook allows you only 5,000 friends, but you can have an unlimited number of fans.
- Facebook business pages are free!

A fan page on Facebook serves as another website for you. "I don't have time to mess with another website!" you might protest. Of course you don't. No one has time. You make time. You make time because of the reasons I listed above.

Much to the consternation of its users, Facebook is constantly changing its interface. I hope that what I share in this edition of the book will be useful for some time to come, but you might need to do a Web search for the most up-to-date information.

Key Elements of an Artist's Fan Page on Facebook

The constant changes on Facebook could distract you. Begin by focusing on these elements on your fan page on Facebook.

The title of your page. Remember what I said above about Facebook pages being indexed by the search engines? You should use keywords like "abstract art," "bronze sculpture," or "landscape painting" in the title of your page. You also should have a page name that is different from your profile name so that fans can easily distinguish one from another. If your profile name is Sherry Law Morris, your fan page could be something like Sherry Law Morris Western Art, Sherry Law Morris Fine Art, Sherry Law Morris Silver Jewelry, Sherry Law Morris Art Studio, or Sherry Law Morris Paintings.

A photo for your profile picture. Although your personal profile probably has a picture of you, the image you select for your fan page should be a piece of your art or a photo of you with your art.

A short descriptive sentence or two about your art. The text in the sidebar of your artist fan page should not be your bio or about your family. It should be about your work. Remember that your fan page is for fans of your art. Greet them with an interesting descriptive phrase of your work. Be creative!

Two of my favorites are:

Wang-eyed pop folk art from a quiet vale in North London
—Tim Bradford

Exuberant Art for the Eternally Optimistic!—Dianna Fritzler

Images of your art under the photos link. When we visit an artist's fan page, we expect to see art. Don't disappoint us or make it difficult for us to find your art by asking us to search, click a link from Facebook to another site, or scroll to see images. Facebook provides nice-sized thumbnails, so we see a good overview of your work by looking under the Photos link—but only if the pictures are there.

If you're worried about the safety of having images of your art on Facebook, then you probably shouldn't be using the site. Having your art online is about sharing, not about holding back. If you're afraid that someone is going to steal your images, you won't use the platform effectively. My next key element should provide some level of protection.

Credit lines. There are two related problems with the main Photos pages on Facebook. The first is that titles do not appear under the image thumbnails. The second is that as users scroll down a single-image page, they lose the artist's name. For this reason, it's critical to have a complete credit line below each image. By complete, I mean that your name, artwork title, media, dimensions, and copyright should be entered in the caption for *every* piece of artwork you post on Facebook. Whenever you post an image directly to your Facebook Wall—rather than adding it under the Photos link—type the credit line into the update before posting. Otherwise, your image shows up in your fans' streams without the credit attached. Pay attention to this detail as you see your art appear in various places on Facebook: your profile, your page wall, your Photos pages or your friends' profiles. Where do the images appear without your name and detailed credit attached? (See Action 7 for a thorough discussion of credit lines.)

Gain Fans

To increase the number of fans on your Facebook page, you can turn your current friends into fans or look for new fans. If you set up a personal profile at first and later added a business page, you should entice friends to join your fan page.

After creating your fan page, the first step in increasing your fan base is to add content to your wall and photos of your art. It should look active and used—even without a large number of fans—before you tell people about it.

Next, send private messages to your 10 best friends on Facebook and ask them if they will please "Like" your page. (When they do this, it turns them into fans. People who "Like" your page are your fans.) Encourage them to write a note on your wall. Comments make the page look livelier.

After you have taken the steps above, post a note to your personal profile wall inviting all of your friends to become fans. Do this at least once a week for the first month and then monthly thereafter.

As soon as you have 25 fans, you can go to facebook.com/username and snag a good URL for your Facebook page. You want something that is easier to remember than the string of letters and numbers that Facebook automatically generates. For example, Lorena Fernandez's fan page is facebook.com/LorenaFernandezArt.

Connect your fan page to your personal profile on Facebook. From your Profile page, click on Edit Profile at the top of the center column. On the next screen, select Education and Work. Add the exact name of your fan page, save changes, and Facebook should automatically create a link for you that appears at the top of your Profile.

Finally, *suggest* your page to your friends on Facebook. From your fan page, click on Suggest to Friends in the right sidebar. Facebook calls up your friends and automatically eliminates all who are already fans.

If your friends are categorized into Lists (see below), you can select a list under Filter Friends. Otherwise, click on specific names or All and send your recommendations.

After you've done all of the above to turn friends into fans, you can think about attracting more fans for your page by using the following tactics.

- Get out of the habit of asking people to friend you on Facebook. Instead, encourage them to become fans. Add your fan page link to your website, your blog sidebar, and your signature block.
- Post daily about your art and art-related stories to your fan page—the updates don't have to be long. Add as many images of your art as possible, and be sure to reply to comments and questions. These readers are your fans! Engage with them.
- Add a Facebook Like plugin to your blog posts and, if appropriate, to pages on your website.

Power Up Your Page on Facebook

Now that your fan page is attracting attention, you want to satisfy your fans. Use some or all of these ideas to make your page a destination.

Add your blog feed. Many artists use their fan pages like a blog, posting images and content directly on the Facebook Wall. But you can also import posts from an existing blog. In other words, you duplicate content from your blog to your Facebook wall.

To add your blog's feed, click on Edit Page from your fan page. Select Apps in the left sidebar and then click on Notes to add the application to your page. From Apps, select Go to App under Notes. Near the bottom of the left sidebar, you'll find Edit Import Settings. There's a slight delay, which sometimes becomes a longer delay, in getting your post to show up after you've published it on your blog. It could be hours, days, or even weeks. There isn't much you can do about this glitch on Facebook, so it's best not to spend too much time worrying about it.

Feature other artists. Your fan page is a terrific place to share your enthusiasm and respect for other artists. It's easy to make an entry on the Wall or by using the Notes feature.

On your wall, write your entry and link to artists' fan pages or directly to their photo albums. Tag them by using @ followed by their fan page name. Just start typing @ and their name while you wait for Facebook to populate your list of connections. You will have to select the name from your list rather than just typing it in order for Facebook to provide a live (blue) link to the page. Artists will know that you have written about them when your post shows up on their walls and in their updates.

The other way to tag someone is by writing about them in the Notes tab, which allows you to use bold and italic text as well as other attractive elements. You can add an image in this feature and edit the note, whereas you can't edit a wall post. However, when the note appears on your wall, Facebook scrunches all of the text together and the formatting is lost. To tag people or their business pages in a note, just add their names in the Tags blank at the bottom of the entry form.

A short but important note about Facebook etiquette: Tagging people randomly just to get your name on their walls is considered spam. Save your tagging for relevant posts.

Extend invitations to exhibits, shows, and sales. Use the Events link to add an upcoming event to your page. The three most important spaces to complete when you're creating notice of an event are the title ("What are you planning?"), the location ("Where?"), and the description ("More info?"). Be precise in each of these lines because limited information appears in the various Facebook locations. For example, the title of the event appears in big letters on the Events page, but is secondary to the description of the event when it appears on your wall.

It's also important to realize that if you add City/Town, it appears on your wall, but not on the main Events page. For this reason, I suggest using the Where line for both the location of the event and the city/state/province. In other words, instead of only adding the city to the

City/Town line, add it to the Where line. If you do this, the location of your event shows up as *XYZ Gallery, Des Moines, Iowa* (rather than just XYZ Gallery). Including the location is much more user-friendly.

The appearance of the location in the Where line is significant because Facebook is international. Most of your friends and fans probably don't live near you. Those who don't live in the same area as you do have no idea where XYZ Gallery is or if they would be able to attend. If no location is visible, they are more likely to dismiss the notice than to click on it out of curiosity.

After you have created notice of the event and have published it to your wall, compare the version on your wall and the one on your events page. Note differences in how the notice shows up and, if necessary, tweak the event description text so that it can be understood immediately upon viewing.

Now, it is time to invite people to the event. You can use any of the following three methods to do so. For all methods, start at the event page you created.

- Click on Select Guests in the left sidebar and complete the process. This option is the best if you know exactly whom you want to invite.
- Click on Update Fans at the top of the page. This method is a better choice for targeting people in a specific location, a certain age range, or even gender. You can also invite all of your fans using this link.
- Click on Share under the event title and send the event invitation as a private message.

"Share" is also available directly from the event as it appears on your fan page wall.

Don't promote your art or events on someone else's fan page. Comment on their posts all you like, but their fan page is *their* page, not yours. Promoting your art and your events on someone's page is considered spamming and could get you banned from a page.

When responding to invitations you receive for events, write a personal note. If you just click on Yes, No, or Maybe, you'll be lumped into a large group of responses. When you write a note, your name and picture appears on that event wall, which all of the other invitees will see.

Save Time on Facebook

Facebook is one of the biggest time-suckers out there—if you allow it to be. To stay focused on what's most important, try any or all of the following tips.

Turn off all notifications. You don't need to be informed the instant someone has posted on your wall or tagged you in a note. Instant notifications are disruptive to your studio and business time. Instead, you can see all activity that has taken place since your last visit by clicking the globe icon on the top left of any page. It's to the right of the Facebook logo.

Use a timer. Set your timer for the minutes (not hours!) you have allotted to an activity and spend no more time than planned. It's amazing what you can accomplish under the pressure of an anticipated buzzer.

Set aside Facebook time in your day. In scheduling your social networking, select a time of day that is best for you and your working rhythms. For instance, if you are most creative from 9 a.m. to noon, don't spend your time on the computer during those hours—unless you use the computer to make your art!

Group your friends into lists. Friends Lists help you organize your Facebook connections. Instead of having hundreds or even thousands of friends' updates in your profile stream, you can select those you are most interested in hearing from at that time.

The most efficient method of creating a Friends List is to process each name when you receive an invitation to connect. After confirming a friend invitation, select Add to List. At this point, you can add to previously created lists or start a new one. I think you will find this method better than having to go through the names later to categorize them.

Another way to create a Friends List is to click on Friends from the left sidebar of your Facebook Home. Then click on the Edit Friends button in the upper right of the center column and then the Create a List button, which is in the same location as the Edit Friends button. A new window will open up with all of your friends in it. Enter a title for your list ("Enter a Name") and begin adding people by typing their names or clicking on their names.

To view your lists, select Home and then click Most Recent at the top center of the page. Click on the blue down arrow and your lists will appear. You may have to select Choose Another if you have a number of lists. Your selected stream will display updates only from the people you included on that friends list.

From here, you can also add people to a list. Click on the Edit List button in the upper right corner. Your list of friends will open, and you can either type names or click on the names and photos of people that you want to add to the list.

TAKE THE LEAD ON TWITTER

Don't join Twitter thinking you're going to promote, promote, promote. The emphasis—the primary purpose—of Twitter is on being social, on making friends. As I said earlier, Twitter is the least promotional of all social media sites.

Most people don't "get" Twitter right away. Until you have been using it consistently for two or three months, you might be flummoxed— and you have every reason to be. Don't look for it to be more complicated than it is or to reveal a deeper meaning. The longer you are on Twitter, the more you will understand the benefits and the more people you will meet. It could become a valuable aspect of cultivating collectors for your art.

Key Elements of an Artist's Twitter Account

In addition to your @name, which I assume you already have, there are five critical items for any Twitter account.

Your profile picture. A picture of you appears on your Twitter Profile page and alongside each tweet you send. You can use a piece of your art for your Twitter avatar, but showing us a picture of your face makes the page more personal.

Your one-line bio. Twitter gives you an extra 20 characters for your bio! Try to differentiate yourself from other artists in a maximum of 160 characters. Tell us about your interests so that we want to follow you. For inspiration, I've listed some of my favorites.

Park ranger turned fiber artist, out to change the world, one felt hat at a time—Carrie Mulligan, @ccmfelthats

The Cycling Artist—London based professional artist, computer geek & perpetual academic—Tina Mammoser, @tina_m

If you like conceptual art, think about honking—Michael Mayer, @studiomayer

Using hammers and a torch to make the world a more beautiful place—Wendy Edsall-Kerwin, @wtek

Your website or blog URL. You are limited to 160 characters for your bio, so let us know where can we read more about you. Twitter gives you a place to add your website address.

Custom Twitter background. It's advantageous to have your art brand as your Twitter background. Do a Web search for "custom Twitter backgrounds" to find the appropriate size and tips for a successful background. The image should be from 1280 x 1024 to 1600 x 1200 pixels. Changing the resolution of your computer screen in your settings will show you how Twitter backgrounds appear on screens of varying resolutions. Make sure vital information doesn't disappear because you have used the wrong image size for your background.

Your location. It's fun and easy to find people by location on Twitter, so be sure to include yours in your Twitter profile. I suggest you choose the closest medium to large city or town because large urban areas are searched more frequently.

All of the above elements plus 20 or more tweets should be in place before you start following people in large numbers. When other Twitter users see that you are following them, they will check to see if they want to follow you back. If you look like a real person with something to contribute, they'll probably return the favor. If there's nothing of interest to them on your Twitter page, there is no reason for them to follow you.

What to Tweet

Every beginning Twitter user faces the same dilemma: What can I say in a maximum of 140 characters that will be interesting to my followers? The bottom line is that there are no rules. Every time I see a formula posted for tweeting, I can quickly point to a successful Twitter user who is doing the exact opposite of what's recommended. With this in mind, aim for variety in your tweets and see what combination works best for you. Below is a menu to choose from.

Entertaining tweets. We all love to smile and laugh! You can provide the fodder for our joviality by tweeting about a funny video or a humorous quote. You will be even more successful if the video or quote is related to art. You could also *be* funny, and that's good enough to win you lots of followers. If being humorous is in your nature, let your personality shine on Twitter. Entertaining tweets are always the top tweets.

Informational tweets. The more you can help people, the more they will return the favor and help you build a following. Because Twitter is social, being helpful earns you extra credit and more friends. You can retweet a link to an upcoming webinar you're attending or an online coupon you discovered. If you hear of a deadline for a show, grant, or residency, tweet it. You can also tweet a link to an online article that might be of interest to your followers.

Inspirational tweets. Post a good quote (referencing the source, of course) or make up one of your own. Links to encouraging videos work well, too. These links are among the most retweeted—at least in my circles. They are also among the most maligned because people tire of them quickly. Unless your passion is to sprinkle the Twitterverse with inspiration, don't overdo it on these tweets.

Inquisitive tweets. People love to give their opinions, so ask questions of your followers. Inquire about resources: "What's the best printer for doing x?" You can also ask seemingly irrelevant, but amusing questions. For example, I once tweeted "Is it biggie or biggy?" This question elicited a load of replies, though no clear winner.

Responsive tweets. You shouldn't always be asking questions and never responding to those from others. Respond to the inquisitive tweets. Answer questions to become part of the conversation.

Contrary tweets. If you want to launch a revolution, take the opposite side. If everyone says the glass is half empty and you insist it's half full, you'll create a stir. This approach isn't for the faint of heart. You must passionately believe in your stance and be able to withstand criticism. Contrary tweets, when backed by passion or evidence, can attract attention.

Congratulatory tweets. If you really want to make friends on Twitter, mention others' accomplishments in your tweets. Think about it. It's like you're a teacher standing in front of a roomful of students and praising one of your students in front of everyone else. Didn't you love it when that happened to you as a child? Adults like accolades, too!

Retweets. Retweeting ("RT" in Twitter lingo) is a courtesy and, again, makes friends for you on Twitter—especially if you're retweeting something another is promoting. Use the retweet button or add a RT within the tweet followed by the person's @name to give that individual credit. Your RTs also show up in contributors' @Mentions columns so they are aware of how kind you were. A retweet looks like this: *RT @abstanfield Is it biggie or biggy?*

Promotional tweets. Aha! We are finally at promoting your art. It's not a mistake that this item is last on the list. You have to send all of the other kinds of tweets in order to earn the right to promote to your followers. If you were constantly promoting, you'd lose friends and followers quickly, but promoting is necessary from time to time. After all, your Twitter followers will be bummed if they are the last to hear about something you have to offer. Remember that everyone who follows you is doing so voluntarily. They have asked to hear from you. A good rule of thumb is to promote 5 to 10 percent of the time. For those of us who didn't like math class, that's once for every 10 or 20 tweets.

Tweet Makeovers

The challenge? Being pithy (and helpful) in a maximum of 140 characters.
The players? You and your Twitter followers.
The scene? Pick one.

Scene 1
You're tempted to tweet: *Congratulations @xxx!*
But you opt for: *Congrats on the photo-video exhibit in May @xxx!*

Why? Unless your followers are following @xxx at the same time you tweet, they will have no idea why you're sending your congratulations. Acknowledge the accomplishment by being specific.

Scene 2
You're tempted to tweet: *New blog post at http://…*
But you opt for: *Artists: Learn how to improve your tweets on the Art Biz Blog http://…*

Why? "New blog post" doesn't tell me anything! All bloggers are pitching their latest post on Twitter. Why should I stop everything to read YOUR blog post? What will it do for me?

Scene 3
You're tempted to tweet: *Great advice for artists at http://mariabrophy.com*
But you opt for: *Artists who want tips for pricing should read this from @mariabrophy http://mariabrophy.com/…*

Why? "Great advice" might not be advice I need or want at the moment. And the link could go anywhere—especially if you're using a link-shortening service like bit.ly and the true URL is hidden. Tell me what I'm going to get if you want me to click on it. Also, if the author of the post you're linking to is on Twitter, be sure to give that person a Twitter plug by adding her @name.

Scene 4
You're tempted to tweet: *This video is hilarious! http://…*
But you opt for: *Cute kitten alert! This video will make you laugh out loud http://…*

Why? See reasoning under Scene 3. In the tempting tweet, I have no idea what the video is about or why I'd want to click on it. Give me something to cling to—something to entice me.

Scene 5
You're tempted to tweet: *Just posted a new work on Etsy, click here …*
But like artist Liz Crain <@LizCrain>, you opt for: *An orange skull jug mixes Halloween metaphors—from my Etsy shop: http:// …*

Why? Again, pique my curiosity. Compel me to look.

Gain Followers

Technically, you can't "get" people to follow you on Twitter. You can't make people do anything they don't want to do. In my experience, these are best ways to attract followers.

- **Be helpful.** Tweet useful information and resources.
- **Be nice.** Say nice things and avoid complaining. Twitter can seem like a giant complaint dump at times. People unload on Twitter—forgetting that their professional reputations are at stake. You can stand out by not joining in the chorus of negativity.
- **Be generous.** In their book *Trust Agents*, Chris Brogan and Julien Smith say that you should promote other people 12 times as much as you promote yourself. Imagine the friends you make when you're retweeting what others say, recommending a blog, or encouraging your followers to follow someone else!
- **Follow more people.** The more people you follow, the more people you will communicate with on Twitter. But use caution and follow a few people at a time until your number of followers catches up to those you are following. It doesn't look good if you are following 500 people but only have 47 followers.

     To find people to follow, try Twellow.com or TweepSearch.com and search by subject or location. You can also try the search function on the Twitter site, although I think you'll find the other search platforms to be more powerful.

Save Time on Twitter

It's more difficult to set aside time for Twitter than it is for Facebook because it only takes a few seconds here and there to post or respond to posts. Twitter is an ongoing conversation that you drop in on whenever you have a minute. But if you find yourself on Twitter too frequently (or staying too long), you might need a defined Twitter time. With this in mind, let's look at four ways to keep you focused while using Twitter.

Look only at what is on the screen in front of you. Tara Reed, of artlicensinginfo.com, has a Twitter philosophy to reduce your stress about this fast-paced site. She calls it the "Zen of Twitter."

> *Don't worry about what you might have missed when you weren't looking, just assume that the tweets you are meant to see are the ones on the screen when you are inspired to look.*

It's wonderful advice, and it might easily be applied to Facebook and other social media sites. Look only at what's on the screen. There's no need to dig for older posts.

Keep your eye on your art. Remember that your focus should be on making art—not being immediately aware that someone has sent you a message or has mentioned you in a tweet. Adjust your notifications under Settings/Notices after you've logged in to Twitter so that you're not interrupted doing your important work.

Create Twitter lists. Like Facebook Lists, Twitter Lists offer you the opportunity to categorize the people you're following. With a click of the mouse, you can tune out a lot of noise in your Twitter stream and get caught up with your favorites. You might create lists based on geography, subjects (metalsmiths, breaking news, humor), close friends, or just the people you don't want to miss.

Use TweetDeck, HootSuite, or Seesmic. Although Twitter's interface gets more sophisticated every day, it is fairly basic and easy to use. It doesn't, however, have the power of platforms you can find at TweetDeck.com, HootSuite.com, or Seesmic.com (there are others as well). These programs, which are available for free, let you keep an eye on multiple lists (similar to the ones you can create on the Twitter site) simultaneously. You can send tweets directly from the program.

One of my favorite features of these platforms is the ability to post-date tweets, which can save oodles of time! Let's say you have an exhibit opening in a week. You can schedule tweets to be sent every day before the opening. Just be sure to vary the time of day the tweets are sent and the content of each post-dated tweet.

TIPS FOR MANAGING SOCIAL MEDIA

Complete your profile. Don't try to connect with a large number of people on a social media site before you have fully completed your profile and have posted some of your own content.

Think thrice before duplicating content word-for-word on these social media sites. Most people won't see your multiple posts, so exposure isn't the problem with duplication. The problem is that each platform has a specific "personality" and purpose. Some items you post to Twitter aren't appropriate for your Facebook wall. Likewise, an item you post on Facebook might not make sense to Twitter followers if it's out of context.

Reset your passwords at least twice a year. Using strong passwords discourages hacking, but changing your password helps you avoid a huge headache. See Passwords in the Resources section at the back of the book.

Turn off all notifications for social media activity. I mentioned this time-saving tip in the discussions for Facebook and Twitter, and I reiterate it here. Don't let social media keep you from your most important tasks—particularly, your time in the studio.

Review your privacy settings. It's your responsibility to know how these sites work. Read the terms and understand what you are sharing with whom.

Act like the world is watching. Approach your online activity with this belief uppermost in your mind: Whatever goes online, stays online and is accessible to the world. You might delete an item at some point, but someone somewhere has archived it. It's no accident that "reputation management" is a growing field these days. Experts are being called in to clean up the misadventures of people who talked too much or spoke without thinking. Don't be one of them.

Monitor your time. It's easy to get caught up in other people's tweets, questions, and photos. Whenever you catch yourself "over-engaged," stop and remember that you intended to spend only 15 to 30 minutes. Ask yourself: Do I really need to spend time on this activity now? Is it the best use of my time? Should I be in the studio? This awareness will pull you back to reality and reminds you what is most important for your art business.

Don't try to be everywhere. Select one site or two that work for you and have fun with them.

Introduce yourself. In "real" life, you could go up to someone at an art opening, stick out your hand, and simply say, "Hi, I'm Sally. Will you be my friend?" But, c'mon. Would you really do that? I doubt it—so why are you doing it online? Wouldn't it more natural—and more polite—to introduce yourself by sharing something that you have in common with the other person?

Instead of using the empty default friend request (Facebook) or "Join my network" (LinkedIn), I hope that you'll take the time to personalize your initial contact with people who may not know you well or at all. It is important that you know your connections because privacy issues are becoming an increasingly serious issue on all social media sites. We want to know who people are before we allow them into our communities.

- To friend or connect with another artist, try this approach: "Hi, Steve. I saw your art in *American Artist* and was impressed. I'd like to connect here." That gives the other person a frame of reference as to why you are requesting a connection.
- To friend or connect with someone in your past: "Hey, Frank. It's been a long time, but we had the same drawing class our junior year in college. I moved away from Ohio (to Oregon)

about 15 years ago, but I'd like to connect with you here."
Mentioning your location (or any other personal detail) gives
the other person some sort of reference. You might even find
out that it's another thing you have in common.

• To friend or connect with someone you don't really know: "Hi,
Mary. I've been admiring your art and blog for a couple of
years now and just found you here on Facebook. I hope we can
connect here." Of course, you have to tell the truth, but sincere
flattery is good for any networking situation.

Think about how you would introduce yourself in an email message
or at a party and use that approach as a starting point. Don't ever presume
that people remember you if you've had only brief contact with them or
if your connection was in the distant past. Summon all of your manners
and do it the right way. After all, you only get one shot at it.

NO-EXCUSE PRINCIPLE

Social media can help connect you to a large community and relieve the
confines of the solitary world of your studio. If you want to amplify your
online presence, social media is your ticket. But you'll be disappointed
if you approach social media only as a promotional tool to benefit you.

NO-EXCUSE ACTION

Use social media to connect and build relationships. Be friendly, be
kind, be generous, and you'll prosper on social media sites. Just don't
forget to set that timer.

Action 9

Send a Newsletter

That Begs to Be Opened

Getting Back in Touch Paid Off for Him
*After years of putting it off, I finally got my newsletter designed,
written, and sent out. The good news is it's already doing its job!
Within a day I had heard back from someone who went to a
solo show of mine several years ago. She had attended with her
sister. While she didn't buy anything, her sister did, and she's
always been jealous. Since I never sent out a newsletter, she
never thought to contact me. But the day after I finally sent out
my newsletter, I got an email from her asking about buying two
pieces. My newsletter was the little boost she needed.*
—Daniel Sroka <danielsroka.com>

Businesses, nonprofits, and entrepreneurs have known for decades that
newsletters are a terrific way to keep in touch and nurture relationships
with clients, customers, donors, members, and volunteers. Are you
taking advantage of this marketing marvel? Writing and distributing
a newsletter (whether by mail or email) is one of the best ways to
continue to air your name and to update your raving fans about your
progress. Interesting solid content can help you make a reputation for

yourself. A well-written newsletter also becomes a valuable promotional piece to include in your portfolio and to hand to guests at your studio and exhibitions.

Writing a newsletter is a commitment and responsibility. There is no sense starting a newsletter unless you intend to keep it up. Once you have committed to a newsletter, you must make it a part of your routine. If you ask people to sign up for your newsletter and tell them when to expect it, they'll be disappointed if you don't deliver.

You don't have to purchase fancy mailing lists or hire slick designers in order to have a great newsletter. All you need is news! And almost anything can be developed into interesting (that's the key: *interesting*) content. One of my favorite newsletters is from my carpet cleaner. My carpet cleaner! It's about eight pages and has intriguing seasonal stories and tips in it—not at all related to carpet cleaning. I read almost every word and even keep the sections I want to refer to.

The main goals for your newsletter are to generate sales and opportunities, toot your horn, provide information to your collectors, and create goodwill by including other columnists and community activities. Even more importantly, the reason you distribute newsletters is to keep your name in front of people. If done well, your newsletter will be a powerful promotional addition to your regular emails, postcards, and letters. If it's really good, it will be kept and shared with others.

> The primary goals for your newsletter are that people share it, keep it, and look forward to each issue.

PLAN IT

Before you begin your newsletter, plan! Planning your newsletter well in advance of its appearance allows you time to get it right. Decide how frequently you will publish your newsletter, make sure the schedule is realistic for you, and add the deadlines to your calendar.

Create an accurate budget and stick with it. After you have worked through this chapter and decided whether you'll distribute a print or email version of your newsletter, consider the costs: design fees, printing, paper/envelopes/supplies, postage, software, photography, and anything else you need to get your newsletter into the hands of readers or on their computer screens.

If the responsibility of a newsletter sounds overwhelming right now, you can take a small step by creating a file labeled "Newsletter Ideas." Stuff it with items you come across that you find interesting, stories you want to tell, tips you'd like to share, and designs you find appealing. You can also make files in your email program to keep your e-ideas. For example, you might create e-folders for "Content Ideas" and "Images." Move incoming emails to the relevant folders so that you can find them when you're ready to start your newsletter.

NAME IT

The title for your newsletter isn't nearly as critical as the content. However, the title you choose should reflect your style or subject matter as well as the newsletter content. It should beg to be opened and read.

If you plan on posting your newsletter on your website, as you should, keywords included in the title will yield better search engine rankings. For example, my former newsletter title ("Do This") wasn't a good title for search engines. Artists looking for marketing help would never search for "Do This"! So it was changed to "Art Marketing Action." As a result, my search-engine placement continues to hover near the top for the phrase "art marketing."

You might consider creating a title for your newsletter along the lines of the following.

> Studio News from Brian Whisenhunt
> Dog Portraits by Frida Munson
> Mark Barron's Garden Ornaments
> Painting Now by Deborah Stevens

Except for the first example, all these titles describe a particular type of artwork. Titles like these are better for search-engine placement since they contain keywords. However, if your newsletter is to be printed only (rather than electronic), the wording of the title is probably not as important. A couple more pieces of advice about titles: (1) I advise you not to use one that is too cute or esoteric in a way that would cause a disconnect with your art; and (2) I encourage you to include your name in the title since that's what you want people to remember.

FILL IT

If you have a good idea of your audience, you can better focus your content. If your audience is primarily young single women, your newsletter will be quite different from that of the artist who seeks portrait commissions from wealthy retirees. Regardless of your audience, your newsletter should have four core components.

The first component is the art. As with all of your self-promotion efforts, your art should be the reason behind the entire newsletter. Recipients would be disappointed in an artist's newsletter that did not include images, so your art should take center stage. A great image can intrigue and elicit inquiries. Be mindful if you are printing in black and white. Black-and-white images should have strong contrasts and reproduce well without the benefit of color.

For a printed newsletter, use images printed at a higher resolution (300 dpi or above). The files for these pieces of art will be huge and, therefore, the documents will also be very large, but the print quality will be noticeably improved. For an electronic newsletter, use photos at lower resolution (72 pixels per inch) and size. There's no sense annoying people with slow-loading attachments. Be sure to credit the photographer and include your copyright as well as the title, date, dimensions (H x W x D in inches or centimeters), and medium.

Next, you have to have news. What do you have to report in terms of exhibits, awards, acquisitions, articles, new retail outlets, or commissions? And how can you make the news entertaining and interesting? (See Action 10 for a closer look at enticing language.)

The third component to consider is items or articles that are of interest to your readers. Including articles that aren't all about you will make your newsletter something special that begs to be read. Viewers are interested in all sorts of things, which is why you should include a variety of content. Men, in particular, like to know how things are made. For them, you can discuss your technique or a new medium, but make sure your writing isn't too dry. If you are writing about technique, write about how yours is different from other artists. You are trying to differentiate yourself from the crowd. Women tend to be interested in the emotional aspects of art. Share the genesis of your inspiration with them in a way they can relate to.

Demonstrate how your art fits into the broader scope of the community. For instance, if you make sculptures of eagles, have the bird specialist at the zoo write a brief paragraph on eagles, invite an Eagle Scout to write about his troop, or note the history of the bald eagle as an American symbol. By bringing others into the process, you are casting a wider net of influence. Collaborations always yield bigger audiences. Your content possibilities double or triple if you have a niche market. Pet portrait artists write about overcrowded animal shelters, new products for dogs and cats, or upcoming television shows for pet lovers. Artists who interpret local scenery can write about land conservation, the opening of a new retail store, or a weather phenomenon that affected the community. Get the idea?

32 Ideas for Newsletter Content

1. Your art technique or medium—if unique, understandable, interesting
2. Expanded information on one of your subjects
3. Your new work and how it is relevant to the community or larger art world
4. New exhibit of other artwork related to your own
5. The history of a color, art medium, or technique
6. Art and politics
7. An upcoming fundraiser for a local arts organization
8. Art education

9. Donations of artwork you made for a charity auction and why
10. Public funding of the arts
11. A new public sculpture in town
12. An interview with a curator or collector
13. Creative projects for those who are not artists
14. Feature article on a nonprofit organization you have donated to or that has a mission you agree with
15. Rebuttal to an art review in the newspaper (while you're at it, send it to the paper as well)
16. A review by you of an art exhibit
17. Anything related to your niche market
18. Kids' projects that relate to your art, such as an outline drawing they can color or a hands-on activity
19. A new material or resource, especially if your newsletter goes out to a lot of artists
20. Review of a book or movie about art
21. Great moments in art history
22. How to care for art
23. Quotes about art
24. Notes about an art lecture you attended
25. Media coverage of the arts (or lack thereof)
26. Calendar of your upcoming exhibits, programs, or events
27. A recent award or honor you received
28. New gallery representation
29. Recent purchases and commissions (only public collections, unless you receive approval from individuals)
30. Great website links, wacky links, or just plain helpful links
31. Top resources or quotes you tweeted or found on Twitter
32. Funny or insightful comments from your fan page on Facebook

Don't be tempted to say everything in the first issue. Slowly reveal yourself to your readers, being careful not to discuss too much in one place. You want to keep readers' attention over the long run. Break down larger topics into a series of articles and you'll have plenty for your next newsletter as well as for your blog. Interact with your readers and viewers by encouraging input from them. But avoid asking questions like "What did you think?" Be creative! Include a provocative question that stimulates thoughtful answers and participation. If you create public sculpture, for example, you might ask: "Do you have a favorite public sculpture or one that you abhor? Write and tell me about it!" If you make wearable art, ask: "What's the most memorable outfit you have owned or that your mother sewed for you?" You can include the answers in your next newsletter or on your blog or Facebook fan page. You might also incorporate them into a gallery installation.

And, finally, the fourth component for your newsletter is a call to action. It would be a shame if you put together a good-looking newsletter and then forgot to include a call to action. Tell readers what to do after reading your newsletter. Do you want them to get a sneak peek of your latest sculpture before it goes to the foundry? Attend your opening with a friend? Buy a reproduction for a holiday gift? Whatever your goal is, be clear and make it easy for your readers to act.

Another way to get readers to act is to include a "teaser" that encourages them to visit your website, attend your exhibition, or visit your studio. Pose a question in a printed newsletter that is answered on your website or include a coupon that is good for a set of free note cards at your next open studio sale.

And don't forget to directly ask your recipients to forward your newsletter.

> *If you have enjoyed this newsletter, I encourage you to share it with anyone and everyone. I am trying to build a bigger audience for my work and can only succeed with the help of friends like you.*

Or . . .

> *I hope you have enjoyed this newsletter and that you will share it with your friends and family. I'd also appreciate your help in spreading the word about my exhibition opening on March 15 (details in the story above). Please come and bring a friend!*

Follow my design rules for portfolio items under Action 6 to create a great-looking newsletter from the ground up.

PRINT IT

In general, printed newsletters appear less frequently than electronic versions, primarily because of the time and expense involved. But printed newsletters have a longer shelf life and are more likely to be kept on the recipients' desks or on their refrigerators.

For the best quality (if you're not printing yourself), take a digital file to your copy center and have copies printed directly from your file. Print your newsletter on white paper, especially if you are using color images of your artwork. Some artists can get by with color paper if they are using black-and-white images. For instance, an artist whose work is rooted in nature, such as a clay artist, might select an earthy or even lightly speckled paper. Artists who create bright funky paintings or sculptures might need colorful paper to convey their message.

People Look Forward to Her Newsletter

Elia Woods is a fiber artist living and working in Oklahoma City. Over a number of years, she worked on a series called Vegetable Prayers, fabulous contemporary quilts with photo-transfer images of the vegetables in her organic garden. She put out a quarterly newsletter called "Earthly Delights." Each issue was based on her most recently completed quilt, which, in turn, focused on a single vegetable. (Shown at right is the Kale issue.)

Elia included the history and folklore of the featured vegetable, along with information about how to grow and cook it. In addition, she added community information (how to get involved with organic and community gardens or the slow food movement, for example). Upcoming exhibits, classes, and open studio events were highlighted. The newsletter was printed in black ink on 100% recycled paper, which reflected Elia's heartfelt concern for a healthier planet. A color postcard image of her art was enclosed with each newsletter and an electronic version was posted on eliawoods.com.

Earthly Delights

art and garden reflections from 32nd Street | Elia Woods

All Hail to Kale

All through my growing up years, I knew I did not like kale. I had never actually tasted it, but I knew, firmly, that I did NOT like kale. Then one day, in an odd moment of culinary open-mindedness, I tried a winter greens soup, and immediately fell in love with kale. I made it three times the following week, and quickly learned a key fact: all kale is not created equal. Some of the bunches I bought were yummy and tender, and some were tough and bitter. This led me to my next conclusion: nothing matches home-grown.

Oh, kale! What a world of wonder I had been missing! Krinkly, curly Scotch kale, purple-tinged Red Russian, bumpy Black Tuscan "dinosaur" kale... the array of colors and shapes is enticing. The brightly colored ornamental kales are actually edible as well, as long as you grow your own or know for certain that they haven't been sprayed.

Kale is one of the easiest to grow members of the brassica family, an ancient group of highly nutritious vegetables that includes cauliflower, broccoli, cabbage, kohlrabi and Brussels sprouts. All are cool weather crops, and some are a bit challenging to grow here in Oklahoma. But kale is a forgiving and easygoing friend in the garden. Plant seedlings in early spring for harvesting through early summer, and again in September for fall and winter meals. Kale will happily carry on through cold winter temps. Indeed, most varieties are sweeter after the first freeze, although Red Russian is tender even in early fall. Pick the outer leaves off the plant, and it will continue to grow and produce. Hot weather brings bitter flavors. Brassicas respond well to very fertile soil; composted leaves are an especially good addition.

Those cute little green inchworms that appear in spring and early fall will quickly devour the leaves on a young kale plant. In a small patch, handpicking and smooshing is quick and effective.

My favorite method of cooking kale is to sauté some garlic, toss in the chopped kale, cover the pan and let it steam in its own juices, then sprinkle with lemon juice or balsamic vinegar. Yum!

Exhibits and Classes

Food for Thought
My solo exhibit *Food for Thought* premiered at the Tulsa Artists' Coalition gallery in October. This body of work celebrates our sources of sustenance and explores the sacred trust we have with the natural world. Special thanks to the TAC volunteers and staff, who made this opportunity possible, and to all of you who were able to attend or encouraged me along the way. Fellow artist Lynn Craigie wrote a lovely review, which you can read on my website, www.eliawoods.com (click on "exhibits").

I was very pleased to have my artworks *Seeing Red*, *Little White Lies* and *Freedom Got the Blues* accepted in Fiber National 2007 at the Lancaster Museum of Art, PA.

Dinner in the Deuce
An exceptional exhibit at Untitled ArtSpace, 1 NE 3rd, Jan. 11-Feb. 23, of handcrafted dining environments created by teams of artists. My team's table is *Poised al Fresco*, and includes my handwoven table napkins and hand dyed silk canopy. www.1ne3.org.

City Arts Center at Fair Park
951-0000 or cityartscenter.org

Café City Arts 2008: Circus Maximus thru Feb. 23
My newest scarves in doubleweave and shadow weave.

My adult **weaving classes** resume Jan. 22.
Tuesdays, 7-9pm or Thursdays, 10am to noon, $104.

Easter Eggs with Natural Dyes: Free Event!
Sat. March 15, 1-4 pm (come and go) All ages welcome (children under 12 must be accompanied by an adult). Bring your own eggs; we'll provide the dyes and show you how to create tantalizingly beautiful designs. This is the first in a series of free intergenerational programs on natural dyes made possible thanks to a grant from the Oklahoma Department of Environmental Quality.

More natural dye classes, and our YouTube videos on indigo dyeing and mud painting, at www.cityartscenter.org.

Oklahoma City Museum of Art
Enroll at 236-3100 x213 or www.okcmoa.com.

Pop-Up Cards With A Heart
Sunday, Feb. 3, 1-4pm: adults and teens, $20-25
Sunday, Feb. 10, 2-4: Kids ages 7-10, $10-15
Make fun and fabulous pop-up Valentines cards!
Transferring Art Nouveau Imagery onto Fabric
Sat. Feb. 16, 10am – 4pm, $40 (members) or $50
Explore the heat transfer method of applying photo imagery to cloth. All materials provided.

This newsletter celebrates the pleasures of being spiritually and physically nourished by the earth... our earthly delights.   **Issue #9 - Winter 2008**

Newsletter design: Patricia J. Velte <whitewingdesign.com>

Kale: *Brassica oleracea var. acephala,* kail, n. [Scot. kale, kail. var. of cole.] a hardy, nonheading cabbage with loose, spreading, curled leaves; cole or colewort.

Pecan Bounty

The pecan harvest this year has brought me to my knees, both in gratitude, and in order to harvest this bumper crop. It's hard to beat the experience of walking around one's own yard, gathering delicious food right off the ground. I never got very far with hand shelling our pecans, so I've been delighted to discover that Farmer's Grain in Edmond will crack and blow pecans for .39 cents/#. After blowing, the pecans are almost completely shelled; you'll still need to pick through and discard pieces of shell. By the way, pecan shells are acidic and make ideal mulch for azaleas and rhododendrons. Toasting the nuts briefly in a skillet helps bring out their flavor. I'm posting my favorite Pecan Sandies recipe on my website, www.eliawoods.com.

For comments, suggestions or to add or subtract a name from my mailing list, contact me at:
Elia Woods
(405) 524-3977
PO Box 60803, Oklahoma City, OK 73146
Elia@eliawoods.com
www.EliaWoods.com

This newsletter is printed on Genesis, 100% post-consumer waste paper, from greenlinepaper.com

Earthly Delights

Elia Woods
P.O. Box 60803
Oklahoma City, OK 73146

Coming in May... **Grounded**
Solo exhibit at Individual Artists of Oklahoma gallery, May 2-30, 2008
Opening reception at IAO, Saturday May 17, 6 - 9 pm
The following weekend will feature an outdoor event at our Community Garden

OK, folks, I'm trying something new. The limitation of doing an indoor exhibit about the world outside is that... well, it's indoors. While being inside can offer us a chance for focus and contemplation, nothing awakens the spirit like wind on skin, the scent of damp soil, or spring's first sweet strawberry nibbled straight from the plant. To that end, I am linking my upcoming exhibit at IAO with an outdoor event at the Central Park Community Gardens, where we are undertaking a new effort to create an outdoor green-art-environment which will encourage visitors to experience directly the beauty, complexity and healing power of the living world. More details soon!

Annual Valentine's Art Sale and Card Making Party

Saturday. Feb. 9, 1 - 7 pm
at my studio
1012 NW 32, OKC
Come shop for one-of-a-kind handcrafted cards, or join the fun and make your own! All ages are welcome.

Newsletter design: Patricia J. Velte <whitewingdesign.com>

SEND IT

Of course, you have to consider how your newsletter will be mailed. Newsletters like Elia's can be set up as a self-mailer with two or three panels, which eliminates the need for and expense of envelopes. All you need is a sticker or tape to secure it for sending. However, if you want to be certain that your beautifully printed newsletter is not ragged after going through the machines at the post office, place it in an envelope. You might even do a test run and mail a few to friends and family to see what it looks like after so many people have handled it.

Make your envelope stand out in a pile of mail so that it begs to be read. Ask yourself: What can I send that will make the recipient open my envelope first? Don't you just love getting envelopes made of specialty papers? Or ones with images or drawings on the outside? Think about the ones that catch your eye—the ones you want to open first. As a visual artist, you should be especially mindful of presentation and its impact on others.

If you have a small mailing list, addressing your newsletter by hand will make it more personal. Handwritten envelopes almost always get opened before those with printed mailing labels.

DISTRIBUTE IT

After you mail your print newsletter to your usual clients, place a stack of leftover copies in venues where casual visitors—perhaps many of them art appreciators—can come across them. Leave some at any of the following sites (always ask permission first).

- A gallery that is showing your work
- Your studio
- Retail space of a family member or friend
- Bulletin boards at coffee shops, art schools, and art centers
- The lobby of an art organization, such as an arts council, artist group, or art center
- Your local chamber of commerce (membership has its privileges)

- Places of work for any of your contributing columnists (another good reason for including more people to help you with content for your newsletter)
- Offices that have your work in their corporate collections
- The local library
- Bookstores
- Hair salons
- Dentists' and doctors' offices

If you have a niche market, ask those venues to display your newsletter. You might even consider coordinating a joint mailing with them or ask if they would include your newsletter as a special insert with their mailings and orders.

EMAIL IT

Although print newsletters have some advantages, many artists prefer to email their newsletters. Before you jump on the bandwagon, consider the following advantages and disadvantages of an electronic newsletter.

Advantages of an Electronic Newsletter

- + It can be sent more frequently because it is often less expensive to produce and distribute.
- + Most people are able to put one together quickly and easily.
- + It is easier to send people to your website, blog, or Facebook fan page with an e-newsletter. With a paper newsletter, they have to take the copy to the computer and type in your URL. With an e-newsletter, all they have to do is click.
- + The recipient can forward it without much effort, reaching beyond the scope of your mailing list.
- + It can be more readily posted on your website, which can increase your subscription rate if you have a great newsletter. People like to know what they're going to get before they sign up for something.

Disadvantages of an Electronic Newsletter

- It might get lost in the overflowing inboxes of busy people.
- The recipients may not be "big" email users. In other words, your patrons might prefer holding something in their hands to reading about you on a computer screen.
- It has a shorter shelf life, which means it's easy to delete and forget about.
- Spam filters make it difficult for some emails to get through. Each week, anywhere between 2% and 15% of Art Biz Coach newsletters are undeliverable. Some people don't even know they have a spam filter on.
- Graphics might be blocked from view. Because of the various email configurations, graphics are not loaded or viewed in almost 40% of all messages—an important consideration for artists. E-newsletters should contain enough plain text that the reader receives all of the important information without having to view any graphics.
- You have limited flexibility with your Internet Service Provider (ISP). You want to reach as many people as possible— to build your mailing list well beyond what you can currently imagine. However, your ISP undoubtedly limits the number of emails you can send at once in order to ensure their customers aren't sending spam. This means you need to break up a large mailing list into smaller portions or, preferably, use a separate mail distribution program. Suggested distribution services are in the Resources section at the back of the book.
- There's just something about getting a real piece of mail these days!

In addition to considering the general advantages and disadvantages of electronic newsletters, you should also be aware of the four options for formatting an electronic newsletter.

1. **Plain text.** Plain text is just that: plain. It does not support formatting such as bold, italics, underlining, or different font sizes and colors. Newsletters in plain text can be read in all email applications. (See example below.) The alternative to plain text is rich text (RTF), which does support the various types of font formatting. I don't recommend sending newsletters in rich text because it won't look the same in all email programs.
2. **HTML (Hypertext Markup Language).** Although unavailable in email programs configured to read only plain text, HTML messages are much more attractive.
3. **MIME (Multipurpose Internet Mail Extension).** In the simplest terms, MIME sends your newsletter in both plain text and HTML. Users' email programs are configured for their preference and will view one or the other. You just don't know which ones are reading which versions, so you're safest sending it out in MIME.
4. **A combination of options 1 and 2.** Send it in plain text and then post a link to the HTML version on your website.

If you send your newsletter only in HTML, post a link to a plain text or online version at the very top. It might say, "If your email program doesn't support HTML messages, you might have to view this newsletter by clicking here."

Use Arial, Courier, Georgia, Palatino, Tahoma, Trebuchet MS, Verdana, or Times New Roman in HTML emails to ensure viewing by all. Most other fonts are not universal. Also, be aware that an 8-point font on your screen might be entirely too small on another screen or for older eyes. Be gentle with your readers.

Remember: Not all mail programs behave the same way! Some people have the option to download messages and attachments before they appear. For others who do not have this choice, the giant files are automatically downloaded for them and delay the arrival of other mail. This method is particularly annoying to those on dial-up connections.

Don't ignore those on dial-up. Be sure your newsletters are fast loading by keeping them well under 1 MB. A survey of artist e-newsletters I've received recently reveals how wide-ranging the sizes are.

One newsletter, sent like option #4 above, was 23 KB and contained no photos.

An HTML (option #2) newsletter with five pictures was 29 KB.

An HTML newsletter with six pictures was 379 KB (probably a fairly standard size for all of those photos).

A brief update with a photo attached was 2.1 MB—far too large for one photo.

Decrease the resolution and sizes of your digital images to shrink the file size of your email. As mentioned above, for a website or e-newsletter, drop the resolution of images to 72 pixels per inch (ppi). Never insert an image in a newsletter and scale it to the size you want. Instead, resize it in a photo-editing program. Reducing the display size of the image does not reduce the file size, which is a critical element for load time. Be sure to credit the photographer and to include your copyright information with the title, date, dimensions (H x W x D), and medium.

Do not ever include file attachments such as Microsoft Word documents in your mass mailings. Web guru to many artists, Patricia J. Velte of WhiteWing Design said, "It is considered poor etiquette to send a file attachment to anyone who has not already acknowledged their willingness to receive file attachments from you. And file attachments should never be sent to people you don't know." Moreover, many corporations block all file attachments. PDF files are preferred if they must be sent that way, but there isn't a good enough reason to send a newsletter as an attachment. You may think your file looks nice, but it is a nuisance to a number of people. Stick to the basics here.

View your HTML newsletter in different screen resolutions. Not everyone's screen looks the same as yours. Many people now have their screens set at higher pixels, which make fonts appear smaller, but others are still using 800 x 600. Know the resolution of your screen, but also find out what your electronic documents look like on both higher and lower settings. You'll be amazed at the differences!

An example of formatting for a plain text newsletter is below. Plain text, while less than exciting, looks the same for everyone who views it.

STUDIO NEWS
from ARTHUR JACKSON

January 10, 2011

This newsletter can also be found online—complete with pictures—at
http://www.arthurjacksonart.art/news

SPECIAL INVITATION
[Put the most important, time sensitive, and valuable information here at the top.]

LEAD ARTICLE

UPCOMING EXHIBITIONS

This quarterly newsletter is sent to those who have subscribed through my website or in my art festival booth. To unsubscribe, please reply to this email with "unsubscribe" in the subject line.

Arthur Jackson
894 N.E. 29 Street
Oklahoma City, OK 73162
(405) 555-3850
info@arthurjacksonart.art
http://www.arthurjacksonart.art

CHECK IT

- ✓ Have you thanked your subscribers?
- ✓ Have you credited everyone whose images, words, or ideas you have used?
- ✓ Did you give credit to your photographer?
- ✓ Is the layout clean and easy to follow? Is your artwork the focus or does it get lost in something that is over-designed?
- ✓ Is there at least one item that makes readers want to keep a copy or forward it?
- ✓ Have you included yourself on the distribution list?
- ✓ Do all of your links for an e-newsletter have http:// in front of them? They won't be clickable in all programs without this prefix.
- ✓ Have you sent a test email to a small group of friends and family? Ask them to click through all of the links to make sure they work.
- ✓ Is there a note on the bottom that tells people how they can subscribe or unsubscribe? This isn't optional. It is required by the CAN-SPAM laws. Make sure you're adhering to all of the laws. See Resources in the back of the book.
- ✓ Is your contact info complete? There should be at least two ways to get in touch with you. You also want to include your social media links.
- ✓ If you're emailing your newsletter, review "Email Tricks" in Action 10.
- ✓ Have you reined in your tendency to be wordy? People are more likely to read shorter paragraphs with bullets and key points highlighted than they are to read longer stories. Try to write copy that keeps the readers' attention and makes it more likely they'll spend a longer time looking at your art.
- ✓ Have you added humor where appropriate? Humor is always a winner. Make your readers smile or laugh and you have them hooked.

✓ Did you tell readers how to take action?

✓ Did you check your spelling? Always use the spell check feature before you send it to your editor. It's common courtesy! And there is no excuse in today's computer age to send out misspellings that a computer program could find instantly.

✓ Has somebody else reviewed it? Regardless of how good of a writer you are, it always helps to have a second set of eyes look over the content. Check for misspellings, grammar, tense, repeated words, clarity, and facts.

✓ Have you posted a sample copy of one of your newsletters on your website?

✓ Have you added a copyright notice? Your words, if wholly original and full of content, should contain a copyright notice just as your images do. To avoid redundancy, you can use something along the lines of the following credit line (note correct format of © followed by date and name).

All images and text ©2011 Frank Gilliland. Please contact me if you would like to reproduce this newsletter in any form.

For an electronic newsletter, you might include a notice like this one.

All images and text ©2011 Frank Gilliland. I encourage you to forward this email as long as it includes this copyright notice. Please contact me if you would like to reproduce this newsletter in any form.

After you've gone through the checklist, you're ready to send it. Getting your newsletter off the ground is a big step, but it is yet another way to keep your name in front of people while building more personal relationships.

Download the Newsletter Worksheet at IdRatherBeintheStudio.com.

SHRINK IT (EMAIL UPDATES)

If an entire newsletter isn't your bag, consider sending brief updates in the form of short emails that tell people what's new. These brief messages are distributed less regularly, but perhaps more frequently, than newsletters, which means that you don't promise to send one out every other month. Instead, you send them out when you have information to share. Below are some examples of email updates, which all contain information about who, what, where, when, why, and how.

Inform Potential Students about Upcoming Workshop

REMINDER
I'll be giving a printmaking demonstration at the Contemporary Museum, downtown at 6th & Carr, this Sunday at 2 p.m. Museum admission fees apply, my demo and secrets are free.

For Museum information, call (405) 555-6216.

Arthur Jackson
894 N.E. 29 Street
Oklahoma City, OK 73162
(405) 555-3850
info@arthurjacksonart.art
http://www.arthurjacksonart.art

Website Has Been Updated

Say something more interesting than "I have posted new pictures on my website." Your goal is to get them to click!

SNEAK PEEK
The 8'x4' sculpture I've been breaking my back over has finally arrived from the foundry! Pictures of the finished piece and all the hard work it took to get to this point are online now at http://www.arthurjacksonart.art/newsculpture.

Please visit to see what I've been up to. Or, better yet, call and come by to see it in person.

Arthur Jackson
894 N.E. 29 Street
Oklahoma City, OK 73162
(405) 555-3850
info@arthurjacksonart.art
http://www.arthurjacksonart.art

Reminder for Opening

It is always nice to send out printed invitations, but an electronic reminder is perfectly acceptable for those who opted to receive your email messages.

> DON'T FORGET to drop by my opening at the New Gallery
> this Friday between 6 and 8 p.m. . . . 894 N.E. 29 Street . . .
> Wine, hors d'oeuvres, and friends . . . Gallery talk at 7 p.m. . . .
> It won't be a party without you!

Arthur Jackson
894 N.E. 29 Street
Oklahoma City, OK 73162
(405) 555-3850
info@arthurjacksonart.art
http://www.arthurjacksonart.art

Share Information with Patrons

Interesting news items are an ideal reason to put your name in front of your patrons in an email—especially those that reflect a personal interest of one or more individual collectors. If the blast is just going to a handful of people, personalize each one with a salutation like the one below.

> THOUGHT THIS MIGHT BE RIGHT UP YOUR ALLEY
>
> Dear Gloria,
>
> A rare exhibition of Bauhaus photography can be seen in nearby Tulsa at the Photo Co-op through April 15.

Call (918) 555-2629 for directions and more information or visit
their website at http://www.photoco-op.art

Maybe I'll see you there!

Arthur Jackson
894 N.E. 29 Street
Oklahoma City, OK 73162
(405) 555-3850
info@arthurjacksonart.art
http://www.arthurjacksonart.art

NO-EXCUSE PRINCIPLE

Newsletters are a prime opportunity to share your art as you'd like it to
be seen. They give you control over how your art is perceived as you're
maintaining relationships with the people most likely to purchase from
you. You're not bothering people if you give them something they want
to know about.

NO-EXCUSE ACTION

Start a file titled Newsletter Ideas. It's your first step to a newsletter that
begs to be read and reread.

Action 10

Take Advantage of Basic Communication

Mail, Email, and Phone

Reconnecting with Patrons Led to Increased Sales for Her
I have noticed that the more I communicate with my existing buyers—either by newsletters or handwritten notes—the more they are communicating back with me. That huge improvement has led to more sales. Since taking your online classes, my website traffic has increased significantly, I show up in the top spots on Google, and I recently had two sales due to organizing my mailing list and sending out my new monthly newsletter.
—Michelle LaRae <michellelarae.com>

For the most part, we do not need coaxing or advice to start or be part of a casual conversation with almost all the people we know and meet, including the stranger sitting next to us on a plane. But somehow when it comes to our businesses, many of us never think of the advantages of communicating more effectively. Communication is the lifeline of your business. In this Action, we will look at the many opportunities for and ways we have of communicating.

I frequently have conversations with new clients that sound like this one.

Me: *Tell me about your mailing list.*

Client: *What mailing list?*

Me: *I guess we'll have to work on that. It's not uncommon, but you need to be aware of how important it is to build a mailing list. In fact, I believe it's your number one asset.*

Client: *Really? What will I do with it?*

Me: *Mail and email stuff to your patrons to keep your name in front of them.*

Client: *What kind of stuff? I can't think of anything I'd send them.*

Me (thinking to myself): *We have work to do.*

In your business, your mailing list—whether you use it for regular mail, email, or phone calls—is your most treasured resource. It's not really what you mail or email to people; it's that you're doing it at all. Through these communications, you are putting your name in front of your audience as often as possible. Regular mail, in particular, is not intrusive. Everyone likes to get real mail these days, especially if it includes amazing images of your art.

We looked at sending newsletters in the last Action. In this one I'll review some of the other formats you can use for mailings. But first, let's make a list of the many opportunities for your mailings. Some of these (like a website or blog announcement) will work better for email because recipients can click through rather than having to go to a computer and type in your address. (For additional guidance on some of the items on this list, see Action 11.)

- Invitation to an exhibition opening, gallery talk, or arts festival
- Christmas, Hanukkah, New Year's, Valentine's Day, or other holiday cards
- Birthday greeting
- Thank-you note
- It-was-nice-to-meet-you note

- Announcement of an award, grant, or honor
- Announcement of art placed in a public or corporate collection
- Notice of a new line of work, new licensing company, or new gallery
- Article or book written about you
- Article or book written by you
- Article about your patron that you cut out of the paper or magazine
- Article of particular interest to one or more of your patrons
- New address for studio or home
- Teaching a class or workshop
- Announcement of new website, blog, or fan page on Facebook
- Audio interview that you've loaded onto CDs
- Just because

Before we go over the various devices you can use to communicate items on the above list, we should say something about a component that is basic to all your communications: your contact information. Use only one physical address, email address, and phone number for your business. Providing a choice of email addresses or phone numbers is confusing. If you do so, recipients won't know which is your preference or which to keep in their address books. Make it easy for them.

If you are at all hesitant about giving out your home or studio address, get a post office box. Some artists who run into a lot of strangers at arts festivals or who live alone are concerned about giving out their home address. You have to feel at peace in your environment. Regardless, you should always post a mailing address on your website, business cards, email, and marketing materials. It makes you look like a real business and indicates that you're going to be around for a while. More importantly, it's another way for people to reach you when email fails—and it's failing more and more frequently. Using a real brick-and-mortar address in your emails is also the law if you plan on sending messages to anyone with whom you have no prior relationship. (See Resources in the back of the book for CAN-SPAM law requirements.)

POSTCARDS

Postcards are easy to design at home, inexpensive to reproduce, and less costly than letters to mail. For those reasons alone, they are extremely popular among artists. Postcards are commonly used to announce an exhibit or sale, to hand out like business cards, to leave in stacks in lieu of brochures or flyers, or to add to a promotional packet.

Postcards Do Double Duty for Him

Some artists make an entire promotional packet out of postcards. Prominent portrait painter Michael Shane Neal did just that. While working with an art director, he realized that a brochure would be too restrictive for his promotional needs. He might grow tired of the selected images or the written text. Instead, he opted for a mini-portfolio. For the jacket, Neal orders a die-cut heavyweight paper, which arrives scored and ready to be folded. He adds a selection of 10 to 12 postcards, a bio, and a business card to the inside before folding it and securing the flap for closure. This packet is perfect for personalizing the content for each potential client. A small piece of paper with his signature is raised in an embossed area of the cover. It's the final, classy touch. See michaelshaneneal.com.

Use a single impressive color image along with your name on the front of the postcard. Your name should be prominent so that people associate you with the image they're looking at.

Postcards usually cost between $65 and $150 for 1,000 full-color cards. If you need a smaller order, print them yourself as long as the result looks professional. If you need to order a large number of postcards, but don't have enough people on your mailing list to use them up in six months, leave the back blank except for your contact info. The white space allows flexibility for you to add handwritten notes or stick-on labels trumpeting upcoming events. (See Resources for printing companies.)

There are specific guidelines for margins and areas on a postcard that should remain blank for processing, so be sure to check the latest postal regulations through your printing company or at usps.com.

ELLEN SOFFER
318.347.3059   Ellen@EllenSoffer.com
4830 Line Avenue, #318
Shreveport, LA 71106
EllenSoffer.com

NEW FROM THE STUDIO

New at EllenSoffer.com
14 works on paper
8 paintings

Postcard design: Patricia J. Velte <whitewingdesign.com>

Above is the back of a sample postcard created for Ellen Soffer. Note the amount of white space she has on the back for adding a message. She printed most of the text in light gray, which recedes into the background when black text (printed or written) is added to the card.

REAL(!) LETTERS

Yes, letters. Real-life, stick-em-in-the-mailbox letters! This is why you need to have a letterhead document ready to go. If you send articles or other items of interest to patrons, you will, of course, include a letter. Granted, a quick, personal note on a small notepad might also work, but sometimes you'll actually need to compose a letter.

For instance, you may not receive notice on official paper that announces your award or grant, which means you have nothing to photocopy and send out. Unless you choose to add the information to a newsletter, you'll have to compose a letter explaining the significance of your honor to recipients. In addition, you'll need cover letters for grant and residency applications, gallery submissions, and much more. (See Action 6 for letterhead guidelines.)

I edit many letters for clients. One of the biggest mistakes artists make is that they write too much about themselves. It's as if they have to establish a lifetime of credentials in a small space. As a former secretary to a U.S. senator (eons ago), I wrote hundreds of letters. You may have received similar ones from Capitol Hill in Washington. Even if the representatives don't agree with your issue, almost every one of them will try to be gracious. These letters usually begin with "Thank you for letting me know your concerns about this issue." See that? A "thank you" in the first sentence.

Consider the following rhythm for any letter, picking and choosing what is appropriate for the circumstance. This outline is a winner that lends itself equally to email messages.

Salutation

Dear Miss Brooks,

> It's good manners to open any letter or email with "Dear," but even if you decide against it, always address the recipient by name.

Opening paragraph

Jessica Neil suggested I write . . .
I was so happy to be in Miami last month to see your exhibit . . .
Thank you so much for your help with . . .

> The first sentence always contains a reference to anyone you have in common with the recipient, a compliment, or an acknowledgment of gratitude.

Body—keep it short

I am writing because . . .

> Get to the point in the body and respond to anything that was requested by the recipient.

Close

I appreciate your time and attention . . .

> Be even more grateful and mention you will follow up, if necessary.

EMAIL TRICKS

Just think . . . fifteen years ago only a few of us were relying on email for our correspondence. It's amazing how much our communications have changed in this short period of time. Email is wonderful because it's fast, it's easy, it's cheap, it lures readers to your website with a quick click of the mouse, and it puts your name in front of people on a regular basis. Whether you love it or hate it, it is the preferred mode of communication today. Email makes life so much easier. As frustrated as we are by spam, viruses, and huge attachments, we could never go back to a world without email.

Many people have become lazy with their emails. And sloppy. Very sloppy. I regularly receive emails from people who don't bother to sign their names or who just use a first name. They want something from me, yet they are too rude to address me by name or to tell me who they are. Email can enhance your professional reputation, but only if it's used properly. Building a business for yourself means acting professional in every way. You can cut corners with your email to close friends, but why even treat them that way? Improve your email habits so they become second nature.

You'll use email to generate interest in your work, to respond to inquiries, and to follow up with leads and with patrons of your art. And, yes, I realize that you undoubtedly know how to send an email message by now, so I won't patronize you with those details. I can, however, share some ideas to make your emails more effective.

One big step you can take toward better branding is to use the email address that comes with your website. Every Web hosting service I know of offers at least one email account to go with it. Use yours for everything. As you're trying to get more recognition, don't hide behind an EarthLink, Comcast, or Yahoo address if you don't have to. If you use fakeartistemail@gmail.com for all of your correspondence, your website address isn't in front of recipients. On the other hand, artistemail@artistsownwebsite.com is instantly recognizable. As a recipient of your email, I'll know you have a professional site at artistsownwebsite.com. You've put your name and website front and center and you'll do it over and over again. If you're still using one of the major providers' accounts, you're promoting them rather than yourself.

Start your message by addressing the person you are writing to. "Hi Barbara" and "Dear Barbara" are much more inviting than no salutation at all. This is especially true when you're writing to someone for the first time or asking the recipient for a favor.

Never send out an email message to more than one person unless you blind copy the addresses. To do this, type your email address in the "To" line and everyone else's in the "Bcc" (blind copy) line. It is rude to reveal email addresses to people who don't know each other. Many people fear having their addresses harvested for spamming. Alleviate this fear by honoring their wish to remain private and use the Bcc line.

Write in complete sentences with appropriate capital letters and correct punctuation. Never ever write an email in ALL CAPS. I think most people these days know that WRITING IN ALL CAPS IS LIKE SCREAMING AT SOMEONE! In addition, it's plain painful to read. Save your ALL CAPS for small sections of text you want to emphasize or use as headlines.

Write like you mean business. That means using black or other dark colored text. Furthermore, patterned backgrounds, smiley faces, cutesy elements, and !!! (exclamation points) look less than professional.

Use spell check. Most email programs have an automatic spell checker, which should be turned on by default. Of course, it won't catch *there* for *their* or *your* for *you're*, but it will help eliminate numerous mistakes that might have gone unnoticed.

A signature block that is attached to the bottom of all of your email messages will be an additional step toward better branding. This block includes your full name, your business name (if you use something besides your name), address, email address, website, and a tag line.

Ann Cunningham
11697 West 13th Avenue
Golden, Colorado 80401-4405
303 238-4760
Ann@acunningham.com
http://www.acunningham.com
Tactile Art—Keep In Touch!

Tommy Thompson | Oil Landscapes & Portraits
Web: http://www.tommythompsonart.com
Twitter: http://twitter.com/thompsonart
Facebook: http://www.facebook.com/TommyThompsonArtist

209 Shirley Drive, Florence, AL 35633 USA
256.767.0422, tommy@tommythompsonart.com

Be aware that if you create your signature in HTML code with pretty fonts, colors, and pictures, it might look like Greek if it's received in plain text, but you'll never know it. For that reason, I would set up a signature so that it looks good regardless of who is viewing it. That means it looks right in both plain text and to HTML viewers. Most email programs allow you to change the format you use to send your messages. Toggle this option to test your signature block.

Think twice before adding one of your images to your email signature. Images will show up just as you had intended for some people, but as an attachment for others. Not everyone is keen on getting attachments if they don't know the sender. Bottom line: You take a chance. I happen to like images in artists' signatures, but I'm highly artist-friendly, as you know. I love seeing new work. If you add an image, make it very small by keeping it to 72 pixels per inch (ppi) and no larger than about 200 x 200 pixels.

Make all of your links "hot" by using http:// in front of URLs in your emails. Get in the habit of writing out all Web addresses with that prefix. If the link isn't hot, chances are slim that recipients will take the time to copy and paste the URL into the address line and visit the site. Why risk it?

Don't scan your postcards or other announcements and send them as attachments to a message that has no text in the body. If you send an attachment, you should include text in the body of the message that provides all of the information the recipient needs without having to open your attachment. The attachment should be considered a graphic design element—a nice surprise— rather than the sole source of information.

Email is powerful! We should not use it without remembering that the power can backfire. It takes no time or effort to type a few lines and hit the *Send* button in haste. Stop. Think. And don't ever respond to a message in anger. If you send your message today, will you be glad you sent it tomorrow? Or will you regret it? Is it kind? Is it necessary? While you can never guarantee that your words will be understood in the way you intended, it's impossible to take back the sent word. Take every precaution to ensure your words are kind, intelligent, and clear. If there is a doubt as to how your message might be received, pick up the phone and call instead of email. There's little mistaking the tone of your voice.

A final note about email. I realize I'm repeating this, but so many people just don't get it unless I say it over and over again: *Don't depend solely on email to communicate with people.* It isn't 100% reliable. Sometimes email gets through to the intended recipient and sometimes it doesn't. Many people have spam filters. Have you ever wondered why so-and-so didn't reply to your desperate message? Always take into consideration the fact that so-and-so might never have received it. If they don't respond a second time, pick up the phone and call.

Entice Me

"Please visit my new website at http://www.isntmyartgreat?.com." "I hope you'll drop in to see my work at my new gallery." These messages are not very enticing, are they? Yet, I receive postcards and emails that say little more than either of these. Without any other words, these are lazy attempts to get me interested in your work. I'm busy! Tell me what I'm going to get! What, exactly, is in it for me? And, c'mon, could you insert a little humor? I've had a rough day and need something to smile about.

It would please me greatly if I could see the smile on your face as I'm reading your message. If I had a dollar for every artist that sent me an email with only "please visit my new website" in it, I'd be rich beyond my wildest dreams. Okay, maybe not rich, but I'd definitely have a new outfit with matching shoes.

If you want an audience for your opening, send an email blast like this one.

> *I know you have probably already framed, hung, and forgotten about the postcard invitation to my upcoming opening, so I thought I'd send this as a reminder. Everyone who is anyone will be at Star Gallery on Friday, February 17, from 6 to 9 p.m. I'm going to be premiering a new body of work inspired by my recent trip to Japan. Wear a kimono and obi and come enjoy some sushi with us. (I'm giving you permission to be fashionably late and arrive at 6:10! I sure hope you can make it.)*

If you want to announce a new website or the update of an old one, send a message along these lines.

> *You may have thought you've lived long enough to see everything, but you were wrong. I have created the ultimate mobiles for today's contemporary home. They're bigger than a breadbox— filling up that entryway that no one knows what to do with. Just imagine the look on your guests' faces when you open the door and reveal this baby! Curious? Visit www.isntmyartwonderful?.com for the latest images.*

Now, aren't those two examples a little more enticing than "Come see my new work"? Language can do miraculous things when you spend time with it. You can't expect to be brilliant the first time through.

Her Announcement Made People Smile
Kelly Borsheim announced the "birth" of her new sculpture, *Stargazer,* a nude female carved from marble. According to the clever mailing in baby-announcement format

(complete with pastel-colored footprints surrounding a photo of the sculpture), "*Stargazer* has all of her fingers and toes. Born fully grown—like Venus—*Stargazer* is 24 inches high x 11 x 17 inches. Like her mother, she loves the night and the moon. She is an adventurous girl and has already left home to take up temporary residence at The Home Retreat . . . Won't you stop by to see our lovely new baby?" See borsheimarts.com.

ON THE PHONE

Sometimes nothing but the phone will do for communicating. We just have to hear the other person's voice to be put at ease, to put her at ease, or to ensure she understands our intent. Use the telephone to clarify an order or situation. Writing can be scattered, but a quick phone conversation can clear up any uncertainties or ambiguities. Have you ever felt, after sending ten emails, that a two-minute phone call would have covered everything you needed? You can also use the phone to ensure something arrived safely. (And when you send out a portfolio or letter and say you're going to follow up in two weeks, you'd better do it!)

On the phone, introduce yourself properly. When someone answers on the other end, respond with: "Hi, this is Rita Banwell. Is Jerry available?" Then, when Jerry gets on the line, tell him exactly who you are and why you are calling. Ask if it's a good time to talk. Some people pick up the phone to stop it from ringing even though it isn't convenient for them to talk at that moment. Asking them if they can talk might eliminate some awkward moments. I continue to be amazed at people who call to ask me for my help and, as with email, fail to give me the courtesy of introducing themselves.

Speaking of courtesies, most of these should go without saying, but I must say them anyway.

- Don't call when you're on a cell phone in a tunnel. Duh.
- Don't call when you're harried or multitasking. Plan to devote your full attention to the person on the other end of the phone.

- Don't use a speakerphone unless a disability makes it necessary. They're annoying and seem impersonal. Additionally, the listener can't be assured he or she is speaking to you and you alone. From their point of view, there's no telling who else might be in the room!
- Don't answer call waiting while on a business call unless you're in the middle of a crisis. Doing so sends signals to the person you're talking to that they're not as important as the call coming in.
- Don't call from your cell phone unless you can guarantee privacy. The entire checkout line doesn't need to listen in on your negotiations.
- Don't forget to turn your cell phone off whenever you enter a quiet place, a meeting, a gallery or museum, or a lecture. This is particularly true if you're meeting with a collector. Are you so important that the phone call can't wait an hour or two?

For a better phone conversation, observe these courtesies.

- Smile when you speak. It's said that a smile can be easily detected on the other end.
- Stand up for more authority. Standing up while you're on the phone grounds you and makes you feel confident.
- If you need to leave a voicemail message, be brief. Say what you need in order to get the person on the other end to return the call. No more, no less. You need to leave your name (recited slowly, clearly), phone number, and reason for calling. You can repeat your name and phone number at the end, if necessary.

Voicemail Recordings and Messages

Make your voicemail recording work for you on your business line. Advertise! Try a version of one of these messages (and keep it short and sincere).

> *Hi, this is Tom. Sorry I missed your call, but I hope I won't miss you at my opening. It's Friday, June 20th, at the Miller Gallery. Please leave a message and I'll call you back with directions.*

Hi, this is Emily. I'm out of the country until September, but you can catch me online at myownartistwebsite.com.

HOLIDAY TIPS

Don't let your mail get lost in the holiday rush. Mailboxes are full during the holidays! Get your mail out early, especially if it contains great gift ideas. If you send early enough, highlight your holiday open house and products appropriate for gifts.

The holidays are about giving. Use your newsletter to relate how artists give back to the community and how others can do the same. If you help care for people living with HIV/AIDS, discuss the organization and provide a cut-out donation card that people can complete and send into the organization with their year-end donation.

If you prefer, be different and send a Happy New Year letter after the first of the year, an "I love art collectors" letter at Valentine's Day, or a birthday celebration letter on your birthday or that of your favorite artist from history.

If mailing, use an envelope that will get noticed in a stack of mail.

NO-EXCUSE PRINCIPLE

Connections are critical. It's not only about the process of meeting people, which we're going to get to, it's about maintaining those relationships. You never know where they'll lead or how precious they'll be to your success.

NO-EXCUSE ACTION

Practice sprucing up your language so that it's more enticing. Grab an old email or letter you sent and try reworking it to make it more interesting.

Action 11

Follow Up, Follow Up, Follow Up!

Did I Mention You Should Follow Up?

Are potential collectors slipping through the cracks? Did someone express interest in your work months ago, but you haven't done anything about it? Have you failed to keep in touch with collectors who purchased pricey art from you last year (aside from that thank-you note you sent immediately, of course)? Most artists admit that not following up with business leads, buyers, and collectors is one of the biggest mistakes they make. Think about it: *Are you following up?*

WHEN YOU NEED A THUMP ON THE HEAD

A good system will help you to follow up with collectors, buyers, and other contacts. If the one you have right now isn't working, fix it. You can set up a system on your computer or on paper. Electronic reminders can be set up on your computer using Tasks or To Dos in Microsoft Outlook and Entourage or Apple iCal or Mail. When your message appears on your computer desktop, you can delay it and asked to be reminded again in an hour or even longer. (You can also set up the reminders in any of these programs as calendar events. Smart phones and iPods can be set with similar prompts.)

There are also a number of mailing list databases that come with reminders as well as websites like HassleMe at hassleme.co.uk.

If you don't trust your computer as much as I do mine, try old-fashioned paper. Add reminders to your calendar or create a leads notebook. Whenever you consider someone a good lead for your artwork or career, act on it and use the notebook to follow up. Insert a new page for each lead. Set up the book chronologically—adding new leads to the back. Make a note on your calendar to review your notebook once a month to check on who you need to get in touch with.

If you're wondering what to put in a leads notebook, the Hot Prospect! Form can be found at IdRatherBeintheStudio.com.

SAY "THANK YOU" AT EVERY OPPORTUNITY

Saying thank you in a genuine way should be ingrained in your business practices. Although there are perfectly legitimate reasons for using email to say thank you, handwritten notes will set you apart not only from other artists but also from most people. (See the section about note cards in Action 6.) The mere fact that you are taking the time to write out a note by hand proves your sincerity. And who isn't delighted to see a personal note in a stack of junk mail? "Thank you" is a big part of many of my follow-up suggestions.

She Recognized the Value of a Sincere Handwritten Note
I have been sending handwritten notes for all of my gallery sales for a little over a year. About a month ago, I got a call from the art director of the gallery that carries my work. She was so excited that a person who had just moved into town had seen my work at another person's home. My collector was so endeared by my "warm" personal note, that she shared it with her friend,

*which moved the friend to want to see my work, and then when
she saw my work ended up purchasing four pieces for her new
home. Of course, both of my collectors received a personal note
and a phone call!*—Michele D. Lee <micheledlee.com>

WHAT TO WRITE

Below are common situations that require follow-up. In response to
each situation, I have given my ideas for action as well as suggested
wording for follow-up notes. As you see, your notes don't have to be
long. Two or three sentences will do. What is important is that they are
(1) personal and (2) sincere.

A Friend of a Friend Admired Your Work

Your response: Send a handwritten "Thank you for your interest in my
work" note with your artwork on the cover. That's it. You're just letting
the individual know that you took notice and were pleased with the
attention. Add the name to your mailing list.

> *Dear Mr. X,*
> *Thank you for your interest in my work. I'm glad Sally
> introduced us. I hope you can drop by my booth at the
> Downtown Art Festival over the Fourth of July holiday.*
>
> *Sincerely,*

A Patron Purchased One of Your Pieces Two Years Ago

Your response: What?! You haven't been in touch with her for two years?
Shame on you. But don't dwell on it. You can't lose any more time. Add
her to your mailing list immediately and vow to be in touch two or
three times a year. Send her a note.

> *Dear Ms. X,*
> *Shame on me for being so out of touch. You're not the only
> person I've been ignoring. No longer. I've vowed to turn over
> a new leaf and hope this finds you in good health and humor.*

I'm enclosing a copy of my latest [brochure, exhibit announcement, article]. I thought you might be interested to know that I'm selling very well in the metropolitan area now. I hope you have continued adding to your collection to keep my work company.

If you're ever in the area, please let me know. I'd love to have you as a guest in my studio. In the meantime, you can visit my website to see my newest work (http://www.carlasanders.com).

Kind regards,

A Friend Gave You a Hot Lead

Your response: I can't think of anything that would please your friend more than to contact the lead immediately to investigate the opportunity. She went to the trouble of trying to help you out. If you ignore her overtures, you send the message that you don't need or want her help. Why would she ever try to help you again? First, contact the lead ASAP. Second, send your friend a handwritten note: "Thank you for helping me build my career and business."

Dear X,

Thank you so much for referring me to Jane's Boutique. I have called them and made an appointment to show my jewelry. I'll let you know what happens. It sure is nice to have friends like you in my cheering section!

Warmly,

You Met a Curator at an Opening and Briefly Discussed the State of Contemporary Art

Your response: Send a follow-up "It was nice to meet you" note immediately. If it was a show he curated, be complimentary. Invite him to your next opening if you have one coming up. Otherwise, extend an invitation to your studio. Add him to your mailing list.

Dear Mr. X,

It was nice to meet you at the opening last Friday night. I am so glad to finally see Y's work in person. Kudos for bringing it to town.

Enclosed is an invitation to my next opening. If you're unable to attend, I'd be happy to give you a personal tour of the exhibit at your convenience or show you around my studio. In the meantime, you can see my mobiles at http://www. pattysgrecci.com.

Sincerely,

A Friend or Follower on Social Media Was Particularly Generous

Your response: Acknowledge it! When people go out of their way to frequently retweet your posts or write nice things on your Facebook wall, take time to acknowledge their kindness. Return the favor by retweeting something they've written or encouraging others to follow them. You could also send a Thank You through email or a direct message on the appropriate social media platform.

If you really want to surprise the good Samaritans, track down physical addresses and send a card in the mail.

Dear X,

Thank you for going out of your way to consistently retweet my posts to your followers. You are generous with your time and I wanted you to know it hasn't gone unnoticed.

With gratitude,

The Head of an Arts Agency Wrote a Recommendation for Your Grant Application

Your response: This is a no-brainer. Handwritten thank-you note. Pronto! Add her to your mailing list.

Dear Ms. X,

Thank you for your sincere recommendation for my grant application. I know how busy you are, so I am particularly grateful for your attention. I will let you know what becomes of this process.

Please let me know if there is ever anything I can do to repay the favor.

Appreciatively,

A Gentleman Saw Your Work in a Private Home and Asked the Owner to Contact You Because He's Interested in a Commission

Your response: Whenever you hear that someone has expressed interest in your work, drop what you're doing and contact him. Use the mode of communication that feels best for the situation: phone, email, or snail mail. Even if you can't help him at the moment, your professionalism and attention to his needs will be greatly appreciated. You never know when he'll have a project just for you. And you don't know what connections he might have.

Dear Mr. X,

Mary Montgomery said you had admired my work in her home. I am honored. I get a great deal of pleasure from those who appreciate my work. She also said you might be interested in a commissioned painting for your new office. I would love to talk with you about that when the time is right for you. In the meantime, I am enclosing my brochure and an article about my work. I also invite you to visit my website at http://www.shellylewisstanfield.com.

Sincerely,

Don't want the commission? No problem. Try this:

Dear Mr. X,

Mary Montgomery said you had admired my work in her home. I am honored. I get a great deal of pleasure from those

who appreciate my work. She also said you might be
interested in a commissioned painting for your new office.
While I am currently unavailable for commissions, I
invite you to view my available paintings online at
http://www.shellylewisstanfield.com. If you need further
recommendations, please contact me at any time. I know any
number of artists who would be pleased to talk with you
about a commission.

Sincerely,

You Haven't Heard from Your Gallery in Months and They Have a Number of Your Works

Your response: Those who run galleries are as busy as you are. A healthy artist-gallery relationship depends on communication from both parties. Call your contact at the gallery and ask what's going on. If your work isn't selling, have a heart-to-heart and inquire as to how you might be able to help move it. Add a note to your reminders to contact the gallery every month in the future. Make sure you document your attempts in writing when it begins to be necessary.

A Woman You Don't Know Sent a Collector to Your Website Because She Just Knew He'd Fall In Love with Your Art

Your response: Ask the collector how he found you. Try to get specific contact information for the woman from him. Send a handwritten thank-you note to the woman.

Dear Ms. X,
Mr. Y said I have you to thank for introducing him to my
work. I very much appreciate your interest in my sculpture.
Please call if you're ever in the area. I would be delighted to
show you my studio and works in progress.

With gratitude,

Follow-up notes that are written immediately are the sincerest notes. Two weeks is the longest you should wait. A month is too long, but is better than no contact at all. Procrastinating and sending your note later ends up being more about selling than about nurturing relationships with people. After you have written your thank-you notes, add the recipients to your mailing list. When you invite those people to your next show, they are more likely to remember you and attend.

NO-EXCUSE PRINCIPLE

Following up shows people you care about them and that you are intent on maintaining your relationship. Without the follow-up, people either forget about you or assume you don't care.

NO-EXCUSE ACTION

Create a system that helps you follow up in a timely manner. Whether your system is in a notebook, on your paper calendar, or in your computer, it's most important that it works for you and that it's easy to access at a moment's notice.

"I don't live in an art town."

When I hear this excuse, I think to myself, *What is an art town? What does it mean to live in an art town? Do art towns exist?* I already know the answers to these questions. Except for a handful of places, I've come to believe that there is no such thing as an art town brimming with enlightened art buyers. Not living in an art town is simply another excuse for inaction. Artists who use this excuse think that they would be more successful if they lived in New York or Santa Fe or Portland or, frankly, anywhere else but where they are. They have convinced themselves that their town "isn't an art town."

Setting aside the argument that some communities are not "art towns," you live where you live—and apparently you would prefer not to relocate. So let's look at the advantages you have. You have a far better shot at becoming known in your current community where you have connections. Even a small number of connections are better than none. Do not write off your community. Until you extend yourself, you do not know what possibilities your community offers. And you may find that when you make a reputation locally, it will be easier to move into other markets.

There are disadvantages to moving to a community that you may think is more of an "art town" than yours. Relocating forces you to start over again—to make connections in an entirely new place. And a second option—traveling frequently to another city—can be taxing. Either alternative presents difficulties because you won't know anyone in the new communities. You'll have to start from scratch.

Some artists choose to live far from civilization. If you are among those for whom the closest town with any venue for showing art might be two hours away, you undoubtedly have realized the enormous possibilities of reaching an audience through the Internet. I hope you study Actions 7 and 8 closely. At the same time, you should take advantage of every means of communication in your region. Whether it's through a newspaper, magazine, county website, statewide arts blog, or town crier, make sure the community is aware of you and your art. Make friends with your local media.

Action 12

Be a Media Magnet
Instead of Watching Others Grab the Headlines

Regardless of whether you think you live in an art-friendly community or not, you are probably surrounded by all kinds of people. Each person has a story to tell. Your city or region probably has some sort of infrastructure that keeps people in touch with each other and that shares local news. Even if there is no town paper, there are more media outlets in your area than you're probably aware of.

WHICH IS THE MEDIA FOR YOU?

For the most part, the media consists of newspapers, magazines, television, and radio. However, more and more news is being gathered from new and untraditional sources—primarily the Internet. To be more specific, news is often generated from blogs and other social media sites. In fact, public relations specialists advise us to write news releases (which we'll get to shortly) for Internet consumption rather than only for traditional media outlets.

Word-of-mouth or viral marketing is becoming even more important than stories carried by traditional media outlets. Sure, we all still like to see a story about us in the paper, but we can't be oblivious to how much less effective it is than word-of-mouth marketing. In his book *The New Rules of Marketing and PR,* David Meerman Scott noted that the primary audience for news releases "is no longer just a handful of journalists. Your audience is millions of people with Internet connections and access to search engines and RSS readers."

Devote your time to the media contacts and outlets that make the most sense for you. It would be easy if you could just send your news items to the arts editor of every publication, but most publications do not have arts editors. Call the editorial desk of your target publication and describe the content of your release. Ask for the name of the appropriate person to receive it—double checking the spelling of the individual's name before you hang up.

Every day, make note of the arts writers in the publications you read and add their names to your mailing list. Even newspapers in large cities often have only one person who writes art reviews. Send your release or kit to both the editor and the writer. (I'll discuss this topic in greater detail below.)

Look beyond arts writers as well. A story about your work might fit perfectly in a home, style, or business section of a publication. Contributors to home and style sections often write about functional crafts, decorative wall pieces, and artists who live in interesting houses. Business sections and business publications are particularly interested in an entrepreneurial angle, such as the introduction of a new line of hand-painted accessories you are taking to regional or national markets. Keep an eye on publications to get ideas of where your story might fit. If you're in the United States, find newspapers in your area at 50states.com/news, which links to more than 3,300 sites. Keep track of your media contacts in the database you set up.

Before you add a media contact to your mailing list, ask yourself the following questions.

Is this a publication I want to be featured in?

Do my potential collectors or prospective business contacts read this publication or listen to this radio show?

Does this person write about art or stories such as mine?

Is there another writer or editor at this publication who might also be interested in my story?

Even if the answer to one or more of these questions is No, you could still add the contact to your list. However, you might choose not to devote much energy to them.

Don't forget media outlets like your college alumni association, which is always looking for interesting stories about alumni. Ditto for your church bulletin. Almost all publications present a possible outlet, and smaller publications might be your most valuable connections.

Be realistic, but hopeful, about media attention. Keep in touch consistently with outlets in which you would like to have your work featured and in which you can envision your work. If you get lucky with your first contact with an outlet, great! But be aware that it usually takes multiple exposures to get noticed. Add media contacts to your list with the realization that you are building a long-term relationship with them. Your job is to unearth the names of people who can best champion your work.

BECOME MORE NEWSWORTHY

Media people aren't simply looking for news. They're looking for new news. News with a twist. News with impact. News that will entice people to purchase their publications or listen to their newscasts. News that will lure advertisers. It's your job to help them out a bit. Be that magnet that attracts the media and give them the type of news they're craving.

In her book *6 Steps to Free Publicity*, marketing expert Marcia Yudkin stressed that editors and reporters are looking for stories that would be interesting to their readers or viewers at this moment. Not tomorrow, but right now. She then broke down this question into its three most important elements: (1) our readers; (2) this story—which must be short and focused; and (3) now—what makes it timely? In other words, those in the media are looking for information that addresses these areas.

I'm sorry to have to say it, but the fact that you make art is not news. Everyone has a job and your job is making art. Because so many people seem to be making some kind of art these days, how do you differentiate yourself? Why should reporters be more interested in you than in Artist X or Artist Y? Don't make them guess. Tell them! If you don't know why the media should notice you, take time to figure it out. Go back to Action 4 on writing your artist statement and spend more time journaling.

The fact that you make art isn't news; likewise, your exhibition opening is hardly news. If you live in one of the hundreds of communities hosting monthly gallery walks, peruse your weekly paper. Notice that reporters can choose from any one of dozens of openings on any given gallery walk date. Again, why is your opening or your exhibition more newsworthy than another opening? If you can't think of a reason, perhaps you need to invent one.

Let me help you out a bit. Perhaps your opening is more newsworthy because it's a retrospective of 30 years. Or perhaps it's a theme exhibit to coincide with Day of the Dead, Valentine's Day, or even something that's been a hot news topic—even controversial—lately. Or maybe you are holding it at a wacky, nontraditional venue like a yacht or a forest. Hey, crazier things have happened. Or you're donating 50% of sales to the American Cancer Society.

Let me take those examples a step further. Which of the following exhibitions seems more newsworthy?

1. An exhibition of heart-related art objects on Valentine's Day?

Or

An exhibition of heart-related art objects on Valentine's Day with a corresponding live auction that raises money for the American Heart Association (with a celebrity auctioneer)?

2: An exhibition of landscape paintings?

Or

An exhibition of landscape paintings conspicuously hung in a nearby woodland area?

Or

An exhibition of landscape paintings conspicuously hung in a nearby woodland area on Arbor Day benefiting a local land trust?

3. An exhibition of art by and about women?

Or

An exhibition of art by and about women with 50% of sales going to Susan G. Komen for the Cure?

Or

Your story as a breast-cancer survivor and your participation in an exhibition of art by and about women with 50% of sales going to Susan G. Komen for the Cure?

See the differences? The media's need for stories varies from day to day. On a slow news week, writers might jump at the chance to write about you. But if big news breaks on a particular day, your story will be blown off the pages. Imagine what happened to coverage of art events and openings after the September 11 terrorist attacks or Hurricane Katrina. They were no longer a priority to anyone. Every community can be rocked by a local crisis. Or there may not be a crisis at all. It might be that a number of other organizations coincidentally planned their events at the same time as yours. It often boils down to lucky timing, but also to which events are more newsworthy.

You can send out the same old news release with answers to who, what, when, where, why, and how, but the most you can probably hope for in this format is a calendar listing. To get a quality story, distinguish your news from all the other releases that are flying in and out of journalists' inboxes. Become more newsworthy!

CREATE AN ONLINE MEDIA KIT

In advance of sending a news release (it's coming up, I promise!), consider adding a dedicated media kit page to your website. It can also be called a media room, press kit, news room, or whatever you like as long as members of the media understand where they can find out more about you when they visit your site. On that page, you'll include the following (must-have items are marked with an *)—in the suggested order from the top of the page down.

*Contact info. Make it easy for journalists to reach you via phone, email, and social media. Put your contact information at the top and the bottom of your media kit home page and each of your other media kit pages.

*News releases. Keep them updated and timely.

*Images. A selection of your images should go along with your news releases. Include low-resolution versions of two or three artworks. At least one should have high contrast and look good in black-and-white print. Add explanatory text such as: "High-resolution images are available within 24 hours upon request," with a link to your email address and a notation of your phone number. In order to protect yourself from theft or reproduction of your work, place the high-resolution images on a hidden page on your website. It can be accessed through a URL that you give only to the media and that isn't linked from any other page on your site. It can even be password protected. Under each image, include the following information.

> Credit: Your name, title of artwork, medium, size
> © Year, your name
> Photography credit: Photographer's name

If you have more than one news release out or more than one event going on, distinguish which images are part of which event. Use subheadings to categorize the images in your media kit or consider an additional credit line that confirms which images go with which news releases.

> *In the exhibition "Deborah Williams: Paintings Fresh from the Studio"*

> *Selected for exhibition in the State Capitol*

Articles. List the articles that are about you or that mention your art. Local coverage is just as important as national coverage. Link to any articles you can find online. If an article is not online and you'd like to use the text on your site, it is okay to provide a synopsis or description of the article that includes quotes. It is not okay to reproduce the entire article on your site without permission. You are concerned about the theft of your copyrighted images, and you should always be respectful of others' copyrighted work.

Art info. This section can include your statement, but only if it is written in a way that would be meaningful for the media. Include facts about your medium or style. Feature a bullet-point version that gets to the hard facts and link it to a longer version if necessary.

*Bio. Not your résumé! This isn't a job interview, so why make journalists piece together your entire career? Pick out the highlights, review Action 6 about writing your bio, and spice it up for the media.

Images of the artist. These pictures should enhance your reputation as an artist. They might show you in your studio surrounded by your art, at work on a new sculpture, or at an art opening beside your work. The media prefers action shots, so make an effort to add interesting photos to your marketing materials. Follow the guidelines for using high and low resolution (see the Images section above).

Artist's blog. Provide a link to your art blog, which, of course, contains fascinating content about you and your work.

Quotes. Tidbits from curators, patrons, critics, and students from whom you have obtained permission to quote.

As with all of the pages on your website, make sure the Media Kit is easy to navigate. It should have its own menu and helpful headings at the top of each page.

WRITE A NEWS RELEASE

Everyone thinks that a well-written news release is the best way to get noticed by the media. Based on my research, it's only a very small part of what makes you attractive to the media. The *pitch* is the critical component. But you have to start with the news release in order to get your facts straight and ensure that your message in your pitch will be understood. It should be brief, but long enough to tell a compelling story.

When writing your release, look it over for the five *W*s and the one *H*.

WHO	Whom is the news release about or who will benefit from the news?
WHAT	What is the specific event or newsworthy item? Describe it.
WHERE	Where is it taking place?
WHEN	When is it taking place (or when did it take place)?
WHY	Why is this event newsworthy?
HOW	How can you be contacted? How can they get more information? How can the contact take action?

You should email your news release in plain text—not HTML or rich text. You want to make sure you see it on your screen exactly as it will be seen by the recipient. An email message is preferred to a paper release almost across the board. Use your release headline in the subject line, making sure it's spiffy and encourages opening. Upon opening, the recipient should see this rhythm of items in the message: *salutation, the pitch* (see below), *your signature,* and *news release.*

News Release Format
FOR IMMEDIATE RELEASE

Contact: *Your name, phone number with area code, email address*

Release date, city, state/province—*[dash followed by] Body of your news release*

In the last paragraphs, specify locations, dates, special events, hours open, and other necessary details. Add a final "For more information" and link to your online media kit.

At the very bottom (to signify the end of your release), type: **—End—**

Below is a media release I worked on with my client Margret E. Short. It was pretty easy to write because Margret had been blogging about the work for about eight months. When it came time to put together a release, all of the words were already written. I just had to try to provide an interesting angle.

SAMPLE NEWS RELEASE

FOR IMMEDIATE RELEASE

Contact: Margret E. Short
503-652-2749
mshortfineart@aol.com

NEW PAINTINGS BY MARGRET E. SHORT EXPLOIT
REMBRANDT'S BLING IN AN AMUSING GAME OF SEEK-AND-FIND

Portland, Oregon, May 20, 2007—For the last year, Portland artist Margret E. Short has been eating with, laboring side-by-side, and dreaming about Rembrandt and other Dutch masters. In particular, she's been studying the historical pigments they used and introducing them into her work. If she were any closer to her inspirations, people would start whispering. But that probably wouldn't deflect her mission.

Short's splendid series of still-life paintings, "Margret E. Short: Lessons from the Low Countries," opens at Portland's Lawrence Gallery on June 1 and runs through June 30. Each work is inspired by the color palette of a select painting in the exhibit "Rembrandt and the Golden Age of Dutch Art," which opens one day later at the Portland Art Museum. Reproductions of the Dutch inspiration paintings will be exhibited alongside Short's completed works, which are finished with detailed reproductions of Dutch period frames. Viewers will enjoy participating in the artist's visual amusements. Not only are the colors reproduced, Short has also quoted, quite accurately, sections of each original work in her homages. It's a game of seek-and-find.

Not content with contemporary colors, Short replicated the 17th-century pigments of the inspiration paintings for this collection by hand-grinding each mineral. Her blog, http://margretshort.typepad.com, has documented the meticulous study of the ancient hues. Luscious colors with magical names like lapis lazuli, cinnabar, and azurite are the focus of each bountiful still life. Delighted with her discoveries, Short says, "There is no comparison to the handling qualities of the modern pigments. Everything about the handmade historic pigments is different from the modern: particle size, thickness, consistency, color, saturation, and on and on."

Throughout the creation of the paintings, Short's exhaustive research led to unexpected findings. Among her favorites is the word "pronk," which she associates with today's "bling." While it isn't often featured in contemporary painting, bling was abundant in The Netherlands of the 17th century. It was a prosperous society and the center of world trade. Diamond cutting, book publishing, textile manufacturing, shipbuilding, fishing, and banking were among a growing number of trades that flourished. The Dutch merchants bartered their goods for imported spices, paper, silk, wine, olive oil and countless other items that enriched their burgeoning economy. There was plenty of bling to go around!

With expanded patronage, art flourished in this environment. Artists flaunted their abilities to capture reflective precious metals, sparkling jewels, and plump flora. Short, who is well known for her attention to delicate lace, has done the same thing in the 21st century. Each canvas is saturated with enough bling to make Short a legitimate heir to a longstanding tradition.

Margret Short has exhibited her work throughout the United States and beyond, including the C. M. Russell Museum in Great Falls, Montana; the Gilcrease Museum in Tulsa, Oklahoma; Weatherburn Gallery in Naples, Florida; and the Florence Biennale in Florence, Italy. She is the recipient of two coveted Salmagundi Club Awards, the Grumbacher Gold Medallion, and many other national honors. She is also a Signature member of the Oil Painters of America, American Women Artists, and the Copley Society.

An opening reception for "Margret E. Short: Lessons from the Low Countries" will be held during First Thursday Gallery Walk night on Thursday, June 7 from 6 to 9 p.m.

The Lawrence Gallery is located at 903 W. Davis Street in Portland, Oregon. It is open Monday through Saturday from 10 a.m. to 5:30 p.m. and Sundays from noon to 5 p.m. More information is available at http://www.lawrencegallery.net or by calling 503-228-1776.

High-resolution images are available at http://www.margretshort.com/mediaroom. For more information, please contact Margret E. Short at 503-652-2749 or mshortfineart@aol.com.

-END-

PITCH YOUR STORY

Think about the hundreds of news releases that find their way into the inboxes of editors and writers. They all must look the same after a while. Your pitch is an opportunity to pique the interest of recipients—to show them you are a true media magnet and to encourage them to look over your entire release. Here's the pitch we used for Margret's news release.

> *Dear Mr. Fitzgerald,*
>
> *For the past year I have been grinding the world's most precious minerals and replicating historical pigments to capture the "bling" in the canvases from the age of Rembrandt. My inspirations were eleven specific 17th-century Dutch paintings, from which I have appropriated the color palettes for my own homages to the Old Masters.*
>
> *These works will be exhibited in the nearby Lawrence Gallery as "Rembrandt and the Golden Age of Dutch Art" opens at the Portland Art Museum. I think you'll find it fun and fascinating to compare my work to the inspiration paintings. In fact you can go to http://www.margretshort. com/mediaroom to see an example.*
>
> *A full press release is below. Please let me know if I can answer any questions or give you a personal tour of the exhibit. I hope you find the story a nice tie-in to the exhibit at the Portland Art Museum.*
>
> *Sincerely,*
> *Margret E. Short*

We had difficulty getting media attention for Margret's exhibit, perhaps because it coincided with the opening at the Portland Art Museum—a bigger news story. However, Margret sold almost 70% of her paintings in the gallery! She did so with the help of the untraditional media. She wrote her release and pitched it to all of her friends and patrons, asking them to forward it. The gallery did the same. I'll show you how to do this at the end of the section.

MEDIA TRICKS I'VE PICKED UP

I want to share with you some of the things I've learned about working with the media. I've read them, heard them, or experienced them. I've undoubtedly learned some of them from making mistakes.

- Follow media outlets on Twitter and Facebook. Respond to their tweets and write on their fan pages. Don't just "like" what they write, but make intelligent (or funny) comments when the opportunity presents itself.
- Be available. If you send a media release, you'd better be checking your phone messages and email regularly. Journalists are on deadline. If they can't reach you, they'll look for another story.
- Develop a list of five to ten questions that a reporter might ask you and write out your answers. Practice your responses. I've discovered that reporters often ask questions that artists think are irrelevant, but that's only because they are unseasoned about art. It's up to you to steer the conversation to what you want to talk about. Practicing your story from different angles can help you.
- A two- to three-sentence email pitch is preferred to a full-blown media release. You have to wow them immediately. One reporter said, "I know within two seconds whether it's something I want to write about or not." Note: That doesn't mean you shouldn't send a release, but that you might keep it waiting in the wings rather than use it for the initial introduction.
- Don't ever try to control a story. Once you contact the media, the story is theirs, not yours. This is especially true of larger media outlets that want to "own" the story. They want to figure it out, so don't write the story for them.

- Do not send attachments to journalists (by which I mean do not attach photos or document files that contain a release). Wary of computer viruses, the recipients who receive messages with attachments are likely to delete them immediately. Of course, you can make an exception if you have a personal relationship with the recipient.
- While listening in on a media panel, I discovered everyone present preferred email to any other form of contact, although the phone was sometimes okay. No one wanted to receive faxes. And printed press kits and press releases were deemed big and bulky—and therefore undesirable as well. Email was the clear winner.
- It's always best to have a contact at the media outlet, particularly in television. If you know someone, go to that individual first. Otherwise, carry out due diligence to understand who the appropriate contact would be.
- Although those in television need only a few days' notice of your event, newspapers want your information "as far in advance as possible"; a monthly magazine needs your information at least eight to twelve weeks ahead of the day of the event.
- Everything is on the record. If you don't want your words to appear in print, don't contact the media or respond to questions. If you say "This is off the record," the reporter quickly loses interest in talking to you.
- One business columnist said he is interested in stories in which people overcome great obstacles, but also those that are abysmal failures. He likes to discuss the growth of a business.
- Don't ever send gifts to a reporter, but do thank them with a personal note or call whenever they mention you. According to journalistic ethics policies, reporters are not allowed to accept gifts.
- If you can't translate your story into one that the media would be interested in, it might be worthwhile to hire a P.R. specialist.

PERSISTENCE PAYS

Just because your story doesn't appear when you pitch it doesn't mean you should give up. Don't be discouraged! It takes time to build a relationship with the media. You have to learn to be persistent without becoming an annoyance.

Follow up on the telephone. Call the recipient of your news release after about a week. Present a verbal pitch similar to the one you sent in the email, reminding the contact of your email message. Don't ask if your original message was received—just assume that it was. Offer to answer any questions, but make the call very brief without pressuring the recipient for coverage.

Invite editors and reporters to your events. Don't forget to put media contacts on your list to receive invitations, newsletters (if you are acquainted), and other mailings. On the invitations, write a personal note encouraging them to attend. Anne Leuck Feldhaus <annesart.com> was featured in the *Chicago Tribune* because the editors received her newsletter. They had previously written a story about her, so she emailed her newsletter to them. By keeping her name in front of the editors, she came to mind when they needed a story.

Send a follow-up news release. It is not a bad idea to send a second release to weekly or daily publications a week or two before the publication's deadline. If your event wasn't covered, you might send another release after the exhibit opening to remind readers not to miss the show before it comes down.

Say thank you. After your event is covered write a special note to the appropriate person to say thank you for the article.

Holiday list. Send holiday greetings to members of the press who have helped you and those you would like to be on your side.

Update your media list and contact names at least once a year. Add notes in your database about the coverage you received or articles journalists have written that were memorable for you. Keeping track of this information will help you personalize your future relationship with them.

Familiarize yourself with PRWeb.com. You should be aware of this site for posting your news release online. Click on archives and search for terms of interest to you such as "Miami art exhibit," "artist Ohio," and "art exhibit California." You'll find all kinds of media releases!

INTERVIEW YOURSELF

Artist Andi Woods-Fasimpaur <mysticspiralstudio.blogspot.com> sent me this dilemma.

> *I was recently approached by the publisher of a small regional magazine about the possibility of being profiled either in their print publication or on their website. After exchanging a couple of email messages, he has now asked me if I would be willing to write the profile myself. I'm horribly uncomfortable with this aspect of self-promotion and I also worry that some of the impact and credibility of the profile will be lost if it was obviously written by me.*

Without knowing much about the publication or Andi's goals, my immediate response is: *Hey, someone wants to run a profile on you. Go for it!* On the other hand, I understand her level of discomfort. We read with suspicion when articles appear to be obviously self-serving and written by the person being profiled. It's wise to be cautious. But see if you can quell the level of discomfort and use the situation to your benefit. Don't miss out on an opportunity just because you're uncomfortable with it. Look at it a different way to see if you might be able to use it to your advantage.

Remember that many publications don't have the staff to write an article about everything of interest. websites are often overseen by one overworked person. A proposal of the sort Andi received is the perfect occasion to mold your story and tell it as you like.

What if, instead of writing the profile, you approached the editor and asked if you could write the article in interview format? You'd ask the questions and provide the answers, but you obtain the editor's permission to use his name as if he were asking the questions. You could even run the questions by him beforehand and ask him to select the ones he's most comfortable with. It's always a good idea to provide options that give him ownership in the story. Another approach might be to ask someone you know to act as the interviewer. (That person's name would appear on the interview.) You write the interview, run it by the "interviewer" for approval, and you're all set. In addition to sharing it with the person who requested a story in the first place, use the interview for your P.R. notebook, portfolio, brochure, and website.

Go to IdRatherBeintheStudio.com to pick up Ten Questions for Your Self-Interview.

SEND YOUR NEWS RELEASE TO EVERYONE BUT THE MEDIA

Remember at the opening of this section I noted that word of mouth, blogs, and online attention are becoming every bit as important as traditional media? Now's your chance to make this work for you. You're going to learn to send enticing email messages that include your news releases: messages that people are more than happy to share with others and post on their blogs, messages that will make you a media magnet! Do such messages really exist? Yes, of course. You've undoubtedly forwarded many of them yourself. But they're rare—as rare as a bona fide Picasso at a garage sale.

If you want people to actually read and to act on your electronic media release, you need to do three things. First, personalize your message to the recipient. A good email distribution program allows you to send mass email messages with each recipient's name. If you don't have such a program, a smaller number of personalized emails is far preferable to those addressed to "Hello everyone." When you're asking for people to do something for you—to act—you must make them feel that you care about them as individuals. This much is fairly self-explanatory, so I'm going to focus on the other two things you need to do to ensure your email gets around: Be very clear in your mind what you want the recipients of your email to do *and* make it easy for them to act.

You might think this advice is obvious, but try to recall how many confusing, half-baked emails you have received. I'm sure you've never ever sent one in your entire life. I, on the other hand, can't begin to count the number of times I've sent an email that was misunderstood by the recipient.

To explain best how to compose a better email blast for your media release, we need an example. Let's say you have a gallery and you've put together a theme exhibit titled "Red, White, and Blue" to coincide with Independence Day. It will consist of artwork composed of those colors or even patriotic themes. Pretty straightforward, right? But sending an email or media release with just the facts is downright boring. Let's see if you can seduce your recipients into visiting your exhibit in the middle of the summer.

Create an Email Message in Four Parts

Part 1: The news release. Although the media release will be at the very end of your email message, compose it first because it answers the major questions: Who, what, where, when, why, and how. It brings clarity to your message. Make it interesting and tie into something else that is timely or is in the news—in this case, the 4th of July. Double-check to make sure you answer all of the major questions your reader might ask. I received a media release that was very handsome, but I couldn't even tell what city the gallery was in! That's too much work for a reader.

Why do you have to write a media release if your email isn't going directly to the media? As I said, we're aiming for untraditional or new media. In short, media releases today are consumed by more than the conventional press. You'll post it on your online media kit and on your blog, where it can be read by everyday folks. It will also be sent to—and this is key—bloggers. Bloggers can be an instrumental ally if your news is of interest to their readers. You find them because, of course, you are blogging yourself. It helps to have a prior relationship with the bloggers, such as leaving comments on each others' blogs. Return to Action 7 for more on blogs.

Part 2: The pitch. The pitch is the essential ingredient you need to go along with the release. It is what you need above all other ingredients. Here's how you might pitch to your friends and patrons.

> *Dear Sandra,*
> *We sincerely appreciate your patronage and hope you can*
> *don your favorite red-white-and-blue outfit for our parade*
> *of patriotic art. Most importantly, we hope you're intrigued*
> *enough to share this message with everyone you know. Here's*
> *what's happening . . .*
> *We at Golden Fine Art are shooting off fireworks of our*
> *own this summer. If you thought you were seeing red, look*
> *again. It's not just red, but red, white, and blue in our*
> *gallery. All of the details are below in a media release. In*
> *a nutshell, we've gone crazy with patriotism and our gallery*
> *is bursting with art in the colors of the flag. Sousa is playing*
> *in the background and we don't want you to miss the*
> *opening reception on Friday, June 28, from 5 to 8 p.m.*
> *It just wouldn't be a party without you. Please come.*

Notice that I have tried hard not to make this news all about me (the gallery). If it's all about what the gallery is doing, recipients will have a hard time figuring out where they fit in. I try to use the word "you" often, as if I am speaking directly to the recipient.

Part 3: The "ask." The "ask" is the most important part of your message. We rarely get what we don't ask for. It's alluded to in the opening paragraph of the pitch, but you should also conclude with something like this "ask."

If you have enjoyed our exhibitions in the past, would you care to help us out? We have made it super easy for you to share this information with your friends, add to a newsletter, or post on a blog. Simply copy and paste the letter and media release below and pass it on. We depend on patrons like you to help get the word out about our gallery. It means a great deal to us and, especially, to our artists.

Thank you, in advance, for your help spreading the word about "Red, White, and Blue."

Most sincerely,

Part 4: The copy-and-paste pitch and "ask." This element goes right below Part 3. It's a critical addition that makes it easy for your recipients to add your news to their emails, websites, newsletters, and blogs. If you only give it to them from your perspective (Part 2), they have to rewrite everything as if it were coming from them. Who has time for that? Here's how you might rewrite the original pitch so that anyone can copy and paste it.

One of my favorite galleries, Golden Fine Art, is shooting off fireworks of its own this summer. If you thought you were seeing red, look again. It's not just red, but red, white, and blue in the gallery. All of the details are below in the gallery's media release. In a nutshell, they've gone crazy with patriotism and they're bursting with art in the colors of the flag. Sousa is playing in the background and they don't want you to miss the opening reception on Friday, June 28, from 5 to 8 p.m.

Throw on your favorite red-white-and-blue outfit for Golden Fine Art's parade of patriotic art. I'm planning on attending and hope you can come, too. (Feel free to share this with anyone and everyone.)

Now you're ready to send your email media release to everyone but the media. You'll send everything in plain text to ensure the formatting is the same for each person who opens it. More importantly, you want to make it childishly easy for people to forward your message. HTML formatting creates all kinds of barriers for those who want to copy, paste, and personalize the email you're going to ask them to share with everyone they know.

To reiterate, your email will be sent formatted in this order.

→ The Pitch and the "Ask"
→ Your Signature, Website, and Contact Info
→ The Copy-and-Paste Pitch and "Ask" (as if your recipient were going to pass it on)
→ The Media Release (with complete contact info and website link)

After you've written it up, print it out and get a second set of eyes to look it over. Send a sample copy to yourself and wait at least a couple of hours before you look at it again. When you're assured everything is just right, start pushing the send button and wait for the fireworks to begin.

NO-EXCUSE PRINCIPLE

No one can promote your work better than you. Fancy P.R. firms may be able to help you out, but even they will have to squeeze the story from you. Stories don't fall from the sky. You have to make yourself a media magnet.

NO-EXCUSE ACTION

Start noticing all the stories about artists written in your local papers. At the same time, pay attention to those about writers, musicians, and performance artists. Which ones appear in the arts section of the paper? Which on the front section? Business section? What are the angles? What makes the story relevant to readers now? How can you expand your idea of the media and use it to promote your art?

"I'm an introvert."

The fourteenth episode of the third season of the NBC hit show *The Apprentice* featured the two teams working with artists. The teams' first job was to select an artist to design a T-shirt. The second job was, you guessed it, to sell the shirts. The winner would be the team that earned the most money from the sale of the T-shirts. Easy enough, right?

Team Magna blew Team Net Worth out of the water! The technique Magna used was an obvious move to anyone attuned to marketing: Team Magna capitalized on their artist's collectors' base. The team had the artist send an email message to his list of 3,000 patrons to tell them that a new limited edition of his work was available. It was so elementary—such basic marketing sense—that the other team should have done the same thing, but they didn't.

Team Net Worth relied on advertising and foot traffic. Team Magna knew that people who already recognized and purchased the artist's work would be much more likely to buy his T-shirt than passers-by. This success shows the power of an artist's mailing list at work. We don't know that the other artist didn't have a good mailing list. We only know it wasn't used. Don't make the same mistake. Build your mailing list in a way that is comfortable for you and then use it.

I know you'd rather stay in your studio. Good things happen there. And it's a much more comfortable environment if you are an introvert and loath to speak up on your own behalf. Remember that if you stay in your studio and hide because you are bashful, that's one less artist in the crowded market. But let me ask you: By this time next year, will you feel okay about using shyness as an excuse for not taking action? What about in five years? Here's the big question: What if you never lived up to your potential because you say you're shy? Of course, I'm not a psychologist. I can't speak to genuine fears. I just want you to do everything possible to overcome excuses. Sharing your art by building on your current connections—like the artist in *The Apprentice*—is much more fun than trying to sell it. Let me show you how.

Action 13

Share, Don't Sell
to Build Your Contact List

One thing I hear frequently from artists is that they don't want to sound like they're running a used-car lot. With due respect to all used-car salespeople, you should have no trouble approaching sales differently. You're selling art, not used cars! Rather than focusing on sell, sell, sell, set your sights on building relationships with people in order to build your contact list. Even if you're truly an introvert, you almost certainly find joy in personal contact. I realize I've said this throughout the book, but now is the time when you have to commit to the concept of building relationships. It's not a magic wand or enchanting pill. It will take hard work. When done correctly, it will pay off.

Take a look at any shelf of marketing books. You'll quickly see that the sales technique for almost everything these days is relationship marketing over sales speak. The hard sell just doesn't work as well and no one, especially artists, likes to engage in it. Building relationships works. It's a process and a commitment, but it works.

People buy art from people they know and like. In case you haven't figured it out already, almost everyone likes to know an artist or two. You (artists) are cool. You conjure the previously unknown and unconsidered with your own hands. People think it's neat that they know you. Ergo, meet more people and cultivate those friendships.

People want to see your art; they just don't know it yet. Until you can muster enough enthusiasm about sharing your work, you're going to have a painful time trying to sell it. If you're at all shy about sharing your work with others, it won't go unnoticed. People can sense discomfort and might mistake it as lack of confidence. Guess what? We don't want to buy art from insecure artists. We want to buy art from artists who believe in themselves and their messages. We want to be swept up in your creativity, ideas, and enthusiasm.

Are you ready to get excited about your work? Are you ready to share it with anyone and everyone? Can you get to the point where you wake up each morning thrilled to share your work with the world? Can you create a fever to connect with more people? If you can't, how can you expect anyone else to get excited about your work? Of course, you'll share your art in exhibitions, but also on your website, blog, and in conversation. And don't forget about sharing your work in newsletters, emails, and regular mailings. All of these will help you build your contact list more rapidly than you think.

MEET MORE PEOPLE (FEARLESSLY)

I'm willing to bet there are a lot of people you run into daily who don't even know you're an artist. If that's correct, you have to do something about it. If you want to be known as an artist, you have to tell people. And you start with everyone you know. Then, after all of your current contacts know you're an artist, you have to get out and meet more people!

I said it before: It is estimated that every person knows 150 people. Consider the sales potential! If you met five new people a week, you could potentially reach 1,250 more people within a year. I know it's not realistic to think that each new person you meet is going to tell all of his or her friends and family about you, but you never know. Growing your audience, building relationships, is a deliberate practice. As I said, it's a commitment. Are you willing to commit to it?

Networking will make more people aware of you and your art. Get more involved in your community. Sit on committees and volunteer for posts that do not have anything to do with art. We've already agreed that no one is going to knock on your studio door and offer you a lifetime contract for happiness and success. You have to knock on their doors. And if they don't answer, you have to knock the darned doors down. You may be the world's most talented artist, but unless you speak up, no one will know you exist.

Aren't you more likely to buy a product or service from someone you know or from someone who was recommended to you by a friend? The same is true for those interested in buying art. They would probably enjoy meeting you, learning about your art, and eventually buying some of it if they just got to know you. Art instantly becomes more meaningful to people when they know the artist. So . . . meet more people!

JOIN AN ARTIST ORGANIZATION

Many artists use the "I'm an introvert" excuse and try going it alone. They might have support at home, but they don't know anyone in their local arts community. Not a soul. Worse yet, some artists don't even have the emotional backing of their friends and family. That hurts. So they just stay in their studios and wait for life to happen. Because art is crucial to their happiness, they trudge on, eventually realizing they must seek camaraderie with those who share their plight. They must get involved.

Getting out of your studio—escaping your shyness and comfort zone—leads to the awareness that you are part of a large community of artists. It continues to amaze that as our communication choices multiply, we seem to be doing less and less communing with each other in person. No computer or Internet chat room can ever take the place of human touch and contact.

Without some kind of support system, you will find yourself beaten down and constantly on the defensive. Sometimes you can obtain such support by getting involved in existing artist organizations. If you aren't familiar with one in your area, contact your local or state arts council, which you can find in the resources of the National Assembly of State Art Agencies <nasaa-arts.org>.

Being around other artists builds your confidence and sustains you emotionally. In addition, you will hear about opportunities you never knew existed if you hadn't been part of a group. You'll hear about them before they are ever published! You will also be eligible to apply for grants, awards, and exhibitions sponsored by the organization; be introduced to new art products and materials; and receive business advice in many areas (software, accounting, taxes, copyright, and more). Most importantly, with the right organization, you'll make contacts that lead to the next step on your career path. As you are learning, contacts play a seminal role in your success.

Before you join an organization, make sure it's a good fit for you. Don't join just for the sake of joining, which can end up being a waste of time and money. Attend meetings as a guest and consider where you might fit in. Before you join an organization, you should do research.

- What is the organization's mission? Is it one you can support?
- Who are the board members? Do you recognize anyone's name?
- Is there a staff member to run the daily operations? Or do volunteers manage it? How responsive has the organization been to your questions?
- Look at the art produced by the members. Do you like it? Is it good enough that it challenges you? Or do you think you have already surpassed the members in terms of quality? Are you impressed by the members' résumés?
- Is it a juried membership, requiring artists to submit artwork in order to be considered for membership? (Juried groups aren't necessarily better—just different.)
- What kinds of programs are offered? What types of exhibitions are organized and what are the venues? How are the artists promoted? Are grants or awards available to members? Is there an updated slide registry?

- Does the organization have a website? Is there an online gallery for members? How is it promoted? How often is it updated and by whom?
- How does the organization stay in contact with its members? Through an email newsletter? Snail mail? Is communication on a regular basis or haphazard?
- What are meetings and events like? Talk to members. Ask them questions. Are they satisfied with the organization and how it is run? What is missing for them? Would you be comfortable in the group?
- Are the fees reasonable for the services you are receiving and the contacts you're making?

You aren't joining just to be a member. You are joining to become involved. If you're uncomfortable in an organization, you won't reap the benefits of your membership. If you can't find the right fit in an existing organization, bring together a group of artists who meet regularly for the purpose of supporting each other. Form your own Art Biz Connection artist salon for more structure (see Action 16).

COUNT YOUR CONNECTIONS

In his book *Living the Artist's Life*, author and gallery dealer Paul Dorrell writes, "Connections will sell anything, including bad work." The right connections can even sell bad work. (Of course, we hope it doesn't come to that because there's enough good work to go around.) Sadly, there are still a few holdouts who refuse to believe that connections are critical. I'd even go so far as to say that connections are often more important to your marketing efforts than the work itself. Sorry, but it's true. You have to do everything you can to get noticed in the vast sea of artists today.

Connections can introduce you to:

- The new museum curator or director who is organizing an exhibit of local artists

- The president of the museum board who just so happens to collect works by regional artists
- The gallery dealer you've identified as being the best fit for your work
- The politician who loves to buy crafts by local artists to give as gifts
- The interior designer who is looking for a mural artist for the wealthy beach homes she's working on
- The artist who will be your mentor

See what I mean? Connections can make your career soar, but only if you recognize their value.

It is much easier to make a reputation locally and then spread out into other markets. You never know what connections you can unearth with your current contacts. Make a list of people you need to know, and then play six degrees of separation with that list. Who do you know who knows them? Who do you know who knows someone who knows them? Start working that list from the ground up if you have to. Read on to get an idea of where to begin.

SEE HOW EASY IT IS TO EXPAND YOUR CONTACT LIST

Start your contact list with Uncle Fred and everyone you know. You may think that Uncle Fred doesn't care much about art, but Uncle Fred knows you and loves you. Uncle Fred wants you to succeed and would probably be delighted to help in any way he can. Guess what? Uncle Fred knows a lot of other people. He wants you to share your art with him! Don't make excuses as to why certain people shouldn't be included on your contact list. Just do as I say and begin with everyone you know. Here are some prompts to get you going.

Start with the easiest and most obvious.
- **Family.** All of them.
- **People at your church, school, and/or office.**

- **Friends of friends and friends of family.** If nothing else, you can send them an invitation to your next opening and add "Have Bruce bring you to my opening. I'd love to see you there!"
- **Neighbors.** Show them what you've been up to behind closed doors.
- **Members of organizations you belong to.** The parent-teacher group at your child's school or the political caucus you're active in.
- **Past customers and collectors.** This is an easy one, but it's amazing how many artists don't keep good records! Given the 80/20 rule for sales (that 80% of your sales will come from 20% of your buyers), it's critical to keep these people updated and on your list.

Next, expand your list to include people in the arts (and related areas).

- **Other artists.** Most artists are really good about supporting other artists. They might not be your buyers, but do you know that artist referrals are one of your best bets for getting into a gallery? That's how important it is to keep in touch with them and nourish those friendships.
- **Gallery owners and art dealers where your work fits.** It's always best to ask someone for something after they know who you are. Keep your name in front of galleries before you ask them for representation.
- **Curators of museums and art centers.** To find the names of curators and directors of art museums, visit your local library for the latest version of *The Official Museum Directory*. The publication is produced annually and is costly, so find one to borrow. Your best bet is a good library at any university or museum, including zoos, botanical gardens, and history and science museums. See officialmuseumdirectory.com.

- **Directors of alternative art venues and nonprofit spaces.** Find these venues in calendar listings or by checking out your local or state arts council website. Confirm the current director's name so you can personalize your correspondence. You can also try the American Art Directory <americanartdir.com>.
- **Art reviewers and critics for magazines, daily and weekly newspapers.** I covered this area in the chapter on being a media magnet. Before you need to contact journalists with a news release, keep them on your list and send them postcards to familiarize them with your name and work.
- **Editors of and writers for publications in which your work might fit.** Art magazines are, of course, a natural fit. But so are magazines and newspapers related to your niche market. If the subject matter fits, don't neglect publications for wildlife, pets, women's issues, home decorating, or gardening.
- **Influential art bloggers.**
- **Heads of local and state arts agencies.** Find U.S. state arts councils at the National Assembly of State Arts Agencies <nasaa-arts.org>. Your state agency should be able to direct you to local organizations.
- **Arts organizations you belong to.** These might include museums, art centers, theater and music guilds, or groups specifically for individual artists.
- **Organizers of arts festivals or other community art events.** It isn't always evident who the organizer is, but with a little digging you'll be able to find out who's who for the happenings you're most interested in.
- **People who share an interest in your subject matter (your niche market).** For example, if you sculpt wildlife, add local wildlife and outdoors organizations. While you're at it, add people who write about those topics and people who contribute financially to their nonprofits.
- **Licensing agents, portrait brokers, or other representatives that can help you with a niche market.**

Remember that we're building a list full of potential. You're not going to use this list to email unrequested newsletters and blasts in bulk. You're just gathering all of your contacts in one place. See Action 2.

Don't forget to add people who use art and buy art.

- **Interior designers.** Some artists think interior designers are the ticket to easy street. I'm sure it happens, but I believe it's rare. Many designers are more likely to purchase art in showrooms, so plan to spend time educating them about art available in galleries and other venues. Interior designers and decorators will be most interested in color and size, so don't send them anything without this information. Contacts can be found through the American Society of Interior Designers <asid.org>.

- **Art consultants.** Think of an art consultant (or art advisor) as an intermediary between the purchaser and gallery or artist. Art consultants represent purchasers, not artists. They are in the business of buying art that fits their clients' tastes and needs. They're not in the business of nurturing artists' careers. Their clients might be individuals, but they're often businesses such as banks, hotels, and hospitals. Sometimes art consultants look for framed reproductions; other times they are seeking sophisticated art. When they buy for public spaces, art consultants are usually looking for specific sizes, colors, and subjects that appeal to a wide audience rather than works that are controversial. You can find art consultants in the yellow pages under Art or Art Dealers or Art Galleries. Start with the ones closest to you.

- **Architects.** Architects usually work with designers to select art for clients, but you might find some who are interested in large-scale sculpture and installations. Many architectural firms specialize in the design of schools, healthcare facilities, or hotels—all of which need art. You can find firms in your yellow pages or through the American Institute of Architects <aia.org>.

- **Landscape architects and landscapers.** These contacts are significant if you make outdoor sculpture or garden ornaments. Find them in the yellow pages or through the American Society of Landscape Architects <asla.org>.
- **Hospital administrators.** Some hospitals have active art programs. Find out who is in charge of the art program in facilities in your area. An art consultant may make the purchases for a hospital.
- **Assistants to CEOs and presidents of companies that have art collections.** Art consultants often make purchases for corporate collections; however, there is usually a vision behind the art consultant and that belongs to someone who is the CEO or who is close to the CEO. Unfortunately, a number of highly public corporate scandals have featured so-called lavish expenditures on art, forcing collections underground. The collections still exist, but aren't as prominent in publicly owned corporations.
- **Private collectors.** These collectors are difficult to find, but if you're out and about as much as you should be, they won't escape notice. Private collectors are featured in local papers or are known to loan artwork to museum exhibitions (read museum labels!).
- **Property managers.** Corporate real estate companies are frequently responsible for displaying art in their buildings. Sometimes the art is displayed only in public spaces and the managers' suites, but the intent is to make the building more attractive for potential tenants. You can find out who owns buildings in your area by reading business and commercial real estate journals.

We're not done yet. Remember to add all of these people who know lots of other people.

- **Politicians.** As I've already mentioned, many political figures like to buy things made in their districts, either for themselves or to give as gifts. Make sure they know about your art.

- **Community leaders who sit on boards.** Find these VIPs by reading the lifestyle and business sections of your paper.
- **Members of the clergy.**

As I've said, it will not always be appropriate for everyone to receive every mailing you send. Regular mail is relatively safe since almost everyone welcomes a piece of mail with art on it. Email messages are less safe and should be personalized or reserved for those who have agreed to receive bulk messages. Be discerning about who gets what.

If it seems like a lot of work to build your list, you're right. It is! But a list tailored to your goals and your career is far more valuable to you than any that you can buy. Purchase mailing lists only under certain circumstances. You might buy a mailing list of art consultants or architects, but adapt it by picking and choosing those most appropriate for you. I'm such a believer in building your own lists that I'm not going to mention resources that sell lists. I have no way of checking on their legitimacy. If you do find one you think is suitable, be sure to ask when it was last updated before you turn over your money.

Collect Email Addresses

Are you having trouble getting people to sign up for your mailing list? No wonder. We are all inclined to guard our contact information more closely than ever. Think about your own situation. As you go through your routines and are asked to give your phone number or email address, do you hesitate? Every time an email address is optional on a form I fill out, I leave it blank. I don't need any more email! So how can you encourage visitors to leave their email addresses on your website?

First, tell them what they'll be getting and how often. People want to know exactly what they're signing up for. Don't command visitors to "Sign up for my email list" in a heading. Instead, try enticement: "Be the first to know." Follow with:

> *If you leave your name and email, I will send you announcements to exhibits, openings, and art-related events. You will receive no more than one email message a month from me, except on the rarest of occasions.*

Next, tempt them with a gift. New subscribers might receive access to free e-cards they can send to friends. Or you might allow them to download a miniature reproduction of your work or a special report you've written about collecting art.

Add a privacy policy. A privacy policy (like the one below) tells people that you won't share or sell their information.

> *I value your trust and respect your privacy. Your name and email are safe with me. They will never be sold to or shared with anyone unless required by law.*

It's short, simple, to the point. Not pages of text to wade through or small print. Add a link to your privacy policy next to sign-up forms on your website and blog.

Finally, don't forget to lure people to your list through social media sites like Facebook and Twitter.

NETWORK AS IF YOUR CAREER DEPENDS ON IT— BECAUSE IT DOES

Congratulations on committing to building your contact list. But now is not the time to take a break. While your mail is going out every so often, you should also be going out every so often—in person.

Networking often gets a bad rap because it calls to mind the stereotypical power networker. He's the person who shows up at everything and can't quit talking about himself. He doesn't care who else is in the room. He just wants to make sure he is remembered. He's only there to benefit his situation and couldn't care less about the other people in the room. Networking shouldn't be like this at all. Effective networking is not all about you. It is a reciprocal relationship. It's about connecting people—you to them, them to you, and them to them—and doing so in a sincere manner. When you network, you are meeting new people and becoming genuinely interested in them. You are building relationships. You are sharing, not selling.

If you network to see what you can get out of it, you won't get much. Yes, you are meeting more people in hopes of receiving leads from new contacts. But in the same vein, you have to be willing to give them something in return—something that you hope will help them in their businesses.

A "lead" is a business opportunity shared with you for the purpose of assisting your career. The lead could be about someone who collects work similar to yours or a public sculpture commission that hasn't been widely publicized or a newly opened teaching position. It is extremely important that you follow up on each and every lead given to you unless the lead is for work in which you are uninterested. Your contact is taking the time to help you and demonstrate she cares about your well-being. You owe it to her to follow up or explain why you aren't interested. Express your genuine gratitude for each lead with a hand-written thank-you note. (See Action 11.)

I can't emphasize this point enough: The more people who know you, the more people there are to buy your art. You must meet more people. They're not going to knock on your door, so it's up to you to get out of your home and studio. Network with other artists at gallery openings, lectures, and other events. While you're out, network with other business owners. Many businesses depend on effective networking, and you can learn a great deal from a hair stylist, lawn care professional, realtor, coach, or retailer. All have to market their businesses and take care of daily activities such as scheduling and book-keeping while juggling these responsibilities with personal obligations and desires. You never know the contacts people have until you take time to talk with them.

There are formal networking groups in most cities. They are often facilitated by chambers of commerce or organizations specifically focused on generating leads for members. Read the business journal postings to find out what's available in your area. Chances are you'd be one of only a small handful of artists involved in a formal networking group. To find a chamber of commerce in the United States, visit uschamber.org. National leads groups include Ali Lassen's Leads Clubs <leadsclub.com>; eWomenNetwork <ewomennetwork.com>; and Business Network International <bni.com>.

If there is a weekly business journal in your area, pick up a copy. You will learn a great deal and there are often articles about art in corporate spaces. Business journals usually come out on Fridays. You can also read abbreviated content at The Business Journals <bizjournals.com>, which is the new media division of American City Business Journals—a U.S. chain of journals and websites in 41 major metropolitan markets. If your closest city isn't listed, there is undoubtedly another business publication that isn't affiliated with American City Business Journals. Search online, visit a bookstore, or ask around to find out the name and where you can pick up a copy.

INTRODUCE YOURSELF

Talking Helped Sell Her Art
After your workshop I was quickly motivated and focused. At the prompting of my greatest fan and supporter, my husband, I started talking out loud about my work. I was shocked when a friend asked if I sold my originals. She thought I only licensed my work. Before I knew it, I had sold four big pieces to her. Lesson learned.—Pamela Luer <pamelaluer.com>

Every person you meet is a potential collector or knows a potential collector and you only get one chance to make a first impression. Be prepared to talk to anyone, at any time, about your art. When someone asks what you do, how do you respond? You need a ten-second introduction ready to go. It is only ten seconds long because studies show that you have only nine seconds to keep someone's attention before their mind starts wandering. (Keep that in mind, too, when you give gallery talks or slide lectures about your art.)

Use descriptive language for your introduction because your words stand in for your art. Your words should be intriguing, so the listener will ask more questions and, eventually, to see your work. Your introduction must be succinct. It's far better to engage people in a dialogue in which they ask more questions than to go on and on about yourself.

Your introduction should include:

- Your name (if you haven't already said it)
- The type of art you make
- Descriptive language that helps the listener imagine what your work looks like

Highlight things in your introduction that will intrigue people. Perhaps it is your technique, colors, sizes, subject matter, or materials. Give enough detail so people can visualize a particular style, but don't overload them with too much information. If you aren't sure what to say, practice and see what works best for you. Return to the discussion of style in Action 6 to get a better grasp on how to describe yours and be inspired by the examples below.

> *I create abstract, dream-like images out of the simple elements of nature, such as fallen leaves, sticks, flowers, and seeds.*
> —Daniel Sroka <danielsroka.com>

> *My work combines drawing, painting and collage to explore memory, history, and personal mythology.*—Kesha Bruce <keshabruce.com>

I think of an introduction as a response to small talk at a cocktail party. You most often need an introduction when someone asks, "So, what do you do?" People will lose interest If you respond with a paragraph or drone on and on about yourself. It has to fit naturally into a conversation.

Write out your introduction knowing that the written word is much different than the spoken word. Some things that look fine on paper sound silly or forced when you say them out loud. When someone asks what you do, your response should roll off your tongue effortlessly, with confidence and enthusiasm. It takes time to come up with a good introduction that fits you. Start now and allow yours to evolve. After you have your ten-second introduction down, you are ready to face the world!

So, what do you do?

REMEMBER PEOPLE

As you're out meeting people, don't assume that they know you or remember you. We all forget faces. We age. We change our hair color or style. We gain and lose weight. And we run into the same people in completely different contexts. All of these things make it difficult to remember people's names. That's no excuse for not trying. But we can help each other out by introducing ourselves each time we meet. Assuming that someone remembers you could result in an awkward situation and make the other person uncomfortable. I make a point of reintroducing myself by full name to everyone that I only see once or twice a year.

A firm handshake, excellent eye contact, and genuine care for the concerns of others will go a long way in all environments. I make my workshop participants practice the handshake and eye contact. When you are meeting someone new, focus on that person as if there isn't another soul in the room. Say her name to yourself over and over as you look at her. Repeat it out loud as you talk with her. People who can remember names are showing others that they care about them and their potential business. Aren't you impressed when someone remembers your name? It seems as though it has become a lost art.

WHAT TO DO WITH ALL THOSE BUSINESS CARDS

I think there is too much pressure to hand out a lot of business cards. If I had to choose, I'd much rather walk away with someone else's card than give my card to that person. Why? Holding someone else's card puts you in control (remember the First Principle of No-Excuse Self-Promotion!). When you have the contact information, it's up to you to make the move. When the other person is the only one with your information, all you can do is sit back and wait. You have no idea what is happening to your business card or if it landed in a garbage can. Think about it!

Upon receiving business cards, follow these four steps.

1. Look at the cards while new contacts are still with you. Say their names out loud and make sure you are pronouncing names correctly.
2. As soon as they're out of sight, turn the cards over and jot down anything that will help you remember them and personalize your relationship. When business booms, it's hard to keep track of everyone you meet. Specifics will help you differentiate among buyers, clients, and collectors. Some cultures apparently consider it rude to write on someone else's business card so, to be on the safe side, wait until the individuals are gone to make your notes.
3. Within one week, send a postcard or nice-to-meet-you card with one of your images on it. Do this quickly before your new contacts forget who you are or how you met. (See Action 11 for details on following up.)
4. Put the cards in your "contact list" file for the time you update your contacts.

Incidentally, just because you are in possession of business cards from new contacts, you do not have permission to bombard them with email messages. As I said earlier, people usually don't mind getting post-cards or invitations with lovely pictures on them in the mail. However, most of us stand watch over our inboxes and abhor unsolicited emails. Be judicious in how you use email addresses you have gathered. You might even ask as you're trading cards, "Would you mind if I emailed you announcements for my exhibits? It's about four to six times a year." If they say yes, you have just been given permission. Honor the boundaries you set.

NO-EXCUSE PRINCIPLE

Waiting on the sidelines never served anyone well. Sharing your work with as many people as possible is one of your primary jobs. No one can do it better than you can. You can play it safe and excuse yourself as an introvert, or you can go out and meet people who can help you further your career goals.

NO-EXCUSE ACTION

Tomorrow morning, wake up with a new excitement for sharing your work with the world. Visualize your success as you recite your ten-second introduction. People are responding positively to your work over and over again. How does it feel? Each time you're frustrated or feeling rejected, remember this feeling and try to recapture it. The enthusiasm has to come from you.

"I'm not rich."

Money, money, money. I won't lie to you: You need it. You need money to make money, but I don't want you to go into debt or max out your credit cards. Quite the opposite. I hope you don't do either of these. My aim is to provide a dose of realism. Businesses can't survive without an influx of cash. And you need it for your future.

You need money for your marketing materials, festival booth, art supplies, framing, website, and much more. Too many artists ignore their financial well-being. I've been guilty of it myself. I started my business with such a small amount of cash I might have been declared legally insane. I would never advise an artist to leave a source of income without a guaranteed two-year salary in reserves and an intelligent business plan.

Although funds are a requirement for any business to survive and thrive, you can also generate innovative marketing ideas to help you save money. Apply some of your creative juices to your self-promotion efforts and the world may just come knocking at your studio door after all.

Action 14

Save Money

and Generate Buzz on a Shoestring

She wanted to go to China. It was a cultural tour and the chance of a lifetime, but the ticket alone was $3,200. How would she pay for it without going into debt?

Karen Bubb, a mixed-media artist and public arts manager for the Boise, Idaho, City Arts Commission, is also a big fan of solving problems with the help of artist-friends rather than trying to do it alone. And it's a good thing she values the input of others. One trusted advisor gave Karen the suggestion that helped her get to China. The advisor recommended that Karen sell "shares" of the experience. If she could sell 100 "shares" at $32 each, Karen could pay for her trip. That's all well and good, but even someone as well connected to her community as Karen was had to ask why people would buy shares of a trip to China they would never take. She had to give them value. And the package she came up with enticed potential shareholders with enormous value for only $32 a share!

In return for $32, here is what Karen promised her "shareholders."

- A "stock certificate" (a hand-pulled print created by Karen that doubled as a thank-you note for their purchase)

- A handmade collaged postcard sent from China
- A small (6″×5½″) encaustic painting based on the trip and Karen's experience in China
- An invitation to attend a private party and slideshow after the trip

Karen committed to the trip in January and was due to leave on May 26. A reporter got wind of her plan and an article appeared in the April 17 issue of the Boise newspaper. Her plan to sell shares to family, friends, and colleagues had just exploded to include anyone who wanted to participate. Before she knew it, Karen had sold 225 shares, 30% of which went to total strangers who wanted to be part of the experience. And she had just over a month to make everything come together.

What started as an adventure to a distant land became something bigger because of the way Karen promoted herself. Her trip was now a performance piece. The connections to her shareholders were powerful and informed every decision. She spent much of the month prior to her departure making the collaged postcards that would be sent from China, as promised, to each shareholder. She used the additional funds to purchase an audio recorder and camera to document the trip accurately and artistically.

Upon her return from China, Karen worked for two and one-half years to produce the promised paintings to her shareholders. When they were completed, the paintings were exhibited as a group before being dispersed. The gallery that had long represented Karen was supportive of her decisions and funding methods. The open dialogue between artist and gallery eased minds and ensured both parties that it was a win-win situation. It also lessened the risk of any surprises in the professional relationship.

Karen says she'd do it all over again and probably pay closer attention to creating a realistic budget. When asked if, given the large amount of work she needed to produce following the trip, she might charge more for shareholders, Karen hesitated and said it wouldn't be above $50 per share. Part of the success and the fun was involving so many people in the process. She clarified:

I gained numerous fans by just completing it and doing what I said I was going to do. I probably lost money in the end in that I did not factor in all of the costs of doing the body of work in terms of material and time, but I gained an incredible relationship with many collectors and community members. I also did a body of work I wouldn't have done otherwise, which was very satisfying indeed.

LOW-COST / NO-COST PROMOTIONS

Karen Bubb devised an unusual way to raise funds in order to create her art and generate buzz around it. You can, too. The only limit to the possibilities is your imagination. Here are some other low-cost or no-cost promotion ideas.

- Order a bumper sticker, car magnet, T-shirt, or hat with your website address or art on it. Check out makestickers.com. Barbara Rush (Roswell, Georgia) had a tire cover for the back of her Honda CR-V made at FASTSIGNS <fastsigns.com>. It features her compelling art and website address, undoubtedly bringing smiles to faces of those stuck in traffic. To see a picture, go to barbararush.com/articlesfrombr.html. (She also received links from a number of blogs after I posted a picture of her car on my blog. Good ideas travel fast and result in free publicity!)
- Don't forget to blog and leave your footprint all over the Internet. See Action 7.
- Add images of your art to your iPod or smart phone. You'll be ready for the time when it's easier to share these than to cart around a mini-portfolio.
- Create the most original e-card ever made and tell all of your friends that you'll send it for them free of charge. Make it a seasonal event and particularly attractive to friends who just can't seem to get around to sending cards by mail in time for birthdays and holidays. Be sure you understand the technology involved and can deliver on your promises.

- Put a gift bag of your products together from CafePress.com and have several bags on hand at all times for hostess and thank-you gifts. Always think of ways you can be putting your images in front of people rather than giving them a candle, bottle of wine (unless your art is on the label), or bouquet of flowers.
- Speaking of wine labels, you can order wine bottles with your personalized labels. Just think: your art on a wine label that you hand out to your friends. Of course, it has your website address on it, too. Unfortunately, shipping alcoholic beverages is not possible in all states.
- An email newsletter won't cost you a thing if you can generate it with the tools you have right now. See Action 9.
- Michael Kelty (Ypsilanti, Michigan) is a painter who has a penchant for marionettes, but his puppets aren't for kids. He produces "bawdy" stage shows in bars and other places where adults congregate. See michaelkelty.com.
- Press releases are virtually free when sent via email, as they should be. See Action 12.
- Have a pre-sale. David Castle (Denver, Colorado) had one for a series of works he was planning to produce during his annual pilgrimage to the Oregon coast. He invited people to select a palette of two colors that he could work into original abstract watercolors he would paint just for them. He marketed his idea through his blog, a special email message, and a mailed invitation to 125 top leads. He priced the small unframed works that he would create at half of the usual cost and offered a money-back guarantee. His efforts led to the sale of seventeen paintings before he left on his trip and an additional nine when people came to his studio to pick up their purchases (they bought more for gifts). He spent less than $50 to market the idea. See davidcastleart.com.
- Acknowledging other people with a sincere thank-you note is one of the best and least expensive ways to promote your art and build relationships. Can't afford the note cards? Send an email. See Action 11.

- Comment, like, follow, and interact on social media. Michael Goettee (Atlanta, Georgia) snagged an impressive interview from a respected news blog in his market just because he "liked" the owner's Facebook site. His Facebook success doesn't end there. He says, "The curator at the Booth Western Art Museum found me on Facebook when I'd commented on a mutual friend's posting. He thought he recognized my name from having heard it from someone else and clicked my profile out of curiosity. He then befriended me and invited me to visit him so we could talk about my work." Not long after that meeting, the Museum acquired one of Michael's paintings for their permanent collection. See michaelgoettee.com.
- Speaking won't cost you a thing except time, and teaching will earn bucks while you're keeping your name in front of people. See Action 5.
- Pippi Johnson offers commissioned painting packages of "the view from your dock, deck, or window" to neighbors in Kenora, Ontario. The package includes one 16″×20″ framed original, three matted and framed prints, and fifty cards with envelopes. See pippijohnson.com.
- Throw a "title party." Pamela Murphy (Sister Bay, Wisconsin) has hosted several. She said, "I'd have a lot more paintings called *Untitled* if it weren't for my friends. Occasionally it seems obvious what a piece should be titled, but most often I really have no ideas. When deadlines loomed, it was always stressful trying to come up with titles so I started asking four to eight friends over. I provided dinner, but before they were allowed to eat, the paintings had to be named. We'd start out in my studio, drink some wine, discuss, and name paintings. It was great fun. Three years ago the party got bigger—100 or so people. Just before my show opened, I'd clean up my studio, hang all the work, and provide food, drink, and pencils. Throughout the evening people would write ideas for titles on pieces of paper pinned next to each painting. At the end of the night, I—along with any people still there—read

through all the suggestions and chose names. It's not a democracy since I have final say. I always get terrific titles and I think everyone enjoys the opportunity to be part of a creative process. For me the parties are fun, entertaining, and a way to relieve the stress of coming up with names." See pamelamurphystudio.com.

TEAM UP WITH NONPROFIT ORGANIZATIONS

Forming a community alliance with a nonprofit organization is another freebie—one that could pay off big. An exhibition or event, designed in tandem, would benefit both of you. I suggest that you work with nonprofits other than those set up to assist artists. Examples of such organizations are the Red Cross, the American Cancer Society, local food banks, groups that help disadvantaged children or the elderly, AIDS charities, pets and wildlife funds, Habitat for Humanity, public television and radio, and many more.

There are at least five reasons to partner with a nonprofit.

1. When you give back to your community, you create goodwill and, I hope, feel a greater sense of accomplishment than if you go it alone.
2. Your marketing efforts are no longer just about you. They take on a communal focus, which will expose your art to more people and, ultimately, to the media, which often sponsors charitable causes. You shouldn't be shy about getting publicity this way. Not only do you bring attention to your work, you are spotlighting a good cause.
3. You will meet people who can help you with your career. Nonprofit organizations are overseen by boards of directors, which are usually composed of the pillars of the community (people who buy art!).
4. Nonprofits that exist in multiple cities might provide you with contacts for those locations in the event you want to branch out in the future.

5. Nonprofits are eligible for more grants and public funding than are artists. At some point, your idea might benefit from these resources.

Do not approach nonprofits with the intent of asking them to assist you. Most nonprofits are understaffed and underfunded. As a result, they are constantly scraping by just to meet operating expenses. As far as you are concerned, *you* are there to help *them*! You must approach any proposal with this attitude, which is why any work with a nonprofit should come from a deep belief in their cause. You must be sincere.

She Was Prepared and Took Advantage of New Connections
Your suggestions for teaming with nonprofits and community groups have been especially important for me. When our local Great Salt Lake Bird Festival organizing committee lost their longtime art show coordinator to cancer, they asked if I would step in on short notice and take over. I knew you would have told me to go for it, so I said I would do it. The first year was very rough, but I did one smart thing I learned from you, which was to place a little stand with my business cards and a brief artist biography next to my own work. Voilà! A reporter from a major Utah newspaper was looking for a community interest story, and profiled my artwork and me within a couple of weeks. And one of my previous collectors saw the story and remembered that he wanted to commission a portrait of his dog, so I got some work out of it, too.—Debbie Goodman <debbiegoodman.com>

Before you consider teaming with a nonprofit, do your homework. Make sure the organization has legitimate tax status and is highly regarded. Your reputation, too, is at stake. In the United States, you can check with the American Institute of Philanthropy, a charity watchdog helping donors make informed decisions. See charitywatch.org.

DONATE YOUR ART?

Although donating art isn't seen as a big expense by most artists, it is something you should consider carefully. Artists are bombarded with requests to donate artwork to charity auctions and drawings. Many of the organizations requesting your donations aren't aware that you are unable to receive tax benefits from your gift. Under current IRS rules in the United States, artists who donate their artwork cannot deduct the fair market value for tax purposes. They can only deduct the cost of materials. Some members of Congress have been trying to change this situation for years, so keep watching for legislation. In the meantime, limit your donations while educating the organizations about the tax laws for artists. It is heartening to see many organizations offering a percentage of the selling price to artists who donate. My opinion is that all art and artist organizations have a responsibility to compensate their artists in this manner.

Donating work can be a good thing for your career. You're helping out a cause while getting publicity. Before you agree to donate, however, ask questions—especially if the request comes from an organization that is not known to you. You should get answers to these questions before you consider donating your art.

Does the organization have official nonprofit status?

How long has it been in existence?

For how many years has the event been held? (Beware of first-time events, which are often run on a shoestring budget by volunteers.)

Is there a minimum bid for the art?

Will artists receive any of the proceeds?

How will the auction be publicized?

Is it a live auction or a silent auction? Who will be the auctioneer and how knowledgeable is that individual about art?

How many other items are up for bid?

Will your work be in a program or catalog?

CONSIDERING A SALE?

I want to express a note of caution about sales and specials. Art world insiders often see discounted art as less than tasteful. If work is discounted, it is usually done behind closed doors and with a whisper. A reputable fine art magazine will never run an "Everything Must Go" ad. Ads that bellow GIANT THREE-DAY MASTERS OF ART SALE appear only in newspapers.

The other reason not to advertise sales and specials is that you don't want to upset people who purchased your art at full price. If they see you are running specials, they might wait until your next sale to buy your work. Or they might not buy it again. If you want to consider offering your art at a discount, a better idea might be to include a "friends' discount" coupon or a handwritten note to select people on your mailing list. Be sure that those who have purchased your art in the past get first choice, which will make them feel special—like they're in on a secret.

NO-EXCUSE PRINCIPLE

There are no rules that say you can't do this and you can't do that to promote your art. Be as creative as your comfort level allows and stay within your financial means. Involving more people in planning an event means sharing the expenses and generating a bigger buzz.

NO-EXCUSE ACTION

Dream up one big fantastic event you can implement in the next two years. Go back over this Action and the previous one. How can you include more people? More people = bigger buzz.

NO MORE EXCUSES

You realize you're out of excuses.

With this book by your side, you can safely venture away from your studio armed with the knowledge you need to make your moves. In fact, you may have too much information. You may be feeling overwhelmed. Don't let that feeling paralyze you. We all have that reaction when faced with the daunting reality of what it takes to run a business. Creativity coach Dr. Eric Maisel said: "Overwhelm is generally a function of not being happy and of having to do too much just to keep meaning afloat. . . . There is actually more to be done in life, not less, including the boring things, but in a context of passionate meaning-making."

You can't do everything at once. You have to set priorities. Do what you can, finding ways to enjoy the process. Most importantly, don't allow too many possibilities to paralyze you into inaction. Be realistic, but challenge yourself with each step. Use the ideas that work for you at this time in your career, realizing that other ideas will be needed next year.

Action 15

Plan Your Attack
on Paper

It always helps me overcome overwhelm when I have a good plan that reveals my priorities. Big abstract ideas are broken down into manageable action steps on a business roadmap. Suddenly, it all seems to make sense. Something magical happens when a plan is on paper. Written words seem official and carry a lot more weight than those floating around in our heads. We're often more committed to our intentions when we take the time to put them in writing.

The purpose of this Action is to create a plan of attack that intensifies and enhances communication with your patrons and potential audience. Although I have given you many ideas throughout the book, it's up to you to edit them. Use what works for your unique needs at this point in your career. New needs and new ideas will arise over time. Review your plan in six months or a year. If you have been taking action, your outlook will certainly change. Every self-promotion or marketing plan should be considered a work in progress. It's created at a precise moment in time. It should be revisited on a regular basis to inject new life into it.

GUIDELINES FOR ATTAINING GOALS

As you're setting your goals and planning for the future, keep these guidelines in mind.

- Goals must be specific and measurable or you won't know when you've reached them.
- Goals must have deadlines. Without deadlines, they are only good ideas.
- Goals should be challenging—going beyond what you would normally do without them.
- Goals should be written down. It makes them real. Write them as if they are affirmations rather than wishes.
- Goals should be shared with at least one other person. It's easier to back out of them if you keep them to yourself. It's clear that I would never have finished this book if I hadn't told thousands of people about it each week in my newsletter and on my blog.
- Goals should be accompanied by a reason. Why do you want to attain your goals? What is your deepest motivation? What will you get in return for achieving them? How will the results make your life better?

If you find setting goals to be difficult, don't think you're alone. Because you're self-employed, it is likely that no one ever asked you to set goals. You're too busy making and marketing your art to think about goals. Yet, setting and attaining goals are crucial to any career success. You undoubtedly know that or you wouldn't have gotten this far in the book. Now I'm going to walk you through a few exercises. The first one is intended to get to the big picture. I want to make sure you have that nailed. Then I'll ask you to come up with a more manageable plan of attack that will help you cultivate collectors *and* preserve your sanity. Ready?

VISUALIZE YOUR FUTURE

What does success mean to you? As you recall, I asked you this question in Action 1—at the beginning of the book. How do you define success in the areas listed in that chapter? Do you know yet? If not, now is a good time to look at that list again. You need answers before you can create a plan for your promotions. If you don't know where you're headed, how can anyone help you get there? How can you help yourself get there? How will you know you've arrived?

Take your definition of success and start visualizing. I'm giving you permission to dream big, bold, seemingly irrational dreams in technicolor. These dreams aren't the stuff of fantasy. These are dreams you can make come true. Just as you have a definition of success that is unique, you also have a path created just for you—one of your own making. Your path may look nothing like that of another artist. That's okay. Allow yourself to feel and to understand what you need most. Listen to your head and your heart and create a plan that has the most meaning for your needs. It's time to dream.

If you could have the life you want, what would it be like? Everyone has dreams, but most of us suppress them in the hurry-scurry of daily activities and task lists. It's time to determine what your dream life looks like. Think about your artwork, your home, your family, and friends. Where do you live? Where do you vacation? Where do you make your art and where do you exhibit it? Spare no details. Consider the colors, textures, sounds, and feelings taking form in your vision.

Saying "I want to make a lot of money" is not visualizing. Try this instead: "By 2014, I am making $100,000 per year selling my art on the Internet." Declaring "I'd like a bigger studio" is a wish, not a vision. Instead: "By 2014, I am working out of a 1,000-square-foot studio within a larger artists' community. It is equipped with [natural light, ventilation, plumbing] and has storefront access. I am easily able to afford the rent and enjoy the company of nearby artists. We often get together for a cup of coffee and discuss art ideas, art history, and art materials." See the difference? With the details, it's easier to imagine that studio and picture yourself there. It's hard to get to where you want to be until you can be precise. Specifics will help guide your direction.

Use visualization to help chart the course of your art career. Perhaps this set of steps might help.

1. **Meditate.** As you listen to peaceful music, create a vision of
    your perfect life. Use an eye pillow to block out the rest of the
    world. Keep returning to the goal of visualizing your future.
    Spare no details in the big picture.
2. **Write it down.** Describe your perfect life in great detail. Use
    journaling to revisit and nourish your dream.
3. **Make a collage, painting, or sculpture that brings your
    visualization to life.** After all, you're a visual person. For a
    collage, start by cutting out representations from magazines
    of all the things you desire from life. Put the words and images
    together in a composition that motivates and inspires you
    each day.
4. **Say it out loud.** Don't be afraid to tell other people about
    your vision, but at the very least say it aloud to yourself
    each day. Believe in each word that comes out of your
    mouth.
5. **Keep it close.** Carry a short version of your vision in your
    pocket or handbag and post it where you run into it every
    morning or evening.

Once you know what you want, you can begin to visualize the small
steps you should take to set you on the path to success.

UPDATE YOUR MARKETING MATERIALS

Return to Action 6. Look at the contents of your portfolio and other
essential marketing materials. What do you have available? What do you
need to produce or update in order to project a more professional
image that will help you attain your goals?

Create a plan for your marketing materials using the table format
below. You don't need every item I included on this list, which is intended
as an inventory of possibilities. "Specific Goal" might be a certain
quantity, design stage, or research that contributes to a larger goal.

Marketing Item	✔ Done	Specific Goal with Deadline	Expenses
Contact list on computer			
Inventory on computer			
Cohesive body of work			
Letterhead			
Business card			
Note card			
10-second verbal introduction			
Artist statement			
Stories			
Résumé			
Biography			
Photographs of art			
Photographs of self			
Brochure			
Flyer			
Postcard			
Website			
Blog			
Fan page on Facebook			
Twitter			
Video			
Email signature block			
Newsletter			
Online media kit			
Voicemail message			
Podcast			

PROMOTIONAL GOALS

I refuse to use the term *promotional campaign* because that phrase implies an effort that has a beginning and an end. My concept (promotional goals) doesn't have either. Self-promotion should be one of those routines we talked about in Action 3. Like your art, it's something that you are aware of each and every day. This is where it all comes together. You can't possibly tackle everything in this book at once, but you can put forth your best effort and do what's right for you at this moment.

What are your goals for promotion over the next one to three years? Although there may be some overlap with the marketing materials goals above, this is a more comprehensive survey of your self-promotion goals. Complete only those that are applicable and ignore the rest.

Samples

	Specific Goals with Deadlines	**Actions with Deadlines**
Contact list	I will have 200 new names on my contact list by the end of the year.	I will add five new names each week. I will create a folder immediately and drop names into it that will be on my list. I will add a sign-up form to my website by 5/1.
Mailings	I will send out a new postcard every four months.	I will make an appointment to talk with Diane about design by 5/16. I will have my new computerized database working by 5/31. I will decide on the content of each postcard by 6/15. I will mail 8/1, 12/1, and 4/1.
Public talks	I will give one public talk about my work by the end of next year.	I will research venues and select the five best possibilities by 7/1. I will create an outline and content plan by 8/1. I will make appointments with programming directors by 11/1.

Now it's your turn.

	Specific Goals (one to three years) with Deadline	Actions with Deadlines	Expenses
Contact list			
Mailings			
Newsletters			
Meeting influential people			
Articles			
Exhibition entries			
Grant applications			
Teaching / Demonstrations			
Public talks			
Open studios			
Gallery representation			
Advertising			
Website			
Blog			
Facebook			
Twitter			
Online audio or video			
Newsworthy events			
Other:			

Grab your Promotional Plan at IdRatherBeintheStudio.com.

You may have noticed that in this book packed with information about promoting your art, I have hardly mentioned advertising. It doesn't even rate a subhead! For years, I have listened to horror stories about large amounts of money flushed down the advertising drain. These anecdotes support my belief that word of mouth, personal recommendations, and legitimate articles touting your work carry a lot more weight than any amount of advertising you can do. For that reason, I usually discourage artists from spending money on advertising. (Shall I say it again? Your contact list is your #1 asset!)

However, advertising *has* paid off for some artists. Whether or not you should advertise depends greatly on where and who your audience is and the possible outlets for reaching them. If you sketch portraits of private homes, it might make sense to advertise in realtor trade publications. Likewise, if you create garden sculpture, advertising in a horticultural magazine or website might work for you. If you choose to advertise, decide where you will place your ads and at what frequency. How much will you devote to advertising? How will your dollars best be spent? You might consider advertising as long as it isn't the sole means of promoting your art. For some artists, advertising is a lazy way out. They think they can buy an ad and sit back until things start moving. They don't want to do any more work. Show me an artist who has built a career based solely on advertising, and I'll gladly rewrite this section.

CREATE A REALISTIC BUDGET

Oh, yeah. Money. You have to think about it sooner or later. Neglect this step at your peril. Many a stupid business decision was born from financial ignorance. You need some sort of a budget if you plan to market your work. You can't depend on money rolling in, especially in your early years. And you undoubtedly want to be aware of all the money that needs to go out.

Remember that you can write off business expenses as long as you are set up as a legal business and can demonstrate you are doing everything possible to sell your work and comply with federal, state, and local tax laws. Check with your accountant.

Before you dive into any promotional strategy, look at the expenses you have decided are necessary, when payments will be due, and whether or not you can afford them at this time. If you are going to have an exhibition, budget for items like printing invitations, postage, and refreshments, in addition to the artwork supplies and framing costs. If you want to make a splashy Web presence, budget funds for design and hosting.

Create a realistic marketing budget that is based on your goals, what you can afford to spend, and what you have spent in past years. This budget is not for your entire business, but for your promotional strategy.

Expense	Budgeted Amount
Advertising	
Blog hosting	
Dues	
Classes and workshops	
Computer and other hardware	
Contract labor (such as Web designer)	
Credit card processing	
Domain name registration	
Email distribution service	
Entry fees	
Hospitality and refreshments for exhibits	
Internet Service Provider (ISP)	
Office supplies	
Photography	
Photography equipment	
Postage	
Printing	
Secure shopping cart	
Shipping	
Software	
Web hosting	
Other:	
TOTAL Expenses Planned for Marketing Artwork	$

The plans for your marketing materials and your promotional goals are set. Now it's time to act.

- **Put all the deadlines in pencil on a calendar.** Are they realistic? Can you complete the tasks in the time you have allotted? Are you pushing yourself enough?
- **Create a contract with yourself.** When you have finished defining and refining your goals and action steps, write out a contract with yourself that you will follow your plan, updating it along the way.
- **Envision your success.** Do everything you can to create positive energy and to envision yourself attaining your goals. Write affirmations in your journal. Tear out gallery shots from magazines and glue your work over the art in the photo. Write newspaper headlines for your exhibition.

NO-EXCUSE PRINCIPLE

Building a successful career and reputation is hard work. There are no shortcuts, no easy ways out. Without a plan, you react to whatever comes along. But with a plan, you're in control.

NO-EXCUSE ACTION

Put your plan on paper, but don't file it in the back of a drawer. Keep it in sight. Add reminders to your calendar to check in on your plan once a quarter. If you're really working it, you'll be checking on it weekly.

Action 16

Maintain Momentum

Day In and Day Out

If you're like me, whenever you get a new idea, you're gung ho. Creative juices hit record levels and you don't want to be diverted by anything else. You don't care if you're supposed to be doing that other thing. The new idea is much more fun! You come up with all kinds of excuses as to why you need to put your previous goals on ice.

That may be how you're feeling now. Your head is swimming with ideas and you can't wait to get started. You have lofty ambitions fueled by great intentions. Deadlines are in front of you and daily tasks are at hand. You know what needs to be done and you're ready and willing to do it. For a while. Then, like many people, you will find other things creeping into your schedule. A portrait commission that you didn't want to pass up, a more efficient way to process credit card sales, or a redesign of your promotional materials. All of these diversions add up and take time out of your schedule. If they're not essential, they keep you from reaching your goals. You'll lose momentum.

Because self-promotion is an ongoing task in your career, you must find ways to maintain momentum that energizes you from day to day. This final Action outlines some ideas to help you do just that.

NURTURE A POSITIVE ENVIRONMENT

Do things that make you feel good and contribute to your mental well-being. For me, more than anything else, that means staying organized. I function noticeably worse when I am not organized, have a messy desk, or don't have goals in mind. Reviewing Actions 2 and 3 should help with disorganization.

It's also important to hold on to your passion. You must be completely devoted to the life of an artist to make a living as an artist. Artists make art. When they're not making art, they think about making art and talk about art. They dream about art. Always return to rediscover this passion when you think it is dying. Write affirmations in a journal, post positive photos, and develop a list of motivational quotes. Read inspirational books and listen to inspirational messages. I have a favorite "self-esteem" audio program that I sometimes fall asleep to. I truly believe the message penetrates my thoughts. Books by coaches and business motivation experts are instant energizers.

Subscribe to newsletters that lift you up. Cheryl Richardson's is terrific <cherylrichardson.com>. I also enjoy The Daily Om <dailyom.com>. Both are free. Cheryl Richardson also offers a "Coach on Call" radio show on Hayhouse Radio. You can listen at hayhouseradio.com or catch any of the other numerous inspirational hosts. Get unsurpassed daily cheerleading from Mike Dooley's *Notes from the Universe* <tut.com>.

SET BOUNDARIES

Be very picky about what you allow into your life. It is, after all, your life. Like your art, no one cares about it more than you. And people will often impose their needs on your time—not because they don't care about you, but because they haven't been given clear boundaries by you. So many people want our time, opinions, art, and assistance. We want to make them all happy. We want to please them. We don't want them to be mad at us. And yet, dropping your priorities when something is requested of you doesn't serve anyone in the long run. Changing your focus because someone else wants your time and energy makes you frustrated. You're mad at yourself for agreeing to the request and at the other person for asking you to do it in the first place. Sure, the new task may be easier than other things you have on your task list, but it pushes you off the path. You've put others ahead of yourself. If you keep giving and giving, you have no reason to be upset at anyone but yourself. But if you set firm boundaries, people will know when and where you can help and when and where you draw the line.

Let me share with you a few of the boundaries I have established.

- As I mentioned early on, I refuse to work with anyone who whines and makes a lot of excuses.
- I do not go into my home office until I am clean and dressed.
- I schedule client phone calls only on Tuesdays, Wednesdays, and Thursdays.
- I don't have time to answer questions from every artist who writes to me needing an immediate response. My policy: I will consider questions for my blog or newsletter so that all artists can benefit from the reply.
- I do not answer my business line after 5 p.m. Period.

What boundaries do you abide by? As you're setting boundaries, remember that it is easier to say No to something and then change your mind than it is to say Yes and then back out. In order to have other people respect your career goals, you must show them that you have boundaries and aren't willing to compromise your aspirations. When you are faced with an opportunity or if someone asks you to volunteer for something, it's up to you to decide how to spend your time. Ask yourself one or more of these questions.

If I do this, will I feel it has been a good use of my time?
If I agree to do this, will I enjoy the process?
If I agree to do this, will I end up resenting someone in the process?
Is there something more important that I should be doing?

Develop a standard rejection line for occasions when you're put on the spot. If you don't have one ready, always say you'll think about it before agreeing to do it.

A simple "Let me think about it and get back to you" gives you time to form a response and craft your words carefully.

Saying No isn't a bad thing. Others are not responsible for recognizing your boundaries. You have to tell them. I think you'll be surprised at how much people respect boundaries when given them.

LIMIT CONTACT WITH NEGATIVE PEOPLE

Here is another imperative: Get rid of the naysayers in your life. Banish people who are jealous, unsupportive, or oblivious to what you want and where you want to go. They're downright selfish. If you can't eliminate them completely (and legally) from your life, deliberately limit your time with them and tell them that certain subjects are off limits. You may find it difficult to do this with family members. One client dreaded every meal she had to spend with her sibling. I suggested that she go to a movie with her sibling rather than face the anxiety of conversation.

If you have naysayers who have been unsupportive of your goals as an artist, tell them how you feel and what your boundaries are. Do it before you become too emotional and before it's too late—before they cause you to lose momentum. Say it plainly, matter-of-factly, and leave no doubt in their minds that if they can't be supportive, you'll have to find other topics to talk about or you will have to restrict your time together.

Cope with Criticism

Author and speaker Cynthia Morris <originalimpulse.com> encourages her clients to cope with criticism by using the following process.

Begin by asking: Is it true?

If yes → Does the critic have credibility?

               If yes → What can I learn?

               If no → Did I do my best?

If no → Why was it said in the first place?

If either, and above all → What can I learn?
How can I share this experience with others?

Cynthia advises:

> *The key here is to deal with it and move on, not to dwell on the criticism or make it the focus of someone else's attention. I want other people to focus on positive things, not criticism I might have received. I think the first and last questions are paramount: "Is it true?" and "What can I learn?" apply to every critical comment you might receive.*

KEEP YOUR PLAN IN FRONT OF YOU

Don't let go of the vision you have for your career and your life. Return to Action 15. Practice the visualization exercises regularly as you are reviewing your promotional plan to maintain momentum and focus.

FIND A BUSINESS BUDDY

When life and the pressure of making a living seem overwhelming, you might begin to feel alone. The walls start closing in and the smallest tasks appear impossible. Very few people achieve success without the help of others. We've looked at joining artist organizations and nurturing community alliances, but sometimes you need more personal, focused attention.

Find a business buddy for success. Do you know the number one reason my coaching clients come to me? It's not because I have all the answers. And it's not because I do the work for them. In fact, I won't do the work for them. Almost all of my coaching clients work with me because I act as their partner. Together, we find solutions and the right path for them. More importantly, I hold them accountable for their goals and actions. That's what a business buddy can do for you if you don't have a business coach.

If your business buddy comes in the form of another artist, fantastic! Make sure that artist is not only gung ho for self-promotion but really has it together. Otherwise, you might fare better with someone who is not an artist—someone who is in another business and has to do a lot of relationship building. Other artists aren't always the best people to teach you about running your business. You can benefit from watching how other businesspeople operate. Hairstylists, realtors, and insurance agents: all are in business for themselves. How do they get clients? How do they keep them? How do they stay motivated?

Here are some characteristics to look for in a good business buddy. In return, your business buddy should expect the same from you.

- Self-employed and eager to self-promote
- Highly motivated
- Full of self-confidence and knowledge
- On par or even a little ahead of you (don't find yourself in the position of always being the teacher and motivator)
- Encouraging
- Able to offer suggestions and feedback (not automatically approve of everything)—a kind of devil's advocate who makes you look at things in new ways
- Connected with the community

In this day and age, a business buddy doesn't even have to be someone you meet with face to face. You might pick up a partner through an online forum or request one through your other contacts. Although email is convenient, try to talk on the phone with your partner once every couple of weeks. I know of two artists who check in with their business buddies at the same time every week. I meet face to face with my mastermind partner each month, which is a terrific boost for momentum. In between, we support each other through emails and phone calls.

FORM AN ART-MARKETING SALON

Imagine a group of artists getting together for the sole purpose of helping each other with their marketing plans. That's what the Art Biz Connection is all about. I created this special website and program to show artists how valuable they are to one another and to help them maintain momentum.

My study of art history led me to learn about the numerous communities that have nurtured artists and expanded what art can be. Some were more formal communities; others were informal salons that met in bars and cafés. In the early 1990s, I had my own salon that included artists, an architect and me, the curator. It was invigorating to talk with them each Thursday afternoon.

The Art Biz Connection provides a structure to help artists work together and support one another. It's all about building artist communities where they don't exist and strengthening them where they're already in place.

You bring the artists. I supply the organization and motivation through a nine-session program that guarantees each and every participant a complete art-marketing plan when it's over. You have all the tricks and tools you need in the pages of this book, and you'll have the support of your artist-friends each and every step of the way. See artbizconnection.com.

CREATE A SCHEDULE

What do you have to do each and every day to maintain momentum, to live your dream? What do you have to do every week? Every month? Every year? Answer these questions, which are similar to those in the effective self-promotion list I asked you to consider in Action 3. But this schedule is for your entire life.

> *What do I have to do every day to accomplish my goals?*
> *What do I have to do every week to accomplish my goals?*
> *What do I have to do every month to accomplish my goals?*
> *What do I have to do every year to accomplish my goals?*

GET OUT OF THE STUDIO

There. I've said it. You might rather be in the studio, but you have to get out—not only to cultivate collectors, but to nourish your creativity. In her series of books that started with *The Artist's Way,* Julia Cameron suggested a weekly artist date for "nurturing your creative consciousness, your inner artist." Visiting museums, galleries, and other artists' studios is always rewarding and inspirational. And, although you might be alone on your artist dates, I argue that the ritual surrounding these visits reminds you that you are not alone. You are a significant part of a greater community and tradition of artists.

NO-EXCUSE PRINCIPLE

No one is going to make you get up in the morning, create your art, or promote your art. The drive has to come from within you. Owning a business is tough, and yet that's what you are: a business owner. And you're competing with other business owners. Find ways to maintain the momentum day in and day out.

NO-EXCUSE ACTION

Stop making excuses. Excuses hold you back. Instead of making excuses as to why you can't or shouldn't be doing something, find reasons to take action.

Resources
The Most Important Stuff

RESOURCES ON IdRatherBeintheStudio.com

Principles of No-Excuse Self-Promotion (poster)
Self-Promotion Routines Planner
Presentation Organizer
Marketing Materials Planner
Newsletter Worksheet
Hot Prospect! Form
Ten Questions for Your Self-Interview (worksheet and audio)
Promotional Plan

NO-EXCUSES ART MARKETING WORKSHOPS

I love to travel and meet new artists during my live workshops. See if they might be a good fit for artists in your community.
<artbizcoach.com/workshops>

BLOGGING RESOURCES

Blogger <blogger.com>
Blog Triage Self Study: Maintaining a Healthy Artist's Blog
<artbizcoach.com/btss.html>
Copyblogger teaches you how to be a better blogger. <copyblogger.com>
Get your picture next to your blog comments with a Gravatar.
<en.gravatar.com>
TypePad <sixapart.com>
WordPress <wordpress.org> or <wordpress.com>

CATALOGS ON DEMAND

Blurb <blurb.com>
Lulu <lulu.com>
Photoworks <photoworks.com>
Shutterfly <shutterfly.com>

EMAIL DISTRIBUTION SERVICES

Use one of these services when you email in bulk and want to send
formatted HTML newsletters.

Campaign Monitor <campaignmonitor.com>
Constant Contact <constantcontact.com>
Email Brain <emailbrain.com>
MailChimp <mailchimp.com>
Topica <topica.com>
Vertical Response <verticalresponse.com>

HTML COLOR CODES

If you need to select a palette for your website, newsletter, or blog, check out
HTML Color Codes <html-color-codes.info> or COLOURlovers
<colourlovers.com>.

LEGAL ADVICE

Artists should be aware of the special legal concerns surrounding intellectual
property. I highly recommend that artists keep a copy of Tad Crawford's

book *The Legal Guide for the Visual Artist* on their shelves. There are variations for your special medium at allworth.com.

Follow the law when you use email for your marketing. The CAN-SPAM law (U.S.), which attempts to reduce unwanted and offensive email, went into effect in January 2004. Among other things, it says you must (1) use a subject line that reflects the content of your email; (2) provide recipients an easy way to opt out or unsubscribe; and (3) include a legitimate postal address. Go to ftc.gov/spam and click on CAN-SPAM Act for details. Be sure to keep abreast of any new local, state, or federal legislation that might affect your business.

MARKETING AND PUBLIC RELATIONS
NEWSLETTERS & PRODUCTS

Marketing Minute—Marcia Yudkin <yudkin.com>
The Publicity Hound—Joan Stewart <publicityhound.com>

ORGANIZING AND PRODUCTIVITY

Get Organized Online Class for Artists <artbizcoach.com/go.html>
Productive Day—Leslie Shreve <productiveday.com>

PASSWORDS

Keep your passwords safe and secure with 1Password <1password.com>.

PRINTING

Whenever you see a printed piece you admire, ask who designed and printed it. Below are printing companies that either I have used or have been recommended by other artists. I encourage you to look at their sites and ask for samples.

Club Flyers <clubflyers.com>
GotPrint <gotprint.com>
Modern Postcard <modernpostcard.com>
MOO <moo.com>
Overnight Prints <overnightprints.com>
Postcard Press <postcardpress.com>

Print for Less <printforless.com>
PS Print <psprint.com>
Streetcards <streetcards.com>
Vista Print <vistaprint.com>

SOFTWARE FOR ARTIST DATABASES

For years I have tried without success to get a sense of the software program that stands out as a clear favorite for artists' special needs. Every artist has his or her favorite with none of these coming out a clear winner, although I can say that Mac users have been very happy with Bento. You'll have to research, talk with other artists, and decide which one will work best for you.

Art & Craft Business Organizer—PC only <jaminmark.com/acbo>
Artist's Butler—PC and Mac <lynnsoft.net>
Bento—Mac only, but not specific to artists <filemaker.com/bento>
eArtist—PC and Mac <artscope.net/eArtist>
Flick!—PC and Mac <arawak.com.au>
GYST—PC and Mac <gyst-ink.com>
WorkingArtist—PC only <workingartist.com>

STATIONERY

Envelope Mall—best for bulk <envelopemall.com>
Paper Source—best for smaller quantities <paper-source.com>

WEBSITE DESIGNERS

WhiteWing Design—Patrica J. Velte <whitewingdesign.com>

WEBSITES FOR ARTISTS

ArtSpan <artspan.com>
FineArtStudioOnline <fineartstudioonline.com>

I'd like to know what other resources you might need for your art career.
Please send an email to alyson@idratherbeinthestudio.com.

Thank you!

Your purchase of *I'd Rather Be in the Studio!*
is very much appreciated.

To help you with your promotional efforts, I invite you to download the following FREE RESOURCES at IdRatherBeintheStudio.com.

The **Principles of No-Excuse Self-Promotion** poster is designed to print out and display where it can motivate you every day.

The **Self-Promotion Routines Planner** offers a menu of self-promotion ideas to select from and incorporate into your plan.

Prepare for speaking and teaching opportunities with the **Presentation Organizer**.

The **Marketing Materials Planner** guides you during the production of your marketing pieces.

Create, send, and distribute your newsletter without missing a step with the **Newsletter Worksheet**.

Keep track of business and career leads with the **Hot Prospect! Form**.

Prepare for interviews or writing an article about yourself with **Ten Questions for Your Self-Interview**.

The **Promotional Plan** puts everything together for you in a guide for your goals, tasks, and deadlines.

Visit IdRatherBeintheStudio.com for these gifts and more.

Index

Accomplishments, 81, 82
Actions, 250, 256, 258
Addresses, 100
  collecting, 219-220
  email, 17, 18, 80, 87, 99, 101, 163,
    168, 219-220, 225
  mailing, 17, 18, 163
  website, 80, 95, 103, 163, 169, 232
Advertising, 63, 115, 207, 237
  horror stories about, 247
  spending on, 248
  teaching and, 59
Affirmations, writing, 250, 252
Agents, 5, 134, 216
Allen, David, 24
Ambitions, 4, 5, 9
American Art Directory, 216
American City Business Journals,
  222
American Institute of Architects,
  217
American Institute of Philanthropy,
  235
American Society of Interior
  Designers, 217
American Society of Landscape
  Architects, 218
Announcements, 65, 163, 164, 178,
  225
  attractive, 171-172
  scanning, 170
Apple iCal, 175

Apple Mail, 30, 175
Appointments, reminders for, 31
Apprentice, The (television show),
  207, 208
Architects, contacts with, 217, 218
Art Biz Blog, 109, 111, 118
Art Biz Coach, 97, 113
  classes from, 11, 15, 27
  newsletters from, 151
Art Biz Connection art-marketing
  salons, 6, 213, 257
Art organizations, 65, 101, 236
  communication by, 213
  contacts and, 215, 216
  joining, 211-213, 255
  newsletters and, 149
  speaking to, 57, 58
Articles, 10, 82, 91-92, 94, 163, 178
  benefits of, 247
  newsletter, 143-145
  online, 191
Artist statements, 47, 80, 91, 94, 98
  benefits of, 41, 49-50
  communicating with, 41, 42
  editing, 51-53
  feedback on, 50
  guidelines for, 39, 41-42, 51
  organic, 42, 53
  promotions and, 39-40
  writing, 37, 38, 39, 40, 41, 43, 44-
    45, 50, 51, 54, 55, 71, 188
Artist talks, 56-59, 65-66, 68

Artist's Way, The (Cameron), 258
Arts agencies, contacts with, 216
Arts councils, contacting, 212
Artwork
  high-quality, 76
  older, 98-99
  organizing online, 98-99
  sharing, 208, 210, 226
  statement about, 46-47
  talking about, 47-48
  understanding/appreciation for, 50
Ask, 202-204
  copy-and-paste, 204-205
  pitch and, 205
Assistants to CEOs, contacts with,
    218
Atkinson, Jas: quote of, 76
Attachments, 167, 169, 170, 198
  downloading, 152
  sending, 153
Auctions, 236
Audience, 60, 63, 76
  blogs and, 105
  building, 47, 57, 61, 171, 210,
    248
  connecting with, 53-54
  newsletter, 145
  target, 66
  teaching and, 59

Be Heard Now! (Glickstein), 68
Beardsley, Monroe: quote of, 47
Berman, Harriete Estel, 52
Biography, 41, 80, 83-84, 91, 94, 99,
    164, 235
  artist statement and, 42
  marketing and, 84
  online, 129, 191
  spicing up, 84-86
Blasts, email, 18, 65, 158, 171, 202,
    217
Blink (Gladwell), 74

Blogs, 54, 65, 96, 97, 117, 129, 144,
    145, 150, 162, 163, 191, 210, 216,
    220, 232
  answering questions on, 253
  audience and, 105
  business on, 119
  coordinating, 120
  email subscription forms on, 111
  goals and, 242
  hosting, 100, 106
  keywords/phrases for, 110
  linking, 100, 110
  mission of, 119
  news, 203
  newsletters and, 112
  posting on, 33, 35, 65, 106-107,
    109, 111, 124, 204
  public speaking and, 56
  resources, 260
  sales and, 105
  starting, 105-114, 124
  visiting, 10, 74, 105, 109-112, 114
Blogspot.com, 106
Body, of letters, 166
Body language, 38
Boise, Idaho, City Art Commission,
    229
Books, 10, 163
  art, 33
  business, 33
  inspirational, 33, 252
  marketing, 209
  self-esteem, 11
Borsheim, Kelly: announcements
    by, 171-172
Bothering people, thoughts on, 115
Boundaries, setting, 7, 13, 252-254
Bradford, Tim, Facebook bio of,
    122
Branding, 74-75, 78, 79, 80, 94
  buyers and, 75
  domain names and, 102-103

emails and, 167-168
online, 95
signature blocks and, 168-169
Brochures, 61, 89-90, 93, 164, 178, 180, 201
Brogan, Chris, 96, 134
Bruce, Kesha A., 105, 223
Bubb, Karen: promotions and, 229-230, 231
Budgets, 248-249
Business buddy, 255-257
Business cards, 19, 35, 87-88, 111, 163, 164, 235
  contact lists and, 225
  letterhead and, 89
  receiving, 224-225
Business expenses, writing off, 248
Business journals, 218, 221, 222
Business Journals, The, 222
Business Network International, 221
Businesses
  building, 5, 18, 71, 178, 221, 239, 258
  filing categories for, 25
  online, 88
Buyers, 117, 183
  branding and, 75
  following up with, 175

CafePress, 101, 232
Calendars, 31, 176, 189, 250
Call, Lisa: on blogging, 112
Call to action, 66-67, 145, 156, 192, 202
Cameron, Julia, 258
CAN-SPAM laws, 155, 163, 261
Canfield, Jack, 34, 35
Careers, 11
  building, 3, 35, 178, 217, 250
  goals for, 226

successful, 4, 75-76, 250
  visualizing, 243-244
Castle, David: pre-sales by, 232
Catalogs, 90-91, 236, 260
CDs, 11, 92-93, 163
Cell phones, 44, 172, 173
Chambers of commerce, 149, 221
Chicago Artist Coalition, 96
Chicago Tribune, 199
Chicken Soup for the Soul (Canfield and Hansen), 35
Classes, 3, 56, 60, 61, 94
  online, 161
  promoting, 65
Clergy, contacts with, 219
Closing, letter, 61, 166
"Coach on Call" radio show, 252
Collections, 9, 83, 218
  corporate, 82
  public, 10, 81, 82, 86
Collectors, 5, 16, 19, 83, 91, 231
  contacts with, 181, 215, 218
  cultivating, 2, 15, 17, 173, 175, 186, 222, 242, 258
Commercial sites, sales on, 96
Commissions, 10, 100, 180-181
Communication, 3, 37, 163, 170, 184, 211
  changes with, 167
  intensifying/enhancing, 241
  nonverbal, 68
  opportunities for, 161
  visual, 79
Community, 143, 183, 184, 211, 231, 243, 258
  alliances in, 234, 255
  art-friendly, 185
  connections with, 117, 256
  groups, 235
Community leaders, contacts with, 219
Computers, 117, 156, 211

Conant, James Bryant: quote of, 2
Confidence, 11, 38, 60, 212
Connections, 7, 19, 74, 119, 121,
    125, 152, 180, 187, 256, 257
  face-to-face, 117
  importance of, 174, 213-214, 235
  making, 40, 53-54, 137, 138
  number of, 183
  private, 10, 137
  sales and, 161, 213
  social media, 10, 115, 117-118,
    137, 138, 186, 190
  success and, 3
Consultants, 5, 17, 217, 218
Contact lists, 17-19, 20
  business cards and, 225
  expanding, 27, 209, 214-220
  updating, 199-200
  See also Mailing lists
Contact page, described, 99-100
Contacts, 115, 175, 180, 198, 215,
    246, 256
  artist/business, 34
  face-to-face, 117
  leads from, 221
  making, 117-118, 210-211, 212,
    213
  media, 187
  personal, 18, 209
Content, 61, 108, 110
Contracts, 20, 250
Conversations, 19, 48, 67, 108, 161,
    210
  beginning, 49
  limiting, 254
  steering, 197
Conversations exercise, 47-50, 51,
    52
Copyright, 80, 93, 98, 104, 142, 153,
    156, 191, 212
Correspondence, 19, 20
Coupons, 131, 237

Cover letters, 20, 80, 165
Craigslist.org, 66
Crawford, Tad, 260-261
Creative Commons license, 104
Creative Habit, The (Tharp), 29, 53
Creativity, 13, 29, 30, 47, 49, 210,
    234, 251
  feeding, 7, 258
Credentials, establishing, 166
Credibility, 75, 255
Credit lines, 98, 122-123
Criticism, accepting, 4, 48, 74, 254-
    255
Critics, 2, 37, 90
  communicating with, 3
  contacts with, 216
  credibility of, 255
  quotes from, 192
Curators, 2, 5, 16, 17, 37, 74, 81,
    213
  artist statement and, 39
  biographies and, 84
  catalogs from, 91
  communicating with, 3
  contacts and, 215
  gallery talks and, 55
  meeting, 178-179
  quotes from, 192

Daily Om, The, 252
Databases, 16-17, 18, 19, 262
Davenport, Liz: on organizing, 24
Deadlines, 40, 57, 242, 246-247, 250
Demonstrations, 56, 62
Design, of marketing materials, 78-
    81
Dialogue, 49, 50, 108, 222
Digital theft, discouraging, 104
Diplomacy, speaking with, 111-112
Domain names, 102-103, 106
Donations, 174, 188, 189, 235-236
Dooley, Mike, 252

Dorrell, Paul: on connections/sales, 213
DVDs, 92-93

e-cards, 220, 231
e-documents, 65
e-newsletters, 97, 153, 155, 156
  advantages/disadvantages of, 150-151
Earthly Delights (newsletter), 146, 147-148 (fig.)
eBay, 3, 96
Editorial Calendar, 109
Editors, 186, 199, 216
Edsall-Kerwin, Wendy, Twitter bio of, 129
Education, 5, 82, 86
Email addresses, 17, 18, 80, 87, 99, 101, 163, 168, 219-220, 225
Emails, 33, 44, 71, 89, 100, 138, 140, 162, 163, 180, 192, 198, 199, 204, 210, 257
  branding and, 167-168
  checking, 197
  communicating with, 151, 170, 190
  distribution of, 201, 260
  enticing, 170-172
  habits with, 167
  newsletter, 150-154
  receiving, 158, 167, 170, 202
  reminder, 175
  rhythm for, 166
  sending, 61, 157, 168, 202, 232
  test, 155
  thank-you, 179
  tricks with, 167-172
  See also Blasts, email
Entrepreneurs, role of, 15
Etsy, 96, 101
Evernote, 108
eWomenNetwork, 221

Excuses, 1-2, 253
  making, 2, 251, 258
  overcoming, 30, 208, 239
Exhibitions, 81, 82-83, 140, 145, 162, 204, 248-249, 250
  applying for, 212
  digital submissions and, 93
  entering, 9
  flyers from, 94
  invitations to, 125
  newsworthy, 187-189, 192
  opportunities for, 105
Eye contact, 224

Facebook, 33, 118, 135, 179, 220
  art on, 122
  business pages on, 18, 96, 120, 121, 123
  commenting on, 233
  connections on, 119, 121, 125, 137, 138
  discussions on, 136
  fans on, 120-121, 123-124
  media outlets on, 197
  official pages on, 120
  posting on, 136
  powering up page on, 124-127
  profile, 119, 121, 123
  saving time on, 127-128
  scheduling time on, 127, 134
Facebook Event, 65
Facebook fan pages, 65, 119, 145, 150, 163
  artists on, 125
  Google and, 120
  key elements on, 121-123
  photos on, 67, 121
  promotions on, 126
  writing on, 35, 197
  See also Facebook, official pages; Facebook, business pages
Facebook Lists, creating, 127-128

Fans, 231
  creating, 59, 110
Feedback, 49, 69, 256
FeedBlitz, 111
FeedBurner, 111
Feldhaus, Anne Leuck, 199
Feminist artists, speaking by,
  58-59
Fernandez, Lorena, Facebook page
  of, 123
Festivals, 2, 81, 94, 111, 112, 162
  business cards for, 87
  contacts with, 216
  digital submissions and, 93
  money for, 227
FileMaker, 16, 109
Files, 16, 20, 21
  creating/keeping, 24-27
  electronic, 24
  organizing, 32, 152
  paper, 24-27
Filter Friends, 124
FineArtStudioOnline, 102
Flickr.com, 96
Flyers, 57, 66, 94, 111, 164
Focus, 13, 31, 66, 110, 222, 255
  artist statement, 53
  changing, 252
  keeping, 127
Follow-up, 18, 31, 35, 175
Followers, gaining, 107, 130, 134,
  136
Fonts, 103, 152, 169
  See also Typefaces
Framing, 23, 227, 248-249
Friendships
  contacts and, 215
  cultivating, 210, 211
Fritzler, Dianna, Facebook bio of,
  122
Future, visualizing, 242-244

Galleries, 2, 5, 16, 17, 48, 74, 83, 98,
  101
  applying to, 41, 76
  biographies and, 84
  catalogs from, 91
  co-op, 3
  contacts with, 117, 181, 217
  digital submissions and, 93
  links to, 104
  newsletters at, 149
  online, 34, 96
  visiting, 33, 34, 258
Gallery dealers, 37, 79, 214
  artist statement and, 39
  brands and, 75
  communicating with, 3
  contacts with, 215, 217
Gallery talks, 55-56, 162, 188, 222
Getting Things Done (Allen), 24
Gilbert, Rita, 77
Gladwell, Malcolm, 74
Glickstein, Lee, 68
Goals, 24, 50, 145, 157, 253
  accountability for, 256
  achieving, 242, 244, 258
  boundaries and, 254
  career, 226
  with deadlines, 242
  delaying, 251
  marketing, 245, 249
  newsletter, 140, 242
  promotional, 246-248, 250
  quotas and, 34
  reasons for, 242
  reviewing, 33, 250
  setting, 4, 242
Goettee, Michael, 233
Goodman, Debbie: on connections,
  235
Google, 106, 110, 120, 161
Google Alerts, 112-114

Google Images, 113
Google Voice, 80
Grammar, 45, 51, 52, 80, 156
Grants, 10, 11, 40, 82, 165, 212, 235
  applying for, 212
  thank-you notes for, 179-180
Graphics, 64, 104, 151
Greenbaum, Joann Wells: on
  feedback, 49-50
Guests, contacts through, 48

Habits, 5, 11, 167
Hansen, Mark Victor, 35, 43
HassleMe, 176
Hayhouse Radio, 252
Holiday greetings, sending, 199
Home pages, 97, 99, 103, 128
Honors, 82, 83
HootSuite, 135-136
Hospital administrators, contacts
  with, 218
Hostess gifts, 232
Hosts, 48
Hot Prospect! Form, 176
HTML (Hypertext Markup
  Language), 152, 153, 169, 192,
  205, 260
Humor, 64, 66, 155

Ideas, 110, 210, 241
  pitching, 61-63
Images, 20, 22, 92-93, 96, 122, 142
  adding, 169
  availability, 23
  color, 164
  digital, 117, 153
  online, 231
  polishing, 74, 94
  posting, 110
  sharing, 93
  theft of, 190, 191

Impressions, making, 74, 222
Improvements, 37, 38, 67-69, 241
Information, 15, 131, 170, 191, 192,
  198, 247
  business card, 87
  contact, 18, 163, 190, 205, 219,
  224-225
  electronic storage of, 20-21
  introductions and, 223
  looking for, 188
  sharing, 65, 158-159, 204, 220,
  239
  tracking, 200
  tweeting, 134
Inspiration, 29, 45-46, 244
Installations, 145, 217
Instructional talks, 56, 62, 65-66
Intellectual property, 104
  See also Copyright
Interior designers, 214, 217
Internet, 71, 99, 111, 114, 115,
  118, 151, 184, 185, 186, 211,
  243
Interviews, 200-201, 233
Introductions, 222-224
Introverts, 207-208, 211, 226
Inventory, 16, 21-23, 32
Invitations, 65, 67, 107, 179, 199
  extending, 125-126
  sending, 157, 158, 178, 232
iPods, 176, 231
IRS, 236

Johnson, Pippi, 233
Journalists, attachments to, 198
Journals, 106, 188
  keeping, 6, 44, 45-47, 49, 69, 244,
  250, 252

Kelty, Michael, 232
Keywords, 21, 110, 142

Landscape architects, contacts with, 218

Landscape artists, speaking by, 59

Landscapers, contacts with, 218

Language, 5, 41, 171, 223

LaRae, Michelle: on communication, 161

LCD projectors, 62, 63

Leads, 175, 178, 221

Leads Club, 221

Lectures, 61, 63, 82
  charges for, 62
  planning, 64

Lee, Michele D.: on notes, 176-177

Legal advice, 260-261

Legal Guide for the Visual Artist, The (Crawford), 261

Letterhead, 89, 165

Letters, 140, 165-166
  cover, 20, 80, 165
  pitches in, 61

Licensing agents, contacts with, 216

LinkedIn, 33, 34, 96, 118, 137

Links, 97, 104, 131, 169
  events, 125-126
  to galleries, 104
  meaningful, 110-111
  minor, 97, 100-101
  photo, 122

Listening, 56-59, 108, 222

Living the Artist Life (Dorrell), 213

Living With Art (Gilbert), 77

Logos, 79, 87, 104

Luer, Pamela: on motivation/focus, 222

Magazines, 184, 185, 200-201, 244
  art, 29, 33, 237
  business, 33

Mailing lists, 63, 117, 140, 162, 164, 186
  building, 18, 32, 34, 177-178, 179, 182
  buying, 18-19, 219
  contact with, 115
  databases for, 176
  newsletter, 149
  relying on, 207
  signing up for, 101, 219
  See also Contact lists

Mailings, 73, 100, 162, 180, 246
  holiday tips for, 174
  opportunities for, 152
  regular, 210, 213
  safe, 219

Maisel, Eric: on overwhelm, 239

Mammoser, Tina, Twitter bio of, 129

Marketing, 7, 9, 13, 39, 76, 80, 97, 115, 207, 234, 242, 248
  biographies and, 84
  budget for, 249
  creative, 50
  filing categories for, 26
  generating, 227
  goals for, 245, 249
  information for, 15
  messages, 66, 74, 75
  newsletters and, 139
  plans for, 6, 241, 244, 250, 257
  research, 48
  routine for, 33-35
  social media and, 118
  strategies, 71
  word-of-mouth/viral, 185, 186

Marketing materials, 71, 74, 89-90, 91, 163
  designing, 78-81
  letterhead and, 89
  money for, 227
  online, 191

portfolios and, 73, 94
rules for, 79-81
spending on, 73
updating, 73, 244
Marketing Materials Planner, 94
Materials, 23, 46, 212
printed, 71, 73, 80
sales, 66
See also Marketing materials;
Promotional materials
Maxemail, 80
Mayer, Michael, Twitter bio of,
129
Media, 78, 79, 98, 234
contacting, 186-187, 197-198
local, 184, 185, 191
news releases and, 201-205
newsworthy, 187-189
relationships with, 187, 196, 199
thoughts on, 185-187
traditional, 185, 201
Media kits, online, 65, 190-192, 198,
202
Media lists, updating, 199-200
Media releases, 34, 40, 54, 65, 107,
200, 232
electronic, 201, 202
email, 204-205
printed, 198
sending, 197, 204-205
writing, 35
Messages, 50, 78
creating, 202-203
downloading, 152
email, 100, 138, 192, 199, 201, 202-
203, 219, 232
inspirational, 252
marketing, 66
reading, 171
receiving, 170, 219
replying to, 170
revamping, 73

sales, 107
sending, 73, 74, 168, 169
MIME (Multipurpose Internet Mail
Extension), 152
Mini-portfolios, 164, 231
Mistakes, 43, 74, 102, 166, 168, 197
Momentum, maintaining, 251-255,
257-258
Morris, Cynthia: on coping with
criticism, 254-255
Morrison, Bruce H.: quote of, 15-16
Motivation, 4, 33, 222, 244, 252, 256
Mulligan, Carrie, Twitter bio of,
129
Murphy, Pamela: title party by,
233-234
Museums, 5, 101, 214
contacts with, 117
digital submissions and, 93
exhibitions at, 55
photographers and, 92
visiting, 33, 258

Names, 80
remembering, 224
National Assembly of State Art
Agencies, 212, 216
Neal, Michael Shane: postcards and,
164
Negative people, limiting contact
with, 254
Networking, 33, 112, 138, 211, 220-
222
*New Rules of Marketing and PR,
The* (Scott), 186
News releases, 191, 196
follow-up, 199
media and, 201-205
online, 200
sample, 193-195
sending, 190, 201-205
writing, 185, 192-195

Newsletters, 199, 204, 210, 217, 253
  advantages/disadvantages of, 150-
    151
  announcements in, 65
  art in, 142
  blogs and, 112
  communicating with, 161
  community and, 174
  content for, 141, 142-145, 259
  cost of, 140, 141
  distributing, 140, 149-150
  email, 141, 150-154, 155, 199, 213,
    232
  forwarding, 145, 155
  goals of, 140, 242
  graphics in, 151
  images in, 142
  mailing list for, 149
  marketing/public relations, 139,
    261
  naming, 141-142
  niche markets and, 150
  online, 100
  opportunities and, 140
  planning, 140-141
  printing, 146, 149
  promotions with, 140, 142
  relationships and, 139, 159
  sales and, 140
  screen resolutions for, 153-154
  sending, 16, 18, 34, 139, 149, 162
  subscribing to, 10, 155
  websites and, 112, 156
  See also E-newsletters
Newspapers, 184, 185
  contacts with, 216
  information for, 198
  photocopying, 91
Newsworthiness, 187-189, 192
Niche markets, 65, 78, 113, 143
  contacts in, 216
  formal talks and, 56

newsletters and, 150
public speaking and, 58
No-Excuses Art Marketing
  Workshops, 259
Nonprofits, 216, 234-235
Note cards, 33, 89, 101, 145, 232
Notebooks, 6, 30, 43, 44, 182
  leads, 176
  P.R., 94, 201
Notes, 7, 23
  communicating with, 161
  follow-up, 177, 181-182, 182
  handwritten, 176-177, 178
  sending, 177, 178-179
  writing, 67, 89
Notes from the Universe (Dooley),
  252

Official Museum Directory, The,
  215
Oklahoma Visual Arts Coalition, 96
Online presence, 95, 96, 105, 138
Open houses, announcing, 174
Opening paragraphs/sentences, 50,
  61, 166
Openings, 33, 52, 94, 117, 145
  reminders for, 158
Opportunities, 7, 105, 140, 152, 161,
  176-177, 199
Organization, 15-16, 48, 60, 63, 66,
  261
Overwhelm, overcoming, 239, 241

Packets, promotional, 57, 164
Paintings
  images of, 20
  pricing, 21
  value of, 21
Paper
  handmade, 78
  photocopy, 80
  specialty, 149

Passwords, 136, 190, 261
Patrons, 16, 163, 167, 203, 204, 207
  communicating with, 3, 161
  information for, 158-159
  notes to, 177-178
  protecting, 83
  quotes from, 192
Persistence, 5, 199-200
Phone calls, 31, 44, 61, 162, 176,
    180, 231, 257
  communicating with, 172-174
  follow-up, 199
  scheduling, 253
Phone messages, checking, 197
Phone numbers, 17, 80, 163, 173
Photographers
  crediting, 155
  hiring, 92
Photographs, 92-93
  adding, 105, 198
  high-quality, 80, 104
Pitch, 192, 203, 204-205
  ask and, 205
  email, 197
  making, 196-197
  verbal, 199
Plain text, 152, 154, 169, 204
Plans, 237, 242
  business, 227
  creating, 243, 250
  focusing on, 255
  improving, 37, 241
Politicians, contacts with, 218-219
Portfolios, 93, 145, 172, 201, 244
  image, 96
  marketing materials in, 73, 94
  mini-, 164, 231
  online, 97
  opening, 99
  paper/electronic, 12
Portrait brokers, contacts with, 216
Positive environment, 252, 255

Post office boxes, 80, 163
Postcards, 94, 140, 146, 165 (fig.),
    225, 230
  color images on, 164
  cost of, 164
  designing, 165
  enticing, 170-172
  scanning, 170
  sending, 61, 115, 164-165
Posts, 71, 233
  consistent, 110
  writing, 109
PowerPoint presentations, 62, 63, 64
Presentation Organizer, 67
Presentations, 12, 62, 93
  improving, 67-69
  preparing, 63-64
  promoting, 65-66
  slide, 56, 63
Pricing, 21, 60, 91, 101
  posting, 104
  sales, 23
Printing, 261-262
Priorities, 13, 34, 241, 252
Privacy, 136
  connections and, 137
  policy, 101, 220
  respecting, 220
Procrastination, 32, 40, 182
Productive Day Success System, 30
Products, 212
  marketing/public relations, 261
Professional groups, speaking to, 58
Profiles, 119, 121, 123, 129, 130
  completing, 136
  website, 200-201
  writing, 200-201
Programs, 236
  scheduling, 58
Promotional materials, 39, 91
  printed/electronic, 79
  redesigning, 251

Promotions, 3, 27, 64, 66-67, 73, 79,
    107, 168, 205, 213, 237
  artists statement and, 39-40
  with deadlines, 246-247
  effective, 34
  goals for, 246-248, 250
  inconsistent, 7
  low-cost/no-cost, 231-234
  plan for, 243
  presentation, 65-66
  strategy for, 248, 249
  students and, 61
  successful, 4
  word of mouth, 247
Property managers, contacts with,
    218
PRWeb.com, 200
Psychological preparations, 11, 30
Public relations firms/specialists,
    185, 198, 205
Public speaking, 55, 56, 82, 246
Publications, 92, 186, 187, 200
  recent, 82
  weekly/daily, 199
Publicity, 26
  donations and, 236
  free, 231
Punctuation, 45, 51, 52, 83, 168

Questions, 44, 145, 201, 213
  answering, 197, 198, 199, 253
  follow-up, 49
  provocative, 144
  stupid, 48
Quick-Start Manual outlines,
    109
QuickBooks, 17

Real estate companies, 218
Real estate journals, contacts from,
    218
Recognition, 2, 9, 12, 47, 75, 167

Recommendations, 112
  personal, 247
  thank yous for, 179-180
Reed, Tara: Twitter philosophy of,
    135
References, 62, 178
Rejection, accepting, 4
Rejection lines, developing, 254
Relationships, 231
  artist-gallery, 181
  building, 118, 138, 199, 209, 210,
    220, 256
  maintaining, 3, 27, 159, 174, 182
  media, 187, 196, 199
  newsletters and, 139, 159
  personalizing, 19, 200, 225
  professional, 230
  reciprocal, 220
  social media, 138
Remembering people, 224
Reminders
  electronic, 175-176
  sending, 31, 158
Reporters
  gifts for, 198
  invitations to, 199
Reputation, building, 92, 119-120,
    136-137, 167, 214, 250
Research, 32, 48, 61, 71
Resources, 6, 17, 89, 91, 101, 151,
    155, 162, 163, 235, 260
  personal, 6
  tweeting, 134
Responses, 48, 197, 198, 199, 253
  forming, 254
  getting, 37, 38
Résumés, 21, 41, 62, 80, 81-83, 84,
    91, 99, 191, 212
  master, 81
  updating, 82-83, 85
Retail outlets, checking in with,
    34

Retweets (RT), 132, 134, 179
Reviewers, contacts with, 216
Rich text (RTF), 152, 192
Richardson, Cheryl, 252
Risks, 2-3
Rituals, 5, 258
Rondina, Hank: on artist statement, 41
Routines, 5, 6, 7, 30-33, 33-35
RT. *See* Retweets
RTF. *See* Rich text
Rule of 5, 35
Rush, Barbara, 231

Sales, 1, 10, 47, 76, 92, 188, 189, 196, 209-210, 211, 227, 232, 237
  blogs and, 105
  connections and, 161, 213
  contacts and, 210
  direct, 97
  filing categories for, 27
  intermediaries and, 3
  invitations to, 125
  newsletters and, 140
  online, 105
  poor, 12
  records, 16, 21
  worrying about, 75
Salutations, described, 166
Saying No, 254
Schedules, 32, 60, 251, 253
  creating, 257-258
  seasonal, 57
Scott, David Meerman, 186
Sculptures, 9, 78, 217, 248
Search engines, 96, 98, 102, 111, 113, 141, 186
Seesmic, using, 135-136
Self-confidence, 4, 13, 256
Self-employment, 13, 242, 256
Self-esteem, 11, 252

Self-promotion, 2-3, 18, 47, 76, 95, 115, 134, 200, 227, 241, 246, 256
  contact lists and, 20
  effective, 257-258
  newsletters and, 42
  no-excuse, 3-4, 10
  routines for, 35
Shareholders, story about, 229-230
Short, Margret E., 56, 107, 108
  media release for, 193-195
  pitch for, 196
Shreve, Leslie, 30
Shyness, 207-208, 211
Signature blocks, branding and, 168-169
Signatures, 169, 192, 205
Site-hosting services, 95
6 Steps to Free Publicity (Yudkin), 187
Skills, 59, 67-69, 78
Slides, 41, 56, 63, 212, 230
Smart phones, 31, 176, 231
Smith, Julien, 134
Social media, 80, 87, 96, 100, 119, 135, 179, 220
  connections on, 10, 115, 117-118, 137, 138, 190
  data from, 18
  interacting on, 233
  introducing self on, 137-138
  managing, 136-138
  marketing and, 118
  mission for, 120
  as promotional tool, 138
Soffer, Ellen: postcards and, 165, 165 (fig.)
Software, 212
  database, 16-17, 262
Spam, 125, 126, 151, 167, 168, 170
Speaking, 61, 63, 67, 233
  dates for, 62
  fear/trepidation of, 69

Speaking, *continued*
  planning for, 57
  practicing, 68
  teaching and, 59
Speaking Circles, 68
Spell check, 80, 156, 168, 186
Spelling, 51, 156
Spirituality, 10, 11
Sroka, Daniel, 80, 139, 223
Stationery, 89, 262
Stock certificates, story about,
    229-230
Storytelling, 84, 85, 86
Students, 157
  attracting, 59, 61
  quotes from, 192
Studios, 10, 48, 149
  cleaning, 32
  getting out of, 258
  nonnegotiable time in, 7
  office space and, 15
  visiting, 258
Styles, 5, 45, 76, 77
Subjects, 45, 76, 254
Subscribers, 109, 155
Subscription forms, email, 111
Success, 7, 55, 75-76, 81, 183,
    211
  achieving, 3-4, 9, 255
  defining, 9-12, 243
  eagerness for, 13
  fear of, 2
  organizing for, 12
  path to, 244
  vision of, 9-11, 226, 250
Success Principles, The (Canfield),
    34
Supplies, 227, 248-249
Support, 22, 211

Tag lines, 79, 168
Tagging, 125

Tasks, 243, 253
  reminders for, 175
  scheduling, 30, 31
  tackling, 31-32, 250
Taxes, 212, 236, 248
Teaching, 56, 67, 69, 82, 221, 233
  advertising and, 59
  audience and, 59, 61
  expertise and, 59
  income from, 60
  learning and, 59
  speaking skills and, 59
Teaching promotional packets,
    contents of, 57
Technology, 4, 31, 114, 231
TED conferences, 68
Testimonials, 94, 100
Thank you, opportunities for, 176-
    177, 199, 232
Thank-you notes, 31, 166, 198, 221,
    229, 232
  handwritten, 178, 179-180, 181
  sending, 67, 175, 179, 182
Tharp, Twyla, 29, 53
Thoughts, organizing, 41, 63
Time magazine, on social warmth,
    117
Title parties, 233-234
Titles, searching for, 21, 22, 233-234
Toastmasters club, 68, 69
Trotter, Deb: on websites, 96
Trust Agents (Brogan and Smith),
    134
TweepSearch.com, 134
Tweet makeovers, sample, 132-133
TweetDeck, 135-136
Tweets, 65, 108, 130-132
Twellow.com, 134
Twitter, 18, 34, 65, 108, 113, 118,
    220
  account elements on, 129-132
  communicating on, 134, 136

coordinating, 120
custom background for, 129-130
following on, 130, 134, 136
media outlets on, 197
philosophy, 135
profile on, 129, 130
reputation on, 119-120
saving time on, 134-136
taking lead on, 128-138
Twitter Lists, creating, 135
Typefaces, 79, 80, 82, 90, 152
TypePad, 106

Unger, John T.: on business cards, 88
URLs, 80, 95, 111, 123, 129, 150,
    169, 190

Velte, Patricia J., 102, 153
  newsletter by, 147-148 (fig.)
  postcard by, 165 (fig.)
Venues, 56, 57, 58, 69, 83, 212, 217
  alternative, 216
  biographies at, 84
  describing, 85
  lecturing, 62, 64
  promotions by, 65
  teaching, 10, 60
Videos, 33, 62
Vision, 9, 11, 243, 244, 255
Visual art, 63, 64, 79
Visualization, 226, 244, 255
Voice recorders, 43, 44
Voicemail, 44, 80, 173-174

Watermarks, 80, 104
Websites, 54, 121, 124, 129, 150,
    153, 162, 200, 201, 204, 205, 210,
    213, 220, 257
  addresses, 80, 95, 103, 163, 169,
    232

announcing, 171
classes/workshops on, 65
creating, 96-105, 262
discussions/passages on, 108
emails and, 167-168
linking, 110
names on, 103
newsletters and, 112, 156
profiles on, 200-201
public speaking and, 56
securing, 95
spending on, 102
tempering background of, 103
updating, 34, 96, 105, 157-158
visiting, 10, 74, 97, 98, 171
Whining, 7, 12, 253
WhiteWing Design, 153
Wildlife artists, speaking by, 58
Woods, Elia, 149
  newsletter of, 146, 147-148 (fig.)
Woods-Fasimpaur, Andi, 200
Word usage, 44, 52
WordPress, 106, 109
Workshops, 3, 56, 60, 65, 94, 157,
    259
Writers, 17, 37, 186
  contacts with, 216
Writing, 3, 50-51, 110, 187, 241,
    244, 250
  first-person, 41
  learning, 107
  mental preparation for, 44
  newsletter, 140
  perfecting, 109
  preparing for, 42-44
  professional, 168
  starting, 44-45

York, Sherrie: on blogging, 109-110
Yudkin, Marcia, 187

Actions

Actions

Actions